First World War
and Army of Occupation
War Diary
France, Belgium and Germany

1 CAVALRY DIVISION
2 Cavalry Brigade
2 Machine Gun Squadron,
'H' and 'L' Battery Royal Horse Artillery and Brigade
Pioneer Battalion
5 August 1914 - 13 March 1917

WO95/1111

The Naval & Military Press Ltd
www.nmarchive.com
Published in association with The National Archives

Published by

The Naval & Military Press Ltd

Unit 10 Ridgewood Industrial Park,

Uckfield, East Sussex,

TN22 5QE England

Tel: +44 (0) 1825 749494

www.naval-military-press.com

www.nmarchive.com

This diary has been reprinted in facsimile from the original. Any imperfections are inevitably reproduced and the quality may fall short of modern type and cartographic standards.

© Crown Copyright
Images reproduced by permission of The National Archives, London, England, 2015.

Contents

Document type	Place/Title	Date From	Date To
Heading	B.E.F. France & Flanders. 1 Cavalry Division 2 Cavalry Brigade 2 Machine Gun Squadron 1916 Feb To 1919 Mar 'H' Battery Royal Horse Artillery 1914 Sept To 1919 Mar 'L' Battery R.H.A. 1914 Aug To 1914 Oct Brigade Pioneer Bn 1917 Jan To 1917 Mar.		
Heading	WO95/1111/1		
Heading	1916-1918 1st Cavalry Division 2nd Cavalry Brigade. 2nd Sqdn Mach. Gun Corps Feb 1916-Mar 1919 Formed 1916 Feb To Lancers Bde Box 1166		
War Diary	Tincques	03/01/1917	10/01/1917
War Diary	Enquin	28/02/1916	30/04/1916
Heading	War Diary of 2nd Machine Gun Squadron. 2nd Cavalry Brigade-for May 1916.		
War Diary	Enquin	01/05/1916	24/06/1916
War Diary	Raye-Sur-Authie	25/06/1916	25/06/1916
War Diary	Mezerolles	26/06/1916	26/06/1916
War Diary	Berteaucourt Les. Dames	27/06/1916	27/06/1916
War Diary	Querrieu	28/06/1916	30/06/1916
Heading	War Diary of 2nd Squadron. Machine Gun Corps July, 1916 Volume No. VI		
War Diary	Querrieu	01/07/1916	04/07/1916
War Diary	Metigny	05/07/1916	11/07/1916
War Diary	Querrieu	12/07/1916	13/07/1916
War Diary	Yille-Sous Corbie	14/07/1916	24/07/1916
War Diary	Querrieu	25/07/1916	31/07/1916
Heading	War Diary of 2nd Squadron, Machine Gun Corps. August 1916 Volume No VII		
War Diary	Querrieu	01/08/1916	10/08/1916
War Diary	Incheville	11/08/1916	31/08/1916
Heading	War Diary of 2nd Squadron. Machine Gun Corps. September 1916 Volume No VIII		
War Diary	Incheville	01/09/1916	07/09/1916
War Diary	La Neuville	08/09/1916	14/09/1916
War Diary	Lannoy Valley	15/09/1916	17/09/1916
War Diary	La Neuville	18/09/1916	25/09/1916
War Diary	St. Georges	26/09/1916	30/09/1916
Heading	War Diary of 2nd Squadron, Machine Gun Corps. October 1916. Volume No IX		
War Diary	St. Georges	01/10/1916	20/10/1916
War Diary	Berteaucourt Les-Dames	21/10/1916	31/10/1916
Heading	War Diary of 2nd Squadron, Machine Gun Corps. November. 1916. Volume No. X		
War Diary	Berteaucourt-Les-Dames	01/11/1916	09/11/1916
War Diary	Preures	10/11/1916	30/11/1916
Heading	War Diary of 2nd Squadron, Machine Gun Corps December. 1916 Volume No XI		
War Diary	Preures	01/12/1916	31/12/1916
Heading	War Diary of 2nd Squadron, Machine Gun Corps. January 1917. Volume No XII		
War Diary	Preures	01/01/1917	31/01/1917

Heading	War Diary of 2nd Squadron, Machine Gun Corps February 1917 Volume No XIII		
War Diary	Preures	01/02/1917	28/02/1917
Heading	Appendix to War Diary of 2nd Squadron, Machine Gun Corps. February 1917 Volume No XIII		
War Diary		17/02/1917	28/02/1917
Heading	War Diary of 2nd Squadron, Machine Gun Corps March 1917 Volume No XIV		
War Diary	Preures	01/03/1917	01/03/1917
War Diary	In The Trenches	01/03/1917	01/03/1917
War Diary	Preures	02/03/1917	02/03/1917
War Diary	In The Trenches	02/03/1917	02/03/1917
War Diary	Preures	03/03/1917	03/03/1917
War Diary	Trenches	03/03/1917	03/03/1917
War Diary	Preures	04/03/1917	04/03/1917
War Diary	Trenches	04/03/1917	04/03/1917
War Diary	Preures	05/03/1917	05/03/1917
War Diary	Trenches	05/03/1917	05/03/1917
War Diary	Preures	06/03/1917	06/03/1917
War Diary	Trenches	06/03/1917	06/03/1917
War Diary	Preures	07/03/1917	07/03/1917
War Diary	Trenches	07/03/1917	07/03/1917
War Diary	Preures	08/03/1917	08/03/1917
War Diary	Trenches	08/03/1917	08/03/1917
War Diary	Preures	09/03/1917	09/03/1917
War Diary	Trenches	09/03/1917	09/03/1917
War Diary	Preures	10/03/1917	10/03/1917
War Diary	Trenches	10/03/1917	10/03/1917
War Diary	Preures	11/03/1917	11/03/1917
War Diary	Trenches	11/03/1917	11/03/1917
War Diary	Preures	12/03/1917	12/03/1917
War Diary	Trenches	12/03/1917	12/03/1917
War Diary	Preures	13/03/1917	13/03/1917
War Diary	Trenches	13/03/1917	13/03/1917
War Diary	Preures	14/03/1917	14/03/1917
War Diary	Trenches	14/03/1917	14/03/1917
War Diary	Preures	15/03/1917	15/03/1917
War Diary	Trenches	15/03/1917	15/03/1917
War Diary	Preures	16/03/1917	16/03/1917
War Diary	Trenches	16/03/1917	16/03/1917
War Diary	Preures	17/03/1917	17/03/1917
War Diary	Noyelles	17/03/1917	17/03/1917
War Diary	Preures	18/03/1917	31/03/1917
Miscellaneous	Appendix I	10/03/1917	10/03/1917
Miscellaneous	Operation Order by Captain L.W.D. Wathen, Commanding 2nd Machine Gun Squadron. Appendix II	15/03/1917	15/03/1917
Miscellaneous	Operation Order by Captain L.W.D. Wathen, Commanding 2nd. Machine Gun Squadron. Appendix III	15/03/1917	15/03/1917
Heading	War Diary of 2nd Squadron, Machine Gun Corps April 1917 Volume No XV		
War Diary	Preures	01/04/1917	05/04/1917
War Diary	Maninghem	06/04/1917	07/04/1917
War Diary	Anvin	07/04/1917	08/04/1917
War Diary	Frevin Capelle	09/04/1917	10/04/1917
War Diary	St. Laurent Blangey	11/04/1917	12/04/1917

War Diary	Previn Capelle		13/04/1917	17/04/1917
War Diary	Rougefay		18/04/1917	19/04/1917
War Diary	Contes		20/04/1917	30/04/1917
Heading	War Diary of 2nd Squadron. Machine Gun Corps May 1917. Volume No XVI			
War Diary	Contes		01/05/1917	12/05/1917
War Diary	Cuhem		13/05/1917	13/05/1917
War Diary	Ecquedecques		14/05/1917	14/05/1917
War Diary	Les Amusoires		15/05/1917	16/05/1917
War Diary	Roelincourt		17/05/1917	22/05/1917
War Diary	B. 15 Central		23/05/1917	31/05/1917
Miscellaneous	Disposition of the Squadron is as follows:- Appendix 1		30/05/1917	30/05/1917
Heading	War Diary of 2nd Squadron, Machine Gun Corps June 1917. Volume XVII			
War Diary	B. 15 Central		01/06/1917	01/06/1917
War Diary	Ecurie		02/06/1917	02/06/1917
War Diary	Les Amusoires		03/06/1917	13/06/1917
War Diary	Ecurie		14/06/1917	18/06/1917
War Diary	In The line. (Gavrelle Sector)		19/06/1917	30/06/1917
Miscellaneous	Appendix I 2nd. Machine Gun Squadron. Fire Programme.		28/06/1917	28/06/1917
Heading	War Diary of 2nd Squadron, Machine Gun Corps. July 1917. Volume No XVIII			
War Diary	Gavrelle Sector		01/07/1917	03/07/1917
War Diary	Les Amusoires		04/07/1917	31/07/1917
Heading	War Diary of 2nd Squadron, Machine Gun Corps, (Cavalry). August 1917. Volume No XIX			
War Diary	Les Amusoires		01/08/1917	27/08/1917
War Diary	Hezecques		27/08/1917	28/08/1917
War Diary	Enquin		29/08/1917	31/08/1917
Heading	War Diary of 2nd Squadron, Machine Gun Corps (Cavalry) September 1917. Volume No XX			
War Diary	Enquin		01/09/1917	30/09/1917
Heading	War Diary of 2nd Squadron, Machine Gun Corps. (Cavalry) October 1917. Volume No 21.			
War Diary	Enquin		01/10/1917	07/10/1917
War Diary	Watten		07/10/1917	08/10/1917
War Diary	Houtkerque		09/10/1917	13/10/1917
War Diary	Enquin		13/10/1917	31/10/1917
Heading	War Diary of 2nd Squadron, Machine Gun Corps, (Cavalry) November 1917. Volume No 22			
War Diary	Enquin		01/11/1917	13/11/1917
War Diary	Bray Area		13/11/1917	14/11/1917
War Diary	Doingt		15/11/1917	19/11/1917
War Diary	Fins		20/11/1917	22/11/1917
War Diary	Metz-En-Coutre		22/11/1917	30/11/1917
Heading	War Diary of 2nd Squadron, Machine Gun Corps, (Cavalry), December 1917 Volume No 23.			
War Diary	Doingt		01/12/1917	02/12/1917
War Diary	E.14. B		02/12/1917	03/12/1917
War Diary	Long Avesnes		04/12/1917	16/12/1917
War Diary	Bray		17/12/1917	23/12/1917
War Diary	Courcelles		24/12/1917	31/12/1917
Heading	War Diary of 2nd Squadron, Machine Gun Corps (Cavalry). January 1918. Volume No 24.			
War Diary	Courcelles		01/01/1918	31/01/1918

Heading	War Diary of 2nd Squadron, Machine Gun Corps. (Cavalry). February 1918 Volume No. 25.		
War Diary	Courcelles	01/02/1918	16/02/1918
War Diary	Courcelles Jeancourt	16/02/1918	21/02/1918
War Diary	Courcelles	22/02/1918	28/02/1918
Heading	War Diary of 2nd Squadron, Machine Gun Corps, (Cavalry) March 1918. Volume No. 26		
War Diary	Cookers Quarry (Ref. 62c. 1/40,000) (Right Subsector)	01/03/1918	09/03/1918
War Diary	Cookers Quarry	09/03/1918	11/03/1918
War Diary	Courcelles	12/03/1918	14/03/1918
War Diary	Roisel	15/03/1918	25/03/1918
War Diary	Bussy-Les-Daours	26/03/1918	27/03/1918
War Diary	Hamelet	28/03/1918	30/03/1918
War Diary	Bussy-Les-Daours	31/03/1918	31/03/1918
Heading	War Diary of 2nd Squadron. Machine Gun Corps, (Cavalry) April 1918 Volume No. 27		
War Diary	Bussy-Les-Daours	01/04/1918	04/04/1918
War Diary	Amiens	05/04/1918	10/04/1918
War Diary	Bachimont	10/04/1918	11/04/1918
War Diary	Galametz	12/04/1918	12/04/1918
War Diary	Predefin	13/04/1918	15/04/1918
War Diary	Fiefs	16/04/1918	16/04/1918
War Diary	Beaumetz-Lez-Aire	17/04/1918	30/04/1918
Heading	War Diary of 2nd Squadron. Machine Gun Corps, (Cavalry). May 1918 Volume Vol 28		
War Diary	Beaumetz-lez-aire (Hazebrouck 1/100,000)	01/05/1918	06/05/1918
War Diary	Dennebroeucq	07/05/1918	21/05/1918
War Diary	Boubers	21/05/1918	22/05/1918
War Diary	Saulchoy	23/05/1918	31/05/1918
Heading	War Diary of 2nd Squadron, Machine Gun Corps, (Cavalry). June 1918 Volume No. 29		
War Diary	Saulchoy (Abbeville 1/100,000)	01/06/1918	05/06/1918
War Diary	Saulchoy	06/06/1918	30/06/1918
Heading	War Diary of 2nd Squadron. Machine Gun Corps, (Cavalry) July. 1918 Volume No. 30		
War Diary	Saulchoy (Abbeville, 1/100,000)	01/07/1918	07/07/1918
War Diary	Saulchoy	08/07/1918	10/07/1918
War Diary	Bealcourt	11/07/1918	11/07/1918
War Diary	Sarton	12/07/1918	22/07/1918
War Diary	Thievres	23/07/1918	31/07/1918
Heading	War Diary of 2nd Squadron. Machine Gun Corps, Cavalry. August 1918 Volume No 31		
War Diary	Thievres (Ref. Map Lens 1/100,000)	01/08/1918	05/08/1918
War Diary	Wargnies	06/08/1918	06/08/1918
War Diary	St. Sauveur	07/08/1918	07/08/1918
War Diary	Caix	08/08/1918	14/08/1918
War Diary	Bretel	15/08/1918	15/08/1918
War Diary	Maizicourt	16/08/1918	19/08/1918
War Diary	Warlincourt	20/08/1918	21/08/1918
War Diary	Sarton	22/08/1918	31/08/1918
Heading	War Diary of 2nd Squadron, Machine Gun Corps (Cavalry). September 1918 Volume No 32.		
War Diary	Maizieres (Ref: Lens, 1/100,000)	01/09/1918	05/09/1918
War Diary	Rebreuve	06/09/1918	15/09/1918
War Diary	Willeman	16/09/1918	16/09/1918
War Diary	Caumont	17/09/1918	17/09/1918

War Diary	Frohen-Le-Petit	18/09/1918	23/09/1918
War Diary	Famechon	24/09/1918	24/09/1918
War Diary	Aveluy	25/09/1918	25/09/1918
War Diary	Moislains	26/09/1918	28/09/1918
War Diary	Hamelet	29/09/1918	30/09/1918
Heading	War Diary October 1918 Volume 33, 2nd Machine. Gun. Squadron		
War Diary	Hamelet Sheet. 62c 1/40,000 K 21.a. Central	01/10/1918	06/10/1918
War Diary	(Sheet 62c)	07/10/1918	07/10/1918
War Diary	L,14.C.8.8.	08/10/1918	08/10/1918
War Diary	Gouy	09/10/1918	09/10/1918
War Diary	Sheet 57 B. V.7. Central	10/10/1918	10/10/1918
War Diary	Le Trou au Soldar	11/10/1918	13/10/1918
War Diary	Cauvigney Fm 62c Q32d	14/10/1918	31/10/1918
Heading	War Diary of 2nd Squadron. Machine Gun Corps, Cavalry November, 1918 Volume No. 34		
War Diary	Cauvigny Fm (Ref. Sheet 62c. 1/40.000-Q.32.d)	01/11/1918	05/11/1918
War Diary	Gravecourt	06/11/1918	06/11/1918
War Diary	Goeulzin	07/11/1918	07/11/1918
War Diary	Mons-En-Pevele	08/11/1918	10/11/1918
War Diary	Wasmes	11/11/1918	11/11/1918
War Diary	Ellignies-St. Anne	12/11/1918	12/11/1918
War Diary	Belloy	13/11/1918	17/11/1918
War Diary	Brugelette	18/11/1918	18/11/1918
War Diary	Naast	19/11/1918	19/11/1918
War Diary	Belloy	14/11/1918	17/11/1918
War Diary	Brugelette	18/11/1918	18/11/1918
War Diary	Naast	19/11/1918	19/11/1918
War Diary	Belloy	14/11/1918	17/11/1918
War Diary	Brugelette	18/11/1918	18/11/1918
War Diary	Naast	19/11/1918	20/11/1918
War Diary	Rougelette	21/11/1918	22/11/1918
War Diary	Namur	23/11/1918	23/11/1918
War Diary	Envoz-Couthuin	24/11/1918	26/11/1918
War Diary	Sprimont	27/11/1918	29/11/1918
War Diary	Ruy	30/11/1918	30/11/1918
War Diary	Sprimont	29/11/1918	29/11/1918
War Diary	Ruy	30/11/1918	30/11/1918
Heading	War Diary of 2nd Squadron, Machine Gun Corps, Cavalry. December 1918 Volume No. 35		
War Diary	Ruy	01/12/1918	01/12/1918
War Diary	Konzen	02/12/1918	03/12/1918
War Diary	Boich	04/12/1918	04/12/1918
War Diary	Gymnich	05/12/1918	05/12/1918
War Diary	Cologne	06/12/1918	11/12/1918
War Diary	Refrath	12/12/1918	12/12/1918
War Diary	Stumpf	13/12/1918	15/12/1918
War Diary	Gologne (Deutz)	16/12/1918	20/12/1918
War Diary	Cologne	21/12/1918	31/12/1918
Heading	War Diary of 2nd Squadron, Machine Gun Corps. Cavalry January 1919 Volume No 36		
War Diary	Deutz Cologne	01/01/1919	31/01/1919
Heading	War Diary of 2nd Machine Gun Squadron From 1.2.19 To 28.2.19 Volume No. 37		
War Diary	Cologne	01/02/1919	28/02/1919
Miscellaneous			

War Diary	Cologne	01/03/1919	31/03/1919
Heading	WO95/1111/2		
Heading	1914-1918 1st Cavalry Division 2nd Cavalry Brigade 'H' Bty R.H.A. Sep 1914-Mar 1919		
Heading	2nd Cavalry Brigade 1st Cavalry Division. Joined 2nd Cavalry Brigade 28.9.14 "H" Battery R. H. A. 28th September to 31st October 1914		
Heading	H. Battery R. H. A. 1st Cavalry Division Vol III. 20.9-31.10.14		
War Diary		28/09/1914	31/10/1914
Heading	2nd Cavalry Brigade 1st Cavalry Division. "H" Battery R. H. A. November 1914		
War Diary		01/11/1914	30/11/1914
Heading	2nd Cavalry Brigade 1st Cavalry Division "H" Battery R. H. A. December 1914		
Miscellaneous	H. Battery R.H.A.		
Heading	1st Cavalry Division "H" Batty. R H A Vol V January 1915		
War Diary		05/01/1915	08/01/1915
Heading	1st Cavalry Division "H" Battery R H A. Vol VI 1-28.2.15		
War Diary		07/02/1915	23/02/1915
Heading	1st Cavalry Division 2nd Cavalry Bde "H" Batty: R H A. Vol VII 1.3-30.9.15		
War Diary		01/03/1915	30/04/1915
Heading	1st Cavalry Division "H" Batty: R H A. Vol VIII 1-31.5.15		
War Diary		01/05/1915	31/05/1915
Heading	1st Cavalry Division "H" Batty R H A Vol IX 1-30.6.15		
War Diary		00/06/1915	00/06/1915
Heading	1st Cavalry Division "H" Batty R.H.A. Vol X July 1-31-7-15		
War Diary		00/07/1915	00/07/1915
Heading	1st Cavalry Division "H" Batty: R.H.A. Vol XI August to Sept. 15		
War Diary		11/08/1915	30/09/1915
Heading	1st Cavalry Division "H" Batty R.H.A. Oct 1915 Vol XII		
War Diary		01/10/1915	31/10/1915
Heading	1st Cavalry "H" Batty R H A. Nov-Dec 1915 Vol 11&12		
War Diary		01/11/1915	31/12/1915
Heading	1st Cavalry "H" Bty R H A. Jan 1916 Vol 13		
War Diary		01/01/1916	19/03/1916
War Diary	Beussent	00/00/1916	00/05/1916
War Diary		01/06/1916	30/06/1916
Heading	War Diary of "H" Battery. R.H.A. for the Month of July. 1916 Volune. XXIV		
War Diary		01/07/1916	24/07/1916
Heading	War Diary of "H" Battery. R. H. A. for the Month of August. 1916 Volume X X V.		
War Diary	Querrieu	01/08/1916	10/08/1916
War Diary	Gousseauville	11/08/1916	19/08/1916
Heading	War Diary of "H" Battery R.H.A 1st Cavalry Division September 1916 Volume No XXVI		

War Diary	Gousseauville	01/09/1916	06/09/1916
War Diary	Allery	07/09/1916	07/09/1916
War Diary	La Neuville	08/09/1916	14/09/1916
War Diary	Carnoy	15/09/1916	17/09/1916
War Diary	La Neuville	18/09/1916	25/09/1916
War Diary	Fresnoy	26/09/1916	30/09/1916
Heading	War Diary of "H" Battery. R. H. A. for the month of October. 1916 Volume. XXVII		
War Diary	Fresnoy	01/10/1916	19/10/1916
War Diary	Boffles	20/10/1916	20/10/1916
War Diary	St Leger Les Domart	22/10/1916	22/10/1916
War Diary	Mesnil	24/10/1916	31/10/1916
Heading	War Diary of "H" Battery Royal Horse Artillery for November 1916 Volume XXVIII		
War Diary	Mesnil	01/11/1916	21/11/1916
War Diary	Rubempre	22/11/1916	22/11/1916
War Diary	Bertaucourt	23/11/1916	23/11/1916
War Diary	St Riquier	24/11/1916	24/11/1916
War Diary	Quilen	25/11/1916	25/11/1916
War Diary	Ergny	26/11/1916	30/11/1916
Heading	War Diary of "H" Battery Royal Horse Art. December 1916 Volume no. XXIX		
Miscellaneous	19th Division No. G.223		
Heading	1st Cavalry Division 2nd Cavalry Brigade 'H' Battery R.H.A. Jan-Dec 1917		
Heading	War Diary of "H" Battery Royal Horse Out January 1917 Volume No XXX		
War Diary	2nd Army Artillery School Tilques	01/01/1919	31/01/1919
Heading	War Diary of "H" Battery Royal Horse Artillery February 1917 Volume No XXXI		
War Diary		26/02/1917	26/02/1917
Heading	War Diary of "H" Battery Royal Horse Artillery March 1917 Volume XXXII		
War Diary	Tilques	01/03/1917	08/03/1917
War Diary	Ergny	09/03/1917	17/03/1917
War Diary	Wierre Au Bois	18/03/1917	31/03/1917
Heading	War Diary of "H" Battery Royal Horse Artillery April 1917 Vol. XXXIII		
War Diary	Wierre Au Bois	01/04/1917	05/04/1917
War Diary	Ergny	07/04/1917	07/04/1917
War Diary	Monchy	08/04/1917	08/04/1917
War Diary	Frevent Capelle	10/04/1917	10/04/1917
War Diary	St Laurent Blangy	11/04/1917	11/04/1917
War Diary	Frevent Capelle	12/04/1917	12/04/1917
War Diary	Linzeux	17/04/1917	19/04/1917
War Diary	Loison	19/04/1917	29/04/1917
Heading	War Diary of "H" Battery Royal Horse Artillery May 1917 Volume No. XXXIV		
War Diary	Loison	01/05/1917	13/05/1917
War Diary	Petigny	14/05/1917	14/05/1917
War Diary	St Hilaire	15/05/1917	15/05/1917
War Diary	Quentin	16/05/1917	17/05/1917
War Diary	Locon	18/05/1917	18/05/1917
War Diary	Le Touret	19/05/1917	31/05/1917
Heading	War Diary of "H" Battery Royal Horse Artillery June-1917 Volume No. XXXV		

War Diary	Festubert	01/06/1917	03/06/1917
War Diary	Locon	04/06/1917	11/06/1917
War Diary	Quentin	11/06/1917	11/06/1917
War Diary	Le Hamel	13/06/1917	18/06/1917
War Diary	Festubert	19/06/1917	19/06/1917
War Diary	Le Hamel	21/06/1917	21/06/1917
War Diary	Petit Sains	24/06/1917	30/06/1917
Heading	War Diary of "H" Battery Royal Horse Artillery July 1917 Vol. XXXVI		
War Diary	Angres	01/07/1917	01/07/1917
War Diary	Petit	03/07/1917	03/07/1917
War Diary	Sains	04/07/1917	04/07/1917
War Diary	Estaires	05/07/1917	15/07/1917
War Diary	Quentin	19/07/1917	19/07/1917
War Diary	Mount Bernenchon	22/07/1917	31/07/1917
Miscellaneous	Copy of Letter Received From G.O.C. Cavalry Corps.	28/07/1917	28/07/1917
Heading	War Diary of "H" Battery Royal Horse Artillery volume XXXVII August. 1917		
War Diary	Mont Bernenchon	01/08/1917	27/08/1917
War Diary	Vincly	28/08/1917	28/08/1917
War Diary	Menty	29/08/1917	31/08/1917
Heading	War Diary of "H" Battery Royal Horse Artillery September 1917 Volume XXXVIII		
War Diary	Menty	01/09/1917	30/09/1917
Heading	War Diary of "H" Battery Royal Horse Artillery October 1917 Volume XXXIX		
War Diary	Menty	04/10/1917	06/10/1917
War Diary	Watten	07/10/1917	08/10/1917
War Diary	Houtkerke	08/10/1917	12/10/1917
War Diary	Ruminghem	12/10/1917	13/10/1917
War Diary	Menty	15/10/1917	15/10/1917
War Diary	Hucqueliers	23/10/1917	29/10/1917
Heading	War Diary of "H" Battery Royal Horse Artillery November 1917 Volume XL		
War Diary	Hucqueliers	10/11/1917	10/11/1917
War Diary	Lebiez	11/11/1917	11/11/1917
War Diary	Barly	12/11/1917	12/11/1917
War Diary	Bavelincourt	13/11/1917	13/11/1917
War Diary	Etinehem	14/11/1917	14/11/1917
War Diary	Courcelles	15/11/1917	19/11/1917
War Diary	Fins	19/11/1917	20/11/1917
War Diary	Marcoing	21/11/1917	22/11/1917
War Diary	Metz	23/11/1917	23/11/1917
War Diary	Metz En Couture	24/11/1917	24/11/1917
War Diary	Boursies	25/11/1917	30/11/1917
Heading	War Diary of "H" Battery Royal Horse Artillery December 1917 Volume XLI		
War Diary	Boursies	01/12/1917	01/12/1917
War Diary	Doignies	03/12/1917	03/12/1917
War Diary	Louverval	04/12/1917	05/12/1917
War Diary	Beugny	07/12/1917	08/12/1917
War Diary	Boucly	08/12/1917	09/12/1917
War Diary	Templeux	10/12/1917	31/12/1917
Heading	War Diary of "H" Battery Royal Horse Artillery January- 1918 Volume XLII		
War Diary	Templeux le Guerard	01/01/1918	23/01/1918

War Diary	Jean Court		23/01/1918	31/01/1918
Heading	War Diary of "H" Battery Royal Horse Artillery February-1918-Volume XLIII			
War Diary	Jean Court		01/02/1918	31/02/1918
Heading	War Diary of "H" Battery Royal Horse Artillery March-1918 Volume XLIV			
War Diary	Jean Court		01/03/1918	14/03/1918
War Diary	Vraignes		15/03/1918	15/03/1918
War Diary	Mons		21/03/1918	21/03/1918
War Diary	Roisel		22/03/1918	22/03/1918
War Diary	Brusle		22/03/1918	22/03/1918
War Diary	Lecatalet		23/03/1918	23/03/1918
War Diary	Brie Barleux		24/03/1918	24/03/1918
War Diary	Berny-En Santerre		24/03/1918	24/03/1918
War Diary	Soyecourt		25/03/1918	26/03/1918
War Diary	Caix		27/03/1918	28/03/1918
War Diary	Castell		29/03/1918	29/03/1918
War Diary	Hangard		29/03/1918	29/03/1918
War Diary	Cachy		30/03/1918	30/03/1918
War Diary	Gentelles		31/03/1918	02/04/1918
War Diary			21/03/1918	02/04/1918
War Diary	Amiens		04/04/1918	09/04/1918
War Diary	Renancourt		10/04/1918	10/04/1918
War Diary	Rougefay		11/04/1918	11/04/1918
War Diary	Aubrometz		12/04/1918	12/04/1918
War Diary	Lis Bourg		14/04/1918	14/04/1918
War Diary	Fiefs		16/04/1918	16/04/1918
War Diary	Greuppe		27/04/1918	27/04/1918
War Diary			12/04/1918	22/04/1918
War Diary	Ergny		01/12/1918	17/12/1918
War Diary	Tilques		22/12/1918	22/12/1918
Heading	War Diary of "H" Battery Royal Horse Artillery April-1918 Volume XLV			
War Diary	St Remy Aux Bois		01/06/1918	30/06/1918
War Diary	Villeroy Sur Authie		30/06/1918	30/06/1918
War Diary	Frohen-Le Grand		01/07/1918	02/07/1918
War Diary	Canaples		02/07/1918	04/07/1918
War Diary	Villers		04/07/1918	06/07/1918
War Diary	Rainecheval		06/07/1918	28/07/1918
War Diary	Thievres		28/07/1918	05/08/1918
War Diary	Havernas		06/08/1918	06/08/1918
War Diary	S: Sauveur		07/08/1918	07/08/1918
War Diary	Glisy-Longeau		08/08/1918	08/08/1918
War Diary	Caix		08/08/1918	09/08/1918
War Diary	Vrely		09/08/1918	11/08/1918
War Diary	Caix		11/08/1918	11/08/1918
War Diary	Camon		12/08/1918	14/08/1918
War Diary	Gezaincourt		15/08/1918	15/08/1918
War Diary	Beauvoir Riviere		16/08/1918	18/08/1918
War Diary	Warlincourt		19/08/1918	21/08/1918
War Diary	Sarton		22/08/1918	25/08/1918
War Diary	Goliy En Ternois		26/08/1918	31/08/1918
War Diary	Etree-Wamin		01/09/1918	16/09/1918
War Diary	Linzeux		17/09/1918	17/09/1918
War Diary	Villeroy-Sur-Authie		18/09/1918	18/09/1918
War Diary	Mezerolles		24/09/1918	24/09/1918

War Diary	Sarton	25/09/1918	25/09/1918
War Diary	Aveluy	26/09/1918	26/09/1918
War Diary	Vaux Wood	29/09/1918	29/09/1918
War Diary	Hamelet	30/09/1918	30/09/1918
War Diary	Roisel	01/10/1918	03/10/1918
War Diary	Hesbe Court	07/10/1918	08/10/1918
War Diary	Gowy-St Martin	09/10/1918	09/10/1918
War Diary	Maretz	10/10/1918	13/10/1918
War Diary	Coulain-Court	14/10/1918	06/11/1918
War Diary	Creve Cover	07/11/1918	07/11/1918
War Diary	Goeulzin	08/11/1918	08/11/1918
War Diary	Mons En Pevele	10/11/1918	10/11/1918
War Diary	Vezon	11/11/1918	11/11/1918
War Diary	Beloeul	12/11/1918	12/11/1918
War Diary	Mortagne	17/11/1918	17/11/1918
War Diary	Lens	18/11/1918	18/11/1918
War Diary	Mignault	21/11/1918	21/11/1918
War Diary	Wagnalee	22/11/1918	22/11/1918
War Diary	Dhuy	24/11/1918	24/11/1918
War Diary	Wanze	27/11/1918	27/11/1918
War Diary	Fraiture	29/11/1918	29/11/1918
War Diary	Moulin-Du Ruy	30/11/1918	01/12/1918
War Diary	Hofen	04/12/1918	04/12/1918
War Diary	Heimbach	05/12/1918	05/12/1918
War Diary	Wissersheim	06/12/1918	06/12/1918
War Diary	Mungersdorf Cologne	12/12/1918	12/12/1918
War Diary	Berg Gladbach	13/12/1918	13/12/1918
War Diary	Kurten	16/12/1918	16/12/1918
War Diary	Cologne		
Heading	War Diary of "H" Battery Royal Horse Artillery May 1918 Volume-XLVI		
War Diary	Cuhem	01/05/1918	06/05/1918
War Diary	Petigny	21/05/1918	21/05/1918
War Diary	St. Michel	22/05/1918	22/05/1918
War Diary		14/05/1918	14/05/1918
War Diary	Cologne on the R.Hine Germany	01/01/1919	20/01/1919
War Diary	Cologne	01/02/1919	31/03/1919
Heading	WO95/1111/3		
Heading	1st Cavalry Division "L" Battery R. H. A. 5th August to 19th October 1914		
War Diary	Aldershot	05/08/1914	16/08/1914
War Diary	France	17/08/1914	24/08/1914
Diagram etc	Rough Sketch To Illustrate Action On Aug 24.		
War Diary		25/08/1914	01/09/1914
Diagram etc	Rough Sketch on Action at Nery on Sept		
War Diary		02/09/1914	19/10/1914
Heading	WO95/1111/4		
Heading	1917 1st Cavalry Division 2nd Cavalry Pioneer Battn Jan-Mar 1917		
Heading	War Diary of 2nd Cavalry Pioneer Battalion for the Month of January. 1917		
War Diary	Tincques	11/01/1917	31/01/1917
Heading	War Diary of 2nd Cavalry Brigade Pioneer Battalion for the month of February 1917		
War Diary	Tincques	01/02/1917	28/02/1917

Heading	War Diary of 2nd Cavalry Brigade Pioneer Battalion for the month of March 1917		
War Diary	Tincques	01/03/1917	13/03/1917

B.E.F. FRANCE & FLANDERS.

1 CAVALRY DIVISION.
2 CAVALRY BRIGADE.
2 MACHINE GUN SQUADRON.
1916 FEB TO 1919 MAR.
'H' BATTERY ROYAL HORSE ARTILLERY.
1914 SEPT TO 1919 MAR.
'L' BATTERY R.H.A.
1914 AUG TO 1914 OCT.
2 CAVALRY PIONEER BN.
1917 JAN TO 1917 MAR.

B.E.F. FRANCE & FLANDERS

1 CAVALRY DIVISION.
2 CAVALRY BRIGADE.

2 MACHINE GUN SQUADRON.
1916 FEB TO 1919 MAR.

'H' BATTERY ROYAL HORSE ARTILLERY.
1914 SEPT TO 1919 MAR.

'L' BATTERY R.H.A.
1914 AUG TO 1914 OCT.

2 ~~CAVALRY~~ BRIGADE PIONEER BN.
1917 JAN TO 1917 MAR.

no ops 1/11/50 1/1111/1

1916-1918
1ST CAVALRY DIVISION
2ND CAVALRY BRIGADE.

2ND SQDN MACH. GUN CORPS

FEB 1916 - ~~DEC 1918~~ MAR 1919

FORMED 1916 FEB

TO LANCERS BDE

Box 1166

Army Form C. 2118

WAR DIARY

INTELLIGENCE SUMMARY

(Erase heading not required.)

Instructions regarding War Diaries and Intelligence Summaries are contained in F.S. Regs, Part II. and the Staff Manual respectively. Title Pages will be prepared in manuscript.

Place	Date	Hour	Summary of Events and Information	Remarks and references to Appendices
			TINCQUES. 2nd Cavalry Brigade Pioneer Battalion	
TINCQUES	3rd January. 1917.		Billets and Huts. Battalion arrived at 2 a.m. and marched to Billets; very indifferent arrangements for detraining horses and wagons. Day spent in cleaning up and settling into Billets.	
TINCQUES	4th January. 1917.		Billets and Huts. Work on Railway; each company being allotted a section of the work. 2/Lieutenant Hunter admitted to Hospital.	
TINCQUES.	5th January. 1917.		Billets and Huts. Parades:- Work on railway continued.	
TINCQUES	6th January. 1917.		Huts and billets. Parades. Work on railway continued: much time lost owing to traffic on railway.	
TINCQUES	7th January 1917.		Huts and Billets. Parades:- Work on Railway; delays again occurred owing to works train having to proceed to siding to allow of traffic on the permanent line. Two Other Ranks to Hospital.	
TINCQUES	8th January. 1917.		Huts and billets. No work on Railway. Men had baths and employed cleaning billets.	
TINCQUES	9th January. 1917.		Huts and Billets. Parades:- Work on railway continued; frequent interruptions of work owing to railway traffic.	
TINCQUES	10th January. 1917.		Huts and Billets. Parades:-G.O.C. 1st Cavalry Division inspected men at work on railway and the billets. Work generally interfered with owing to traffic on railway.	

Place	Date	Hour	Summary of Events and Information	Remarks and references to Appendices
ENQUIN	28/2/16		The 2nd Machine Gun Squadron came into being on this date and formed a unit in the Machine Gun Corps. Captain L.C. Haslam was appointed to command with the following officers as section leaders.	

Lt. J.A. Anglewood 4th Dragoon Guards
Temp 2/Lt G. Dent 4th Dragoon Guards
Lt. D.F.G. Duff 9th Lancers
2/Lt. S.H. Le Roy Rokeising 9th Lancers
Lt. C.H. Miller 18th Hussars
2/Lt F.W. Pink 18th Hussars

4317 S.Q.M.S. F.E. Sharp, 9th Lancers was appointed Squadron Serjeant Major.
5216 Serjeant A.J. Hargreaves 4th D.G's was appointed S.Q.M.S.
3838 Shoeing Smith Corporal J. Little, 18th Hussars was appointed Farrier.

The H.Q. of the Squadron was established at ENQUIN, as no suitable area could be found for the Squadron

Army Form C. 2118

WAR DIARY
or
INTELLIGENCE SUMMARY
(Erase heading not required.)

Instructions regarding War Diaries and Intelligence Summaries are contained in F.S. Regs., Part II. and the Staff Manual respectively. Title Pages will be prepared in manuscript.

Place	Date	Hour	Summary of Events and Information	Remarks and references to Appendices
ENQUIN	28/2/16		The section was distributed as follows:— Lt. Aylewood with the H.Q. 4th D.G's at BERNEUILLES. Lt. DENT — ENQUIN. Lt. MILLER with the H.Q. 18th Hussars at ALETTE. 2/Lt. PINK — ENQUIN. Lt. DUFF — SEHEM. 2/Lt. LeRoy Lewis — LE ROCQUE.	JCA.
"	29/2/16		Training commenced on this date with equitation in the morning, mechanism revenge finding in the afternoon. The C.O inspected the pack-saddlery of the 4th D.G section at 9-0 A.M.	JCA.
"	1/3/16		Equitation, driving drill and section drill was undertaken in the morning; in the afternoon Range finding class judging distance.	JCA.
"	2/3/16		Training was continued on this day before. At 11-0 A.M. the G.O.C. held a casting parade for the Brigade at BEUSSENT.	JCA.

Army Form C. 2118

WAR DIARY
or
INTELLIGENCE SUMMARY
(Erase heading not required.)

Instructions regarding War Diaries and Intelligence Summaries are contained in F.S. Regs., Part II. and the Staff Manual respectively. Title Pages will be prepared in manuscript.

Place	Date	Hour	Summary of Events and Information	Remarks and references to Appendices
ENQUIN	2/3/16		Ten out of seventeen horses thrown up by the squadron were disposed of.	JCH
"	3/3/16		Route march was undertaken in the morning - route BEUSSENT - BOIS RATEL - PREURES - ENQUIN. 6861 L/C FISHER & T. D.G's & 22227 H/C ROBINSON 18th Hus ars left for a Vickers course at WISQUES.	JCH
"	4/3/16		The Squadron took part in a brigade route march, rendez-vous the T roads ENQUIN. Marching order.	JCH
"	5/3/16		Detachment of the two sections at ENQUIN attended Church parade at PREURES.	JCH
"	6/3/16		Driving drill, equitation section drill took place in the morning. Trench digging, Range finding class a elementary drill in the afternoon.	JCH
"	7/3/16		Route march was undertaken, route DOUDEAUVILLE, DALLE, ENQUIN	JCH

WAR DIARY
or
INTELLIGENCE SUMMARY

Army Form C. 2118

Place	Date	Hour	Summary of Events and Information	Remarks and references to Appendices
ENQUIN	8/3/16		Training was continued with driving drill. Range Practice. Saddle inspection after stables. Trench digging & range finding in the afternoon.	JCA
"	9/3/16		Driving drill, section drill, elementary mounted action in the morning. Kit inspection in the afternoon.	JCA
"	10/3/16		Training was continued as the day before – at 12-30 the C.O. inspected the horses of the two gth Lancer sections.	JCA
"	11/3/16		The Squadron took part in a divisional route march route Y words N of BERNEVILLES out main war – SEQUIERES – ROLET – ENQUIN – Purdey – war × rds W of ENQUIN.	JCA
"	12/3/16		Church parade at PREURES. Lt Anglesmore & Lt Miller moved their section into their billets at DALLE.	JCA
"	13/3/16		In the morning action drill, mounted action & squadron drill. afternoon Rangefinders class, Trench digging – mechanism.	JCA

WAR DIARY
or
INTELLIGENCE SUMMARY

Army Form C. 2118

Place	Date	Hour	Summary of Events and Information	Remarks and references to Appendices
ENQUIN	14/3/16		The Route march arranged for the day was cancelled owing to the weather. Section from this date were attached from A to F. in the new 4th D.G's, 9th Lancers, 18th Hussars.	JCH.
"	15/3/16		Elementary range practice was undertaken in the morning, range finding class, machine gun and return in the afternoon by C.O.	JCH.
"	16/3/16		Section drill, mounted action, squadron drill and action by C.O. In the afternoon Judging distance and Kit inspection. Two men to temporary hospital.	JCH.
"	17/3/16		Route march - BEUSSENT - MONTCAVREL and back.	JCH.
"	18/3/16		Range practice. Saddle inspection.	JCH.
"	19/3/16		Church Parade. 2/Lt. HARTNELL was selected to attend a course of telephony at Div. mounted H.Q. commencing 20th.	JCH.

Army Form C. 2118

WAR DIARY
or
INTELLIGENCE SUMMARY
(Erase heading not required.)

Instructions regarding War Diaries and Intelligence Summaries are contained in F.S. Regs., Part II. and the Staff Manual respectively. Title Pages will be prepared in manuscript.

Place	Date	Hour	Summary of Events and Information	Remarks and references to Appendices
ENQUIN	20/3/16		Twice daily training commenced with section drill, dismounted action and squadron drill in the morning. Range finding class & mechanism in the afternoon.	JCA
"	21/3/16		Route march, a marked improvement is now evident in the march discipline in the Squadron.	JCA
"	22/3/16		Elementary Range practices. The C.O. inspected the horses of B and E Sections at 12-0. noon.	JCA
"	23/3/16		Section drill, dismounted action, squadron drill was carried on in the morning. Lecture by C.O. of judging distances in the afternoon.	JCA
"	24/3/16		Route march. At 2-30 the horses of B & F Sections were inspected by the veterinary Officer. Three men to temporary hospital.	JCA
"	25/3/16		Range practice and saddle inspection.	JCA

WAR DIARY or INTELLIGENCE SUMMARY

Army Form C. 2118

(Erase heading not required.)

Place	Date	Hour	Summary of Events and Information	Remarks and references to Appendices
ENQUIN	26/3/16		Church parade, the O.C. inspected the horses of A & E section during stables.	JCA
"	27/3/16		Driving drill, Squadron drill dismounted action in the morning, range firing class Standard test in the afternoon.	JCA
"	28/3/16		A Route march was carried out via PARENTY – DOUDEAUVILLE – BEZINGHEM	JCA
"	29/3/16		Driving drill was continued also range practices in the morning. Range finding class and vehicles in semaphore during the afternoon.	JCA
"	30/3/16		Mounted drill, driving was undertaken in the afternoon also the waggons of the Squadron were inspected at ENQUINKHUS by the O.C. A.S.C.	JCA
"	31/3/16		Route march. The C.O. inspected the harness everywhere.	JCA

J. Haslam Captain
31.3.16

Army Form C. 2118

WAR DIARY
or
INTELLIGENCE SUMMARY
(Erase heading not required.)

Instructions regarding War Diaries and Intelligence Summaries are contained in F.S. Regs., Part II. and the Staff Manual respectively. Title Pages will be prepared in manuscript.

Place	Date	Hour	Summary of Events and Information	Remarks and references to Appendices
ENQUIN	1/4/16		Training in Driving drill - Range practices. Saddle inspection in the afternoon, the divisional marathon took place	JCH
"	2/4/16		Church parade. The Royal Wilts Yeomanry machine gun section received the training. They were billeted at BERNEUILS, Lt. RICE was the officer in charge.	JCH
"	3/4/16		Driving drill section drill, mounted action war scheme in the morning. Mechanism - range finding - class in the afternoon. One man to temporary hospital.	JCH
"	4/4/16		The O.C. inspected the lines of A + E section at 8.30 a.m. section by C.O. to the Wilts Yeomanry section during the afternoon. One man to temporary hospital.	JCH
"	5/4/16		The Wilts Yeomanry were inspected by C.O. in section drill and mounted action. in the afternoon Judging distances and foot drill.	JCH
"	6/4/16		The Squadron was practised in ceremonial drill for the inspection by the G.O.C. 1st Army.	JCH

WAR DIARY
or
INTELLIGENCE SUMMARY

(Erase heading not required.)

Army Form C. 2118

Instructions regarding War Diaries and Intelligence Summaries are contained in F. S. Regs., Part II. and the Staff Manual respectively. Title Pages will be prepared in manuscript.

Place	Date	Hour	Summary of Events and Information	Remarks and references to Appendices
ENQUIN	3/4/16		The Rehearsal for the inspection by G.O.C 1st Army took place. The brigade rendez-vous at X rds ¼ mile W. of HUBERSENT and marched to DANNE. Practice parade took place on the Sands. Two men to temporary hospital.	DLH
"	6/4/16		Squadron horses were given light exercise after the hard day's march on the 7th. The wills-from any were inoculated on the range by the C.O.	DLH

Army Form C. 2118

WAR DIARY
or
INTELLIGENCE SUMMARY
(Erase heading not required.)

Instructions regarding War Diaries and Intelligence Summaries are contained in F.S. Regs., Part II. and the Staff Manual respectively. Title Pages will be prepared in manuscript.

Place	Date	Hour	Summary of Events and Information	Remarks and references to Appendices
ENQUIN	9/4/16		Church parade	JCH.
"	10/4/16		The Wilts Yeomanry section were instructed by C.O. in dismounted action behind features of the ground. The use of cover etc. The remainder carried out mounted action gradience range finding class was commenced under Lt Pink. In the afternoon section classes in semaphore were also started under the trained signallers.	JCH.
	11/4/16		The mounted manoeuvre for today was interrupted by the weather, sections were dismissed on reaching BEUSSENT. The CO inspected the H.Q. transport at 8·15 a.m.	JCH.
	12/4/16		Range practice for all sections in the morning. The Wilts Yeomanry section firing. We entrained the C.O. inspected the Wilts Yeomanry section - firing. We entrained all the horses of the Squadron. At 11·0 a.m. the D.D.V.S. inspected all the horses of the Squadron. Semaphore classes were carried on in the afternoon. A.C. six pack fine JCH arrived from the base.	JCH.

Army Form C. 2118

WAR DIARY
or
INTELLIGENCE SUMMARY
(Erase heading not required.)

Instructions regarding War Diaries and Intelligence Summaries are contained in F.S. Regs., Part II. and the Staff Manual respectively. Title Pages will be prepared in manuscript.

Place	Date	Hour	Summary of Events and Information	Remarks and references to Appendices
ENQUIN	13/4/16		Both morning section drill, mounted drill and advanced musketerie was continued. The semaphore class worked in the afternoon.	JCA.
	14/4/16		All section parades with their waggons at ENQUIN, ceremonial drill was practised in view after inspection by G.O.C. 1st Army with 17th Semaphore Class in the afternoon. Two men to Tenguay hospital.	JCA.
	15/4/16		Range practice was held in the morning, afternoon saddle inspection. Two men returned from Tenguay hospital.	JCA.
	16/4/16		The section attended Church Parade	JCA.
	17/4/16		The squadron took part in the inspection by the G.O.C. 1st Army on the sands N.W. of DANNE. Brigade gave the General Salute in line, then the march past at the trot finally forming up in Brigade Mass. N.G. Squadron turn out was six guns in lines. The eighteen limbers behind in three lines.	JCA.

Army Form C. 2118

WAR DIARY
or
INTELLIGENCE SUMMARY
(Erase heading not required.)

Instructions regarding War Diaries and Intelligence Summaries are contained in F. S. Regs., Part II. and the Staff Manual respectively. Title Pages will be prepared in manuscript.

Place	Date	Hour	Summary of Events and Information	Remarks and references to Appendices
ENQUIN	18/4/16		The Horses were given a light exercise, however carried out range practice in the morning. In the afternoon a test of semaphore signalling was held – all men fifteen were du minere. One man rejoined from hospital.	JCH.
	19/4/16		Training in Squadron drill, dismounted action and advance range firing was carried on in the morning. Backward men in Signalling carried on their training. The men amid practiced Description occupation of objects. In the memory	EK.
	20/4/16		The training was identical with the day before. In the afternoon twelve men paraded for foot-drill.	JCH.
	21/4/16		Good Friday. The sections attended Church parade. One man to hospital.	JCH.
	22/4/16		Range practices were gone through & the range finders. Class was renewing my officer from hospital. held. The M.G. Section Duke of Hanee &/w/ Freeman arrived detaining	JCH.

1875 Wt. W593/826 1,000,000 4/15 J.B.C. & A. A.D.S.S./Forms/C.2118.

WAR DIARY
INTELLIGENCE SUMMARY

Army Form C. 2118

Place	Date	Hour	Summary of Events and Information	Remarks and references to Appendices
ENQUIN	23/4/16		The section attended Church parade. Divisional Service conducted by Divisional Commander. Temporary hospital. DESVRES. Two changes and one pack horse came up from the base.	Lt.
	24/4/16		Easter Monday was granted as a holiday by Divisional Commander. O.C. Man discharged from hospital. Two men rejoining from base temporary hospital.	Lt.
	25/4/16		The squadron took part in a Divisional scheme. The 1st Brigade — the 2nd Brigade were White. The White force advancing from the East were opposing Khaki forces invading from the West. Special there White was to deny the crossing of the River from ENQUIN to RECQUES. Khaki — the 2nd Brigade seizes the high ground at CAMP RACQUET with the 4th DG's in advance — but failed to gain possession of the whole ridge after enemy it provide from crossing at BEUSSENT & RECQUES. The 18th Hussars were ordered to stop its advance to ENQUIN HAUT. Mitrailleuse Squadron was detailed to each Regiment — the machinery throw were under the O.C. Squadron. One section came into action on the ridge BOIS DE CARROY & provided the attack on	

1875 Wt. W593/826 1,000,000 4/15 J.B.C. & A. A.D.S.S./Forms/C. 2118.

Army Form C. 2118

WAR DIARY or INTELLIGENCE SUMMARY

(Erase heading not required.)

Place	Date	Hour	Summary of Events and Information	Remarks and references to Appendices
ENQUIN	25/4/16		An ENQUIN HOUT with covering fire. Attacks was undertaken by Ptes Khamun & envelopes. The enemy's left via PARENTY.	JCLy.
	26/4/16		Several discharges from enemy's hospital. Enemy injuries from [?] hospital. Advanced Range practices class was continued under Lt. Pirele. Two Rifle Grenades + Germany was included in section drills and air mortar action by the C.O. In the afternoon signalling for rearward men stopping balance. Lecture on the flight of the bullet thro' the German section by C.O. German to hospital.	JCLy.
	27/4/16		Range practices by all sections including the Germany section. Kit inspection start drill in the afternoon. Lecture in afternoon on indirect fire to German section by C.O. German to Empress hospital.	JCLy.
	28/4/16		The hut summer meeting plan came into free from this date. British warren are evacuated and enough pad reserves from sand. Two men return for men in inlet rifle powder spirit in turn here bags. That arriving under taken was the same as for the 26th inst.	JCLy.

1875 Wt. W593/826 1,000,000 4/15 J.B.C. & A. A.D.S.S./Forms/C. 2118.

WAR DIARY
or
INTELLIGENCE SUMMARY

Army Form C. 2118

Place	Date	Hour	Summary of Events and Information	Remarks and references to Appendices
ENQUIN	29/4/16		Asquilum Competition was held in the morning - the following were the clises 1. 2 best horses at man above for section. 2. Section jumping one per section. 3. Packhorse. Two per section. (point of the horse, turning in leading & jumping wire (udged on) 3 per section. 4. Best horses at broken wheres.	J.Ct.
	30/4/16		The Yeomany section carried out range practices. The Section attended Church parade. One NCO rejoined from hospital.	J.Ct. J Harlowe Capt 2nd Kings SR OC 2nd Kings 30.4.4.

Army Form C. 2118

● WAR DIARY
—or—
INTELLIGENCE SUMMARY
(Erase heading not required.)

War Diary
of
2nd Machine Gun Squadron
— 2nd Cavalry Brigade —
for
May 1916.

J.C. Hogan Captain
Comdg 2nd Machine Gun Squadron

WAR DIARY
or
INTELLIGENCE SUMMARY

(Erase heading not required.)

Army Form C. 2118

Instructions regarding War Diaries and Intelligence Summaries are contained in F.S. Regs., Part II. and the Staff Manual respectively. Title Pages will be prepared in manuscript.

Place	Date	Hour	Summary of Events and Information	Remarks and references to Appendices
ENQUIN.	May 1st	Morning	Training — Scheme on the Camp Rac @ Det Ridge. 1 section of the Duke of Lancaster's Machine Guns, attached for training took part in the scheme	J.C.H.
"	2nd	Morning	Training. — All actions carried out long range machine gun practice. The C.O. took the D. of L. Yeo; section in long range firing	J.C.H.
"	"	afternoon	" — Foot-drill.	J.C.H.
"	3rd	morning	" — Advanced Range finding and dismounted action. Also a saddle inspection	J.C.H.
"	"	afternoon	" — Semaphore for backward men.	J.C.H.
"	4th	morning	" — Brigade scheme.	J.C.H.
"	5th	morning	" — Stables.	J.C.H.
"	"	afternoon	" — Range practice, D. of L. Section took part. Practice was interrupted by weather.	J.C.H.
"	6th	morning	" — Saddle inspection	J.C.H.
"	"	afternoon	" — Church Parade. V.O. inspects remounts that had been isolated & passed them fit for duty.	J.C.H.
"	7th	morning	" —	J.C.H.
"	8th	morning	Weather prevents Training. Heavy Rains.	J.C.H.
"	9th	"	" —	J.C.H.
"	10th	morning	Training — Each section carried out Range practice. Semaphore. "C" Section isolated owing to a case of German measles.	J.C.H.
"	"	afternoon	" —	J.C.H.
"	11th	morning	" — Advanced range finding & Section drill.	J.C.H.
"	"	afternoon	" — Semaphore.	J.C.H.

Army Form C. 2118

WAR DIARY
or
INTELLIGENCE SUMMARY
(Erase heading not required.)

Instructions regarding War Diaries and Intelligence Summaries are contained in F.S. Regs., Part II. and the Staff Manual respectively. Title Pages will be prepared in manuscript.

Place	Date	Hour	Summary of Events and Information	Remarks and references to Appendices
ENQUIN.	May. 12th		Training. C and D Sections carried out a short scheme with B and F sections. Section officers umpired.	JCH
"	13th	morning	Squadron Leader and signalling attended a Divisional scheme. Bulk of Squadron given reference to their work. Epérou and Stable. Range practice. D section carried out bombing practice.	JCH
"	14th		Church Parade at PREURES.	JCH
"	15th		Exercise + stables. Rain interfered with training	JCH
"	16th			JCH
"	17th	morning	Squadron scheme, around DOUDEAUVILLE. A competition was held, including the following classes. 1. Best limber and team (1 per section) won by A. Section. 2. Best pack horse + man (one per section) won by B section. 3. Best troop horse, won by E section. 4 Section jumping won by F. Section. R.C.O. jumping won by Capt. Bull.	JCH
"	18th		Sections carried out mounted field practice, taking up positions for the defence, having particular regard to the features of the ground.	JCH
"	"	afternoon	Range finding and signalling	
"	19th		The squadron took part in a divisional scheme.	JCH
"	20th		Brigade horse show. The squadron won 1st prize in the Pack-horse class, and 3rd in both limbers and troop horse.	JCH
"	21st		Church Parade. C section carried out inspection by Capt. Bull.	JCH
"	22nd	morning	A + E Sections carried out long range firing, with the light + heavy tripod. The remaining sections carried out field work	JCH
"	"	afternoon	Squadron Feadron practice and inspection of B+F sections limbers on the reduced scale	
"	23rd	morning	B+F. Long range practice. Remainder. Field work.	JCH
"	"	afternoon	Feadron practice and inspection of A + E sections limbers on the reduced scale	JCH

WAR DIARY
or
INTELLIGENCE SUMMARY

(Erase heading not required.)

Army Form C. 2118

Instructions regarding War Diaries and Intelligence Summaries are contained in F.S. Regs., Part II. and the Staff Manual respectively. Title Pages will be prepared in manuscript.

Place	Date	Hour	Summary of Events and Information	Remarks and references to Appendices
ENQVIN.	May 24th	morning	All sections fired on the 25 yds range.	JCH.
"	"	afternoon	Flexation practice and inspection of C & D sections limbers on the reduced scale	HCH.
"	25th	morning	All training cancelled owing to heavy rain	
"	"	afternoon	Flexation practice. The Vet. O. inspected the horses of A, E & C sections	JCH.
"	26th		C & D Sections fired on the long range.	JCH.
"	27th		All sections practiced on the 25 yds range	JCH.
"	28		Divine Service	JCH.
"	29th	morning	The G.O.C. 1st Cav Div. inspected the squadron. A small scheme was undertaken.	JCH.
"	"	11-0 am	9 horses were cast by the G.O.C.	
"	"	afternoon	Stables.	
"	30th		A and E Sections moved from DALLE, into bivouac at ENQVIN, also D Section moved from SEHEN to bivouac at ENQVIN. The whole squadron is now together. B & C Sections, carried out long range practice.	JCH.
"	31st	morning	The Squadron H.Q. and Section officers, took part in a tactical ride under the G.O.C. The problem of consolidating a position in defence was undertaken, and the intercommunication between the guns & H.Q. & totl.	JCH.
"	"	afternoon	Bombing practice for B & C Sections. The remaining sections continued their arrangements in their new billets.	

J Maskern Captain
Comdg 2nd M.G.S. June 1915

WAR DIARY of 2nd Squadron 1 & 2 Machine Gun Corps

Army Form C. 2118

INTELLIGENCE SUMMARY

Morehead Capt. Comdg.

June 1916

Place	Date	Hour	Summary of Events and Information	Remarks and references to Appendices
ERQUIN	1st		A-E sections fired the remainder of their men on the long range. B.C.D.+F section leaders with squadron Capt. paraded at Erquin & carry out a tactical ride with the G.O.C. The defence of a position was undertaken, + intercommunication tested.	
"	2nd		C-B sections fired on the long range in the morning. The remainder took part in a squadron scheme.	
"	3rd		The whole of the Echelon 'A' on the reduced scale paraded in the morning. + also went a route march. Stables in the afternoon. All sections carried out range practice, with saddle inspection after stables.	
"	4th		The squadron attended memorial service at PREURES.	
"	5th		Owing to raining weather work was interfered with. Sections carried out short individual training in the morning. In the afternoon the G.O.C. inspected the Brigade Echelon 'A' on reduced scale at 3pm at Xrords S of PRENTY.	

WAR DIARY or INTELLIGENCE SUMMARY

Army Form C. 2118

Place	Date	Hour	Summary of Events and Information	Remarks and references to Appendices
Etrepagny	July 6		Owing to bad weather, the Divisional scheme arranged for to-day was cancelled.	
"	7th		The tactical scheme proposed from yesterday took place. The main point carried out were Rapid reconnaissance and intercommunication both by signals & aeroplane.	
"	8th		There was a Divisional Scheme with troops undertaken. The general idea was that the enemy line had been broken & an Infantry Division was ordered to increase the head by rolling up the enemy to the left of the gap. The 1st Cavalry Division was detailed to protect the left flank of the infantry. Aeroplanes co-operated. G.O.C. 1st Army inspected the Operation at 9 a.m. at 12 noon. After walking down the line he inspected the packs. One section came into action, & the operation then filed past in half section.	MS
"	9th		The Divisional Horse Show took place to-day. The operation got third in the section jumping & third in the machine gun competition. Owing to the inspection the day before, most of the	

WAR DIARY
or
INTELLIGENCE SUMMARY

Army Form C. 2118

Place	Date	Hour	Summary of Events and Information	Remarks and references to Appendices
EROUIN	10.7.16		entries had to be cancelled. MS	MS
"	11.7		The squadron attended Divine Service at the large tent at EROUIN.	
"	12.7		A small scheme took place in the morning with the 9th Lancers. The M.G. Ogdn. & our Ogdn. & the 9th lighting a rearguard action defended the high ground between HUCQUELIERS (EROUIN against an (Cavelry Regt.) Owing to bad weather oper-	
			-ations stopped early. MS	
"	13.7		Owing to bad weather the scheme arranged for today was cancelled. The squadron went a route march instead.	MS
"	14.7		"A" & "B" sections carried out long range firing in the morning. The remaining section leaders took their N.C.O.s in a tactical ride. In the afternoon, semaphore signalling two men per section. MS	
"	15.7		A scheme was carried out in the morning - the attack - Reference to a position	MS

WAR DIARY or INTELLIGENCE SUMMARY

Army Form C. 2118

Place	Date June	Hour	Summary of Events and Information	Remarks and references to Appendices
ENQUIN	16th		C & D sections carried out long range practices. The remainder took part in a tactical ride. For Officers & N.C.O's in the afternoon signalling.	
"	17th		Owing to rain, practice was cancelled	HS
"	18th		A detachment from the Squadron attended a memorial service at SAMER to Lord Kitchener	HS
"	19th		In the morning the G.O.C. 1st Cavalry Division inspected Echelon A-B on the reduced scale. Signalling during the afternoon. The Division stood to at ½ hours notice from noon today.	HS
"	20th		A tactical ride was carried out by the C.O. with the Officers & corporals. Signalling in the afternoon.	HS
"	21st		There was no parade this morning as orders re evacuation of ophthalmic store prior to moving had to be done. Signalling plan obtained during the afternoon.	HS
"	22nd		The Squadron turned out in marching order for a route march in the morning.	HS

WAR DIARY or INTELLIGENCE SUMMARY

Army Form C. 2118

Place	Date	Hour	Summary of Events and Information	Remarks and references to Appendices
ENQUIN	June 23rd – 24th		600 ceased. Preparation for the impending move was carried on. The squadron left billets at Enquin at 7.30pm. The Brigade rendezvous was at MONTCAVREL at 9.0pm. The line of march was via AIX-EN-ISSART - BRIMEUX - CAMPAGNE - LES HESDIN - LAMBUS FORTE- FONTAINE to RAYE-SUR-AUTHIE arriving at 5.0am where the squadron billeted.	MS
RAYE-SUR-AUTHIE	25th		A move was made to Brigade rendezvous at LABROYE at 1.00pm. Line of march AUXI-LE-CHATEAU to MEZEROLLES arriving at 3.15am.	MS
MEZEROLLES	26th		Brigade rendezvous at LE QUESNEL Farm 1 mile N.W. of OUTREBOIS + marched via AUTHEUX - FIENVILLERS - CANAPLES to BERTEAUCOURT-LES-DAMES where the went into billets.	MS
BERTEAUCOURT LES-DAMES	27th		Capt. R.M.R. BROCKLEBANK 9th Lancers has arrived + took over command of squadron. Brigade rendezvous at 9.0pm 2 miles S. of village + marched via VIGNACOURT - FLESSELLES - BERTANGLES - COISY - ABBEVILLE to QUERRIEU arriving 2.30am. Camped in Park.	MS
QUERRIEU	28th		Heavy rain, no move.	MS

WAR DIARY
INTELLIGENCE SUMMARY

Army Form C. 2118

Place	Date	Hour	Summary of Events and Information	Remarks and references to Appendices
QUERRIEU	29		Weather still stormy. No more made. The day was spent in cleaning up. (as)	
"	30		No more. Day spent in cleaning & inspecting.	AS

Neurochtent
Capt. Comdg.
2nd M.G. Squadron

30.6.16

Army Form C. 2118.

WAR DIARY
or
INTELLIGENCE SUMMARY.
(Erase heading not required.)

CONFIDENTIAL.

WAR DIARY

OF

2nd SQUADRON, MACHINE GUN CORPS

JULY, 1916

VOLUME No. VI

McMocullowh
Captain Commanding
2nd Squadron Machine Gun Corps

Army Form C. 2118.

WAR DIARY
of
INTELLIGENCE SUMMARY.
(Erase heading not required.)

Instructions regarding War Diaries and Intelligence Summaries are contained in F.S. Regs., Part II. and the Staff Manual respectively. Title pages will be prepared in manuscript.

Place	Date July	Hour	Summary of Events and Information	Remarks and references to Appendices
QUERRIEU	1st		Reveille at 5am. Marched at 5.30 am. via FRANKVILLERS to BRESLE. Halted at BRESLE all day. Marched back to camp in QUERRIEU area at 6.30pm.	
"	2nd		No move. Men cleaning their harness & equipment. Horses at exercise from 4.30pm to 6.20pm.	
"	3rd		No move. Heavy rain. Squadron routine work.	
"	4th		Parade 5.45am. Marched via AMIENS, DREUIL, PICQUIGNY, SOUES, LE QUESNOY to METIGNY where the squadron bivouaced in a field with cookhouse in barn. Officers in house in village this day.	
METIGNY	5th		Kit & equipment inspection at 12 noon.	
"	6th		Clothes kit 12.30pm. Ordinary squadron routine 9 to 10am. Exercise 9 to 10am.	
"	7th		Limbers washed, white horses were at exercise. Limbers inspected. Beauvais horses then exercised.	
"	8th		Ordinary squadron routine. Parade of recruits under their leaders at 9am. Mounted squadron routine.	
"	9th		Sunday. Church parade 9am. Ordinary routine.	D.H.S

WAR DIARY
or
INTELLIGENCE SUMMARY.

(Erase heading not required.)

Army Form C. 2118.

Place	Date July	Hour	Summary of Events and Information	Remarks and references to Appendices
METIGNY	10th		Parade & actions under their leaders at 8.30am mounted. Brigadier visited Squadron in afternoon.	
"	11th		Parade & actions under their leaders at 8am, mounted.	
		6pm	Orders received to rendezvous at 7.55pm, marched from METIGNY via LE QUESNOY SOUES PICQUIGNY DREUIL AMIENS to QUERRIEU.	
QUERRIEU	12th	3.30am	Reached QUERRIEU + went into bivouac in northern area. Routine work all morning.	
"	13th		FRANVILLERS BRESLE BUIRE-SUR-L'ANCRE to VILLE-SOUS-CORBIE arriving there at 8.30pm. Went into bivouac in avenue of poplars close to the AYCRE.	
VILLE-SOUS-CORBIE	14th		Standing to from 3am. Routine morning clothes etc. to move.	
"	15th		Standing to from 3am. Routine work. Blessing of	
"	16th		Officers 16 from 6am. Cloth. Voluntary church parade. to move.	
"	17th		Routine work, cleaning etc. Orders to move at 2 hours notice.	Maps

Army Form C. 2118.

WAR DIARY
or
INTELLIGENCE SUMMARY.

(Erase heading not required.)

Instructions regarding War Diaries and Intelligence Summaries are contained in F.S. Regs., Part II and the Staff Manual respectively. Title pages will be prepared in manuscript.

Place	Date	Hour	Summary of Events and Information	Remarks and references to Appendices
VILLE SOUS CORBIE	18th May		Routine work. Inspection of iron rations, haversacks & "Public Star" & Steel helmet. Horses at exercise. No move.	
"	19th		Routine Exercise stables. Elementary gun drill for all sections for one hour. Semaphore signallers being instructed in afternoon. No move.	
"	20th		Mounted parade & gun drill. Inspection of smoke helmets & clothing. No move.	
"	21st		No move. Horses grazing & at exercise. Semaphore signallers exercised in afternoon.	
"	22nd		No move. A & B sections carried out practice firing at 25 yds range. Other sections gun drill.	
"	23rd		No move. Voluntary church service at 9am & 11am. Inspection of stripped saddles after stables.	
"	24th		Squadron paraded at 8.30am & marched via war at L.I. Regiment of the Brigade via FRANVILLERS to QUERRIEU (AMBREVEA) where it arrived (at 11.30am & went into bivouac.	maps

Army Form C. 2118.

WAR DIARY
or
INTELLIGENCE SUMMARY.
(Erase heading not required.)

Place	Date	Hour	Summary of Events and Information	Remarks and references to Appendices
QUERRIEU	25th		No more. Horses at exercise + grazing from 8.30 to 10.30am. Routine	
"	26th		No more. Routine work. One of the Signallers received in afternoon.	
"	27th		No more. Section paraded under section officers at 8.30 a.m. for gun drill. Foot parade with rifle + bandoliers from 2pm to 3pm. All soldiers washed 1 spur. 1 man attended to Army gooseshod.	
"	28th		No more. C-D sections carried out practice firing from Quarry near ABLONVILLE ROAD. One two three + four two fired the guns. Other sections at gun drill. Transport and Headquarters horses received 2 shoes - 2 men attended gas school.	
"	29th		No more Sections at grazing from 8 to 6. Details (?) + of 8 Mobo h + were exercised. Range finders paraded. Lect O.C. squadron. 2 there + 2 men under supervision of O.C. squadron. The squadron were medically attended gas school. The squadron were medically inspected at 2pm.	
"	30th		No more. Voluntary church service started 11am to 12.30pm	days

Army Form C. 2118.

WAR DIARY
or
INTELLIGENCE SUMMARY.
(Erase heading not required.)

Place	Date	Hour	Summary of Events and Information	Remarks and references to Appendices
OVERRNEZ	July 31st		No more Squadron arrived at evening trenches close to BOIS ESCARDONEUSE under O.C in command. O.C. Squadron attended Brigade Office ride round. ST GRATIEN. Semaphore signalling copied at 2 pm. Exam. Exam Wireys (to front No 8 Battery) Night General Idea.	

N. Brocklebank
Captain 9th Lancers
2nd Squadron Machine Gun Corps

Commanding 2 Squadron Machine Gun Corps

Army Form. C. 2118.

WAR DIARY
or
INTELLIGENCE SUMMARY.
(Erase heading not required.)

Vol 1

CONFIDENTIAL

WAR DIARY
OF
2ND SQUADRON, MACHINE GUN CORPS.

AUGUST 1916

VOLUME No. VII

McMcClelland
Captain
Comdg. 2nd Squadron, Machine Gun Corps.

Army Form C. 2118.

WAR DIARY
or
INTELLIGENCE SUMMARY.
(Erase heading not required.)

Instructions regarding War Diaries and Intelligence Summaries are contained in F. S. Regs., Part II. and the Staff Manual respectively. Title pages will be prepared in manuscript.

Place	Date August 1916	Hour	Summary of Events and Information	Remarks and references to Appendices
QUERRIEU	1st		No move. Lectures carried out small Tactical schemes. Stables 11-12.30	
	2nd		Foot Parade in afternoon.	MS
			No move. Two Sections at practice firing against bank. Range-finders exercised.	MS
	3rd		Sections at Grazing & Exercise. Semaphore signalling. Red and White flag men paraded at 9.15 am for Brigade scheme in signalling & communication in neighbourhood of BOIS DE TAI to ALLONVILLE. Mechanism class in afternoon. Lieut K.V. Mida, Queens Bays, joined as Second in Command.	MS
	4th		No move. Squadron exercised at crossing trenches close to BOIS ESCARDONEUSE. N.C.O.s at Foot Drill and Signallers exercised with Semaphore flag.	MS
	5th		Sections at Grazing & Exercise. All Linten wagons (packed) inspected at midday. Sergeants & Corporals instructed in map-reading in the field by O.C. Squadron.	MS
	6th		No Move. Voluntary Church Service. Stables 9 - 10.30 a.m. Kit inspection	MS

Army Form C. 2118.

WAR DIARY
or
INTELLIGENCE SUMMARY.
(Erase heading not required.)

Place	Date 1916 August	Hour	Summary of Events and Information	Remarks and references to Appendices
QUERRIEU	6th		at 10.30 a.m.	MS
	7th		No move. Gun Drill under Section leaders. O.C. attended Divisional Staff ride from ALLONVILLE to beyond CORSY. Mechanism classes 3.30 p.m. Horse cooking parade 2.30 p.m.	MS
	8th		No move. Sections paraded under Sections experts for grazing. All officers attended Brigade staff ride similar to previous day. Awkward squad instructed in mechanism. Parade of signallers. Signallers.	MS
	9th		Squadron paraded at 3.45 a.m. marching order and marched to PONT REMY via AMIENS & north bank of R. SOMME through ETOILE. "A" & "B" Echelon both brigaded.	MS
	10th		Reveille 3.15 a.m. Bde 5.15 a.m. marching order. Marched to INCHEVILLE via GAMACHES. Bivouacked in meadow between Railway Station & River La BRESLE.	MS
INCHEVILLE	11th		No move. Lectures on Exercise & Grazing. Inspection of Gums & accoutres & smoke helmets.	MS

Army Form C. 2118.

WAR DIARY
or
INTELLIGENCE SUMMARY.
(Erase heading not required.)

Instructions regarding War Diaries and Intelligence Summaries are contained in F. S. Regs., Part II. and the Staff Manual respectively. Title pages will be prepared in manuscript.

Place	Date 1916 August	Hour	Summary of Events and Information	Remarks and references to Appendices
INCHEVILLE	12th		No move. Sections at Exercise + Grazing. Stablemen classes at 3.0 p.m.	WS
	13th		No move. Voluntary Church service. Stables 9.30 to 11.0 a.m. Stripped saddle + harness inspection at 11.0 a.m.	WS
	14th		A + B Sections Practice firing in quarry on road from BEAUCHAMPS to EMBREVILLE. Afternoon - Sports - wreathing on horse back, Tug of War. Inter-section football.	WS
	15th		No move. Riding school dummy thrusting. Afternoon Sports postponed on account of rain	WS
	16th		Sections exercised and grazed under leaders. Afternoon - Sports - VC race. Servants tug of war. Cooks' race. Musical chairs. Inter-section football.	WS
	17th		No move. Riding school + Dummy thrusting. Afternoon. NCO's Tent Pegging with sword. Potato race ½ mile flat race. Stopped race. Inter-section football. Inspection of all rifle covers.	WS
	18th		No move. Voluntary Church Services Stables 9.30 to 11.0 a.m.	WS

Army Form C. 2118.

WAR DIARY
or
INTELLIGENCE SUMMARY.
(Erase heading not required.)

Place	Date	Hour	Summary of Events and Information	Remarks and references to Appendices
INCHEVILLE	18th		Sergeants and Corporals at Riding School. All scouts instructed under Lieut. Mead. Rangefinders instructors under Lieut. Park. All Semaphore signallers exercised. Remainder of Squadron exercises and grazed. Afternoon - Aquatic Sports in lake - Combination race, relay race, 100 yards open, 220 race open - Diving, walking greasy pole, 200 yards race. Intersection for sale.	
	19th		Turnout inspection - Section by section in drill order. Squadron attended Gt Lewers' Sports in afternoon.	AS
	20th		Church Service at 11am. 5 men per section under Orderly Officer. Inspection of very dirty, buckles on stirrup leathers, girths + surcingles, and horn rations. 13 re-inforcements issued.	AS
	21st		No more. B Section carried out short tactical scheme under Second-in-command. Rest of Squadron at Riding School. Dummy thrusting & jumping. Mechanism classes under section leaders in afternoon. Lieut. R.R. Pelly, M.G.C. joined.	AS

Army Form C. 2118.

WAR DIARY
or
INTELLIGENCE SUMMARY

(Erase heading not required.)

Place	Date	Hour	Summary of Events and Information	Remarks and references to Appendices
INCHEVILLE	1916 August 22nd		No move. Camp moved from meadow to a field close to the Chateau, as the meadow was very damp. Rest of Squadron at exercise. Reports sent in from Sections regarding number of eyefringes and sunshades required to complete.	
	23rd		No move. Squadron marched to & fell by the Sea. Sea bathing and horses swimming. Reached camp again at 4.30 p.m. Tenders marched under orders of officer.	HS
	24th		No move. Turnout inspection parade, Section by Section. Backward men at Mechanism class Semaphore signallers exercised in afternoon.	HS
	25th		No move. Riding School and Gunnery knowledge. Foot drill and rifle exercises in afternoon.	HS
	26th		No move. Scouts instructed under 2nd in Command. Semaphore signalling exercised under N.C.O. Sergeants & Corporals instructed in map reading under O.C. Squadron. Rest of Squadron exercised and grazing.	HS

Army Form C. 2118.

WAR DIARY
or
INTELLIGENCE SUMMARY
(Erase heading not required.)

Instructions regarding War Diaries and Intelligence Summaries are contained in F. S. Regs., Part II. and the Staff Manual respectively. Title pages will be prepared in manuscript.

Place	Date August 1916	Hour	Summary of Events and Information	Remarks and references to Appendices
INCHEVILLE	27th		No move. Church service at 11.0 a.m. 5 men per section under orderly officers. Blowing articles inspected:- haversacks, waterbottles, entrenching tools & blouses, strap buckles, bridling & brass pieces dubbined.	
	28th		No move. Rain all morning. Mechanism classes in afternoon.	AYS
	29th		No move. Squadron marched to Ault for sea bathing & swimming horses. Limbers marched under orderly officer. Heavy thunderstorm and rain in afternoon. Reached camp 4.30 p.m.	AYS
	30th		No move. Heavy rain all morning and afternoon. Horses watered fed. 1 N.C.O and 12 men joined from base.	AYS
	31st		No move. Lieut. H. White, M.G.C. joined from base. Sections at exercise under leaders. Rest of squadron cleaning up lines. Afternoon spent in drying clothes & cleaning up.	AYS

Van Strochebrouch
Captain, 9th Lancers
Comdg. 2nd Squadron, Machine Gun Corps.

Army Form C. 2118.

WAR DIARY
or
INTELLIGENCE SUMMARY.
(Erase heading not required.)

Vol 8

WAR DIARY

OF

2ND SQUADRON, MACHINE GUN CORPS.

SEPTEMBER 1916.

VOLUME No. VIII

PH Woodcock
Major.
Commanding 2nd Squadron, Machine Gun Corps.

Army Form C. 2118.

WAR DIARY
or
INTELLIGENCE SUMMARY.
(Erase heading not required.)

Place	Date 1916	Hour	Summary of Events and Information	Remarks and references to Appendices
INCHEVILLE	Sept. 1st		Sections paraded under their leaders for tactical scheme inspection of gear & helpers in afternoon. Stableyard men exercises in sections.	
	2nd		No move. Signals topograph & topreading under Squadron leader. Rangefinders under First Link. Scouts under 2nd in C. Signallers under topsat Rathbell. Rest of Squadron exercised & ragged.	
	3rd		No more. Church Service @ 11-30 am. Stripped saddle inspection.	
	4th		No more. Gun drill under section leaders - rapid action. Observation & recognition of targets.	
	5th		No move. Gun drill under section leaders advancing across country. 2nd in C inspected all harness, Signallers & range- finders. Backward & mechanism class.	
	6th		Marched at 10-30 am via GAMACHES & ARHNES which was reached at 5 pm. Bivouaced. Came on "Gap formation" again.	
	7th		Marched at 10-30 am via OISEL, PICQUIGNY - where 1st relieves AMIENS, DREURS & LA NEVILLE which was reached at 6 pm. Bivouaced.	

WAR DIARY or INTELLIGENCE SUMMARY

Army Form C. 2118.

(Erase heading not required.)

Place	Date 1916	Hour	Summary of Events and Information	Remarks and references to Appendices
La Neuville	Apr. 8		Exercise & Grazing. Troops helmets & box respirators identify trees &	
	9		Field dressings inspected.	
			Exercise Exercise & Grazing.	
	10		No move. Stables 9-30 – 11-0am.	
	11		Reserve Stables. Exercise & Grazing. Morning. Inspection of shoes, kits etc in afternoon.	
	12		Squadron drill in morning. Inspection of clothing afternoon. Brigade conference.	
	13		Divisional Conference. Turned out tackle essence in evening into action as a Squadron. Inspection of smoke Hombs in afternoon.	
	14		Marched from LA NEUVILLE at 6 am via BONNAY – MORLANCOURT, where we off-saddled & watered – to CARNOY VALLEY which was reached about 3.0pm Bivouac.	
Carnoy Valley	15		Standing to – Saddled up all day.	
	16		Standing to at 4 from noise. Two shells landed in camp badly wounding 6 men. Pieces between the men horses of D Section. Two horses	

Army Form C. 2118.

WAR DIARY
or
INTELLIGENCE SUMMARY.
(Erase heading not required.)

Instructions regarding War Diaries and Intelligence Summaries are contained in F. S. Regs., Part II. and the Staff Manual respectively. Title pages will be prepared in manuscript.

Place	Date	Hour	Summary of Events and Information	Remarks and references to Appendices
Corbylle	16th Sept 1916		XSE wounded + Evacuated, and one Section Staffords. All the Horses were caught - No men hurt.	
	17th		Gas Hell attack last night. Men ordered to don Helmets on the Gas Van Extinguisher. Effect only just noticeable. Helmets off in 1/4 of an hour. Church Service at 10.a.m. Stables and Sunday routine. Marched at 7.25 p.m. via Morlancourt — Bonnay. Back to La Neuville and Bonnay.	
La Neuville	18th		Rain all day. Horses exercised for half an hour. Bivouac all mud. Rum ration.	
	19th		Rain all night. Horses exercised for 1/2 hour.	
	20th		Rain all day. Horses exercised for 1/2 hour.	
	21st		Rain all morning. Clear in afternoon + all arms inspected by Section officers.	
	22nd		Fine. Exercise with Saddles. Empty packs. Every man on parade.	
	23rd		Parade at 6.45 a.m. Marched via Pont Noyelles — Amiens — N. bank of Somme — L'Etoile to Bouchon where Squadron bivouacked in Stubble field.	

2353 Wt. W2514/1454 700,000 5/15 D. D. & L. A.D.S.S./Forms/C. 2118.

Army Form C. 2118.

WAR DIARY
or
INTELLIGENCE SUMMARY.
(Erase heading not required.)

Place	Date 1916	Hour	Summary of Events and Information	Remarks and references to Appendices
	Sept. 24th		Parade at 8.15 a.m. Marched via AVRI-LE-CHATEAU - BUIRE-AU-BOIS to FILLIEVRES where Squadron bivouacked in Stubble Field.	
	25th		Parade 6 a.m. Marched to SAINT GEORGES where Squadron bivouacked in Stubble Field opposite CHATEAU MATTEVILLE.	
St Georges	26th		Exercise & Grazing. Afternoon spent in cleaning equipment & saddlery.	
	27th		Horses on Saddle from 6.30 - 10 a.m. All kit & sort inspected by Section Officers in afternoon.	
	28th		Sections at arm drill under their leaders. Morning across country. Coming into action, rapid change of position. Inspection of saddlery in afternoon. 20 men sent to HESDIN & Rollo under Orderly Officer.	
	29th		Squadron parade for Squadron Drill at 10 a.m. Gen. Squallers telephone men & officers in afternoon. Horses scrubbed & ammunition in Bandoliers inspected. 30 men to HESDIN to Baths under Orderly Officer.	
	30th		Exercise & Grazing under Sector Officers. O.C. A.S.C. 1st Corps Div. inspected transport at 2pm at VIEILLE-HESDIN.	

Van WoodWard
Major, 9th Lancers,
Comdg. 2nd Squadron, Machine Gun Corps.
NoSS

Army Form C. 2118.

WAR DIARY
or
INTELLIGENCE SUMMARY.
(Erase heading not required.)

Vol 9

CONFIDENTIAL

War Diary
of
2nd Squadron, Machine Gun Corps.

October 1916.

Volume No. IX

W S Wathen
Lieut.
Commanding 2nd Squadron, Machine Gun Corps.

Army Form C. 2118.

WAR DIARY or INTELLIGENCE SUMMARY.
(Erase heading not required.)

Instructions regarding War Diaries and Intelligence Summaries are contained in F. S. Regs., Part II. and the Staff Manual respectively. Title pages will be prepared in manuscript.

Place	Date 1916 October	Hour	Summary of Events and Information	Remarks and references to Appendices
St GEORGES	1st		Clock put back one hour during night. Church Service at 11.0 AM. 4 men for section under Orderly Officer. Put out targets for field firing.	
	2nd		3 Sections carried out field firing close to Bivouac, firing one belt for each gun, other 3 sections at gun drill. Rain all afternoon.	
	3rd		Rain all day.	
	4th		Heavy rain all morning. The A.D.V.S. 1st Cavalry Division inspected Squadron horses at 9-0 am. Sections then exercised. D Section moved to billets at SAINT GEORGES. Band & E Sections to billets in SAINTE AUSTREBERTHE. Men under cover, but horses in open. Rain all night. Exercise and Graze under Section Officers. 45 men went to baths at HESDIN. Rain during night.	
	5th		Section Officers took their N.C.O's out for map-reading, fire orders, recognition of targets. Sections exercised under Sergeants. Afternoon spent cleaning steel work and Saddlery. Evening Stables now put to 4-0 pm.	
	6th			
	7th		Sergeants and Corporals at Map-reading under Squadron Leader.	

W.O.T.C.

WAR DIARY or INTELLIGENCE SUMMARY

Army Form C. 2118

Place	Date 1915	Hour	Summary of Events and Information	Remarks and references to Appendices
ST. GEORGES	Oct 7th		Rangefinders under Lieut. W. Peak. Signallers and Semaphors under Bst. Hartwell. Remainder of Squadron exercise and Horse branding horses in afternoon. Headquarters moved down into billets at CHATEAU NATIEVILLE from bivouac in field.	M.W.H.
	8th		Stables 9.30 am. Church Service at 11.0 am. A.C. and F Sections moved into billets, the first in SAINT GEORGES, the latter two into STE AUSTREBERTHE.	
	9th		Field day postponed on account of heavy rain. Exercise, fixing up billets, cleaning saddlery.	
	10th		Squadron Leaders attended Brigade Conference at H.Qrs. at 10.0 am. E Section fired on rifle range outside HESDIN. Other Sections at gun drill under Reg'tl Officers. Mechanical classes (Stoppages) in afternoon. 40 men proceeded to HESDIN for baths.	
	11th		Divisional Field day in direction of WILLEMAN - ECLIMEUX. 68 men (30 mounted) proceeded to HESDIN for baths. Troops reached billets about 3.30 pm. off field day.	
	12th		B & D Sections firing on range outside HESDIN. Other sections at drill. Rifle exercises and marching in afternoon. 70 men proceeded to HESDIN for baths. Signallers attended Divisional gun drill Headquarters for scheme.	
	13th		Field day against 9th Cavalry Brigade in neighbourhood of ESTRUTALLIE CHATEAU. Troops returned to billets at 12.30 pm. Rest of day spent cleaning. O.C. attended Brigade tactical scheme between 1st and 9th Brigades.	
	14th			

WAR DIARY or INTELLIGENCE SUMMARY

Army Form C. 2118

Place	Date 1916	Hour	Summary of Events and Information	Remarks and references to Appendices
ST GEORGES	Oct 15th		Stables 11.0 a.m. Section Officers inspected Smoke Helmets, 2 man rations per man, British Warm coats.	
	16th		Fanl. A. Section fired on range outside HESDIN. Other sections at gun drill. Dismounted party being instructed. Sections carried out foot drill in afternoon.	
	17th		Sections at Disposal of Officers – E Section fired on range outside HESDIN. O.C. Squadron attended conference at Brigade Headquarters at 10.0 a.m. Kitchen classes in afternoon.	
	18th		Rain all day. Routine work only.	
	19th		Squadron paraded at 8.30 a.m. and marched via BUIRE-AU-BOIS to FORTEL. Horses picketed out – men in barns.	
	20th		Squadron paraded at 9.0 a.m. and marched via FROMEN-LE-GRAND, BERLCOURT, MONTIGNY, BEAUMETZ, DOMART, ST LEGER to BERTEAUCOURT-LES-DAMES. Horse picketed out, men in barns. Lieut. S.H. LE ROY LEWIS left to join Cavalry Machine Gun Training Centre, UCKFIELD, ENGLAND for 6 weeks.	
BERTEAUCOURT LES-DAMES	21st		Sections at exercise Arms inspection in afternoon.	
	22nd		Lieut. E.E. ROBERTS, Kelsh Horse, joined Squadron. Smoke Helmets and Iron rations inspected. Sunday Routine.	
	23rd		Exercise under Section officers. Inspection of all ammunition in belts and bandoliers. Run.	
	24th		Exercise under Section Officers. Inspection of first field dressings.	[signature]

Army Form C. 2118

WAR DIARY
or
INTELLIGENCE SUMMARY
(Erase heading not required.)

Instructions regarding War Diaries and Intelligence Summaries are contained in F. S. Regs., Part II. and the Staff Manual respectively. Title Pages will be prepared in manuscript.

Place	Date 1916	Hour	Summary of Events and Information	Remarks and references to Appendices
BERTEAUCOURT LES-DAMES	24th		and Identity discs. Foot drill parade in afternoon. Rain. Exercise under Section officers. Rain. Harness cleaning.	
	25th		Brigade parade cancelled owing to rain. Lectures exercised. Cleaning of harness and steel work in the afternoon. Captain (temp. Major) R.L.R. Brockbank proceeded to Lewis Gun School LE TOUQUET.	
	26th			
	27th		Squadron Drill. Lectures to Sections on Indirect Fire Semaphore. Class exercises. Rangefinders dismissed.	
	28th		Squadron Scheme under G.O.C. 2nd Cavalry Brigade. Lieut. E.M.D. NATHEN joined to take over command of the Squadron from AMBALA Machine Gun Squadron.	
	29th		Sunday Routine. Rain.	
	30th		Scheme for Corporals Sub-Brigade. Inspection of Brass name cards. Rain all afternoon.	
	31st		Scheme for Sergeants, Corporals L'Corpls. Remainder of Squadron to exercise. Rangefinders & Semaphore Signallers exercised.	

W.S. Nathen
Lieut. (8th Hussars)
Commanding 2nd Squadron, Machine Gun Corps.

Army Form C. 2118.

WAR DIARY
or
INTELLIGENCE SUMMARY
(Erase heading not required.)

CONFIDENTIAL.

WAR DIARY

of

2ND SQUADRON, MACHINE GUN CORPS.

NOVEMBER, 1916.

VOLUME No. X

Vol 10

WAR DIARY
INTELLIGENCE SUMMARY
(Erase heading not required.)

Army Form C. 2118.

Instructions regarding War Diaries and Intelligence Summaries are contained in F.S. Regs., Part II. and the Staff Manual respectively. Title pages will be prepared in manuscript.

Place	Date	Hour	Summary of Events and Information	Remarks and references to Appendices
BERTEAUCOURT-LES-DAMES.	1/8		Exercise in morning. Divine Inspection in afternoon. Rain.	
	2/8		Exercise in morning. Guns fired in afternoon to test them. Rain.	
	3/8		Exercise in morning. Rangefinders who have not been dismissed, exercised.	
	4/8		H and B sections inspected in Marching order by Commanding Officer. Brigade Scheme for 2nd in Command of Regiments and Squadrons.	
	5/8		Usual Sunday Routine.	
	6/8		C.D.E.F. Sections inspected in Marching Order by Section Leaders. Map-reading exercise for H and B sections of Serjeants and Corporals under 2nd in Command. Afternoon rain.	
	7/8		Rain all day. Squadron under orders to move next day. Ref. Map LENS 100,000.	
	8/8		Rain. Brigade marched via ST OUEN, MIXECOURT, ABBEVILLE, to NOUVION-EN-PONTHIEU. Ref. Map. ABBEVILLE 100,000.	
	9/8		Marched continued via MONTREUIL to permanent Hunter billets in area PREURES, CAILLET, LA RENOIRE, LE FAYEL, and LE BOIS RATEL. Billeting party reached PREURES at 4-15 p.m. and Squadron at 5.30 p.m. Very little billeting could be done before dark. Ref. Map. CALAIS 100,000.	
PREURES.	10/8		Billeting continued. Squadron H.Q. and "C" Section in PREURES. "A" and "D" sections in LA RUE NOIRE. "B" Section at LE FAYEL. "E" and "F" Sections at LE BOIS RATEL.	
	11/8		Squadron employed in improvement of billets. Clipping started. Rain.	

EWSH Capt.

WAR DIARY
or
INTELLIGENCE SUMMARY

Army Form C. 2118.

(Erase heading not required.)

Place	Date	Hour	Summary of Events and Information	Remarks and references to Appendices
PREURES	12/6		Usual Sunday Routine	
	13/6		Squadron Exercise. Improvement of billets continued	
	14/6		Squadron Exercise. All saddlery oiled.	
	15/6		Squadron Exercise. Cleaning of saddlery continued. 1 Officer and 6 other ranks proceeded to DOZINVILLE for instruction in making straw mattresses. 1 other rank left the unit to proceed on ordinary leave to ENGLAND.	
	16/6		Squadron Exercise. Clipping, cleaning of saddlery, equipment and improvement of billets continued.	
	17/6		Squadron Exercise. Cara Sook.	
	18/6		Troop ordered Squadron exercise. Conference of Runners mess at Brigade H.Q. to meet O.C. of Division.	
	19/6		Usual Sunday routine. No church parade owing to ill-health of Chaplain.	
	20/6		Exercises. Work continued in repairing billets	
	21/6		Exercise. 2/Lt H. WHITE and Sgt. SALT proceeded to Divisional School of Instruction	
	22/6		Exercise. Conference of M.G. Section Commanders at Divisional HQ	
	23/6		Exercise.	
	24/6		Exercise. All billets, monumends, cook-houses, latrines to separate inspected by M.O.	

W.R.W. Capt.

WAR DIARY
INTELLIGENCE SUMMARY

Army Form C. 2118.

Place	Date	Hour	Summary of Events and Information	Remarks and references to Appendices
PREVRES.	25/11		Exercise. Pouring wet day.	
	26/11		Usual Sunday routine. No church parade owing to exercises of Chaplain during the preceeding fortnight. Much work was carried out in clothing lines, repairing kits, cleaning harness, painting harness, and all arms of the Squadron were inspected by Sqdn. Sgt.	
	27/11		Exercise. Farm all day. Horse cooking parade for other than veterinary reasons - 4 horses cast.	
	28/11		Exercise.	
	29/11		Exercise. Veterinary Officer NC Sqdron inspected all horses. Capt. D.H. Shea proceeds to England for instructional duty with Cavalry Machine Gun Training Centre, UCKFIELD.	
	30/11		Exercise. Gun Drill for "C" section in afternoon.	

30/11

R.W.S. Watters
Capt. (&? Sqn.)
Commanding 22 Sqdn. M.G.C.

Army Form C. 2118.

WAR DIARY
or
~~INTELLIGENCE SUMMARY~~
(Erase heading not required.)

Vol XI

CONFIDENTIAL.

War Diary.
of
2ND Squadron, Machine Gun Corps.
December 1916
Volume No. XI.

Army Form C. 2118.

WAR DIARY
or
INTELLIGENCE SUMMARY
(Erase heading not required.)

Instructions regarding War Diaries and Intelligence Summaries are contained in F. S. Regs., Part II. and the Staff Manual respectively. Title pages will be prepared in manuscript.

Place	Date	Hour	Summary of Events and Information	Remarks and references to Appendices
PREURES	1 12/16		Exercise. Gun drill in afternoon.	
	2 2/16		Exercise. Rain. Concert in Evening. 3 O.R. proceeded to UK on leave.	
	3 13/16		Sunday Routine.	
	4 12/16		Exercise. Squadron's transport inspected by C.O. Lecture for all ranks on Mechanism.	
	5 15/16		Equitation. Mechanism in afternoon. 2 men proceeded to UK on leave.	
	6 12/16		Equitation - Lecture on animal management	
	7 17/16		Equitation. Lecture on characteristics of Machine Gun and Equitation.	
	8 2/16		Gun Drill Saddle Inspection	
	9 19/16		Exercise. Presentation of Medals by G.O.C. 1st Cavalry Division at 11.0 am at BEUSSENT. Sergeants Platts, Bull and Baker received Military Medals.	
	10 20/16		Sunday Routine. Mechanism - stoppages. Training of Rangefinders Equitation. Capt. L.F.D. Matthew and one O.R. proceeded to U.K. on leave. Lieut. C.H. Miller assumed Command of Squadron. One horse struck off Strength. (died of fractured neck.)	
	11 21/16			

MWSW

Army Form C. 2118.

WAR DIARY
or
INTELLIGENCE SUMMARY.
(Erase heading not required.)

Instructions regarding War Diaries and Intelligence Summaries are contained in F.S. Regs., Part II. and the Staff Manual respectively. Title pages will be prepared in manuscript.

Place	Date	Hour	Summary of Events and Information	Remarks and references to Appendices
PREUVRES	12/2/16		Equitation for 3 Sections. Tactical ride for N.C.O's and remaining Sections. Afternoon, Lecture on Indication and recognition of Targets.	
	13/2/16		Equitation. Training of Scouts. Afternoon - Mechanism.	
	14/2/16		Equitation for 3 Sections. Judging distance during exercise for remainder. Lecture on Indication and recognition of Targets.	
	15/2/16		Equitation 3 Sections. Training of Scouts. Advanced Gun drill and Physical Drill. Three O.R. proceeded on leave to U.K.	
	16/2/16		Exercise before breakfast. Saddle, Kit, and Arms Inspection.	
	17/2/16		Usual Sunday Routine.	
	18/2/16		Exercise combined with indication and recognition of Targets. Lecture on indirect fire.	
	19/2/16		Exercise combined with judging distance. Scheme for Squadron Signallers. Advanced Gun drill in afternoon. Lieut. W. WHITE and Sgt. J. SALT returned from course at Divisional School. One O.R. proceeded to U.K. on leave.	

RWW.

Army Form C. 2118.

WAR DIARY
or
INTELLIGENCE SUMMARY.
(Erase heading not required.)

Place	Date	Hour	Summary of Events and Information	Remarks and references to Appendices
PREURES	20/12/16		Practical instruction for all Section Sergeants in detail of Equitation. 3 Sections Equitation. Remainder Exercise.	
	21/12/16		Lecture on overhead fire. Bell filling. Squadron paraded in full marching order for inspection by G.O.C. Cavalry Corps. Owing to bad weather, parade was cancelled after Squadron had started for rendezvous. Horse inspection by A.D.V.S in afternoon at 3 p.m. "A" Section inspected, too dark to see remainder.	[initials]
	22/12/16		Instruction in equitation for Section Officers and Sergeants. Lecture on overhead fire. Capt. L.W.D. Wathen returned from Leave and assumed command of Squadron. 11.0 A.M. Exercise before breakfast. Stripped saddle inspection. A.D.V.S. "B" section not seen on 21st inst. A.D.V.S.	
	23/12/16		A.D.V.S. inspected horses, etc. of horses, Very good. "C" Section report on condition etc. of horses. Very good. "C" Section not so good as others.	
	24/12/16		Church Parade. Xmas Service, at 11.45 A.M. Exercise on Blankets before breakfast. 3 O.R. proceedes to U.K. on leave.	
	25/12/16		Xmas day. Guard Mounted 10.30 A.M.	[initials]

Army Form C. 2118.

WAR DIARY
or
INTELLIGENCE SUMMARY
(Erase heading not required.)

Place	Date	Hour	Summary of Events and Information	Remarks and references to Appendices
PREVRES	26/12/16		Exercise at 6.0 A.m.	
	27/12/16		Squadron inspected in full marching order at PREVRES at 9.0 A.m. by G.O.C. 1st Cavalry Division, who later inspected Men's Billets	
	28/12/16		Equitation. Lecture on Overhead fire. Two O.R. proceeded to U.K. on leave.	
	29/12/16		Equitation. Lecture on indirect fire.	
	30/12/16		Squadron inspected in marching order by C.O. Great improvement shewn by all seating since Ypres inspection. 1 horse died of fractured neck.	
	31/12/16		Sunday Routine.	

W. Wathen
31/12/16
Capt. (6th D.G.)
Commdg. 7th Squadron, Machine Gun Corps.

WAR DIARY
or
INTELLIGENCE SUMMARY.
(Erase heading not required.)

Army Form C. 2118.

CONFIDENTIAL

War Diary.
of
2ⁿᵈ Squadron, Machine Gun Corps.

January 1917.

Volume No. XII

Army Form C. 2118.

WAR DIARY
or
INTELLIGENCE SUMMARY
(Erase heading not required.)

Place	Date	Hour	Summary of Events and Information	Remarks and references to Appendices
PREURES.	1-1-17		C.D.T and B Sections took Provided 1/2 Section complete. Parade 9.0 am. N. O. ENQUIN. News drive (Robt WAKEFIELD) proceeded. On the whole a good form of drill with a few casualties (from Wakefield) preceded seven limbers (to proceed with Horses. Battalion engaged in mending Order by E.O.C at 10.0 Am at PREURES. Three limbers were despatched to regiments at 5.0 p.m. Sgts. Miller and B. Tomkins attend veterinary Course by A.D.V.S. for fourteen days at recurring rooms. 18th Hussars lasting 14 working days. In the evening a squadron concert in the school PREURES.	
	2-1-17		All Sections Equitation in morning. 3 Sections dismounted drill and Manual Exercises. 1.N.C.O. to Divisional Signalling Course lasting 14 days.	
	3-1-17		All Sections Equitation. Afternoon spent in cleaning saddlery and stables etc. R. Petty and Sgt. Baker joined 1st Cav. Div. School for course lasting one month.	
	4-1-17		Inspection by G.O.C 2/? Cav Bde of B. and D. Sections in Marching Order at PREURES at 10.Am. Turn out very good. Remainder Equitation. 3 Sections dismounted Drill and Manual Exercises at 2 p.m.	
	5-1-17		All Sections Equitation. Medical Officer inspected all men of H.Q. and 3 Sections in afternoon. Saddle Inspection.	
	6-1-17		Exercise in morning. Kit Inspection. All Billets and Cook houses inspected by C.O. Good in most Sections. Veterinary Officer inspected all horses on strength.	
	7-1-17		Sunday Routine. Church Service at ENQUIN for 3 Sections moved by Lt. Miller at 11-30 Am.	

MRW

WAR DIARY or INTELLIGENCE SUMMARY

Army Form C. 2118.

Place	Date	Hour	Summary of Events and Information	Remarks and references to Appendices
PREVRES.	8-1-17	9 AM	C. and D. Sections firing on Range at LE ROQUE. Range about 200* good	
			E " F " " " " " BOIS RATEL " " 25*	
			B " A " " " " " LE PAYEL " " 75*	
			No.s 1, 2, 3, and 4 gunners fired in each case. Exercise Remainder at 8.0 A.m. In afternoon Signallers visual work. All drivers belt filling by hand machine. 2 other ranks proceeded on leave to U.K.	
	9-1-17		Guns impossible to shoot. All ordered exercise in morning. Afternoon stripped saddle inspection.	
	10-1-17		Routine same as yesterday.	
	11-1-17		Range practice at same places as on 8th inst. No.s 5, 6, and 7 gunners fired in each section. In afternoon stoppage classes for all gunners and gun-helmet drill. Commander.	
	12-1-17		Range Practices arranged. Bonnet. Exercise. Medical Officer inspects all men in sections and H.Q.	
	13-1-17		Exercise on Blankets at 8.0 am. Veterinary Officer inspected all horses on the strength.	
	14-1-17		Sunday Routine. Voluntary Church Service at PREVRES at 6 p.m. Heavy snow to extent and incorporated to M.G. School. CAMIERS for 15 days Course.	
	15-1-17		Inspection by C.O. of all transport at PREVRES at 11.0 am. Full allowance for fatigues etc. Turnout good. Remainder exercise 8.0 am. Ride Frozen and Snow. In afternoon Stoppages and mechanism classes.	
	16-1-17		Exercise 8.0 am. Afternoon preparation for transport inspection. Stones.	
	17-1-17		Inspection of all transport by O.C A.S.C and Brigades at 11.0 am PREVRES. Private ____ offends owing to unfit teen, but held at 12 noon. Turn out Very bad weather - Snow. Signallers at visual work in morning and afternoon. 1 Officer and 2 other ranks proceeded to England on leave.	

WAR DIARY or INTELLIGENCE SUMMARY

Army Form C. 2118.

Place	Date	Hour	Summary of Events and Information	Remarks and references to Appendices
PREURES	18/1/17		Service at 9.0am. Afternoon lecture to Gunners. Keyalless at work and Gunner Exercise.	
	19/1/17		Signallers sent on holiday. Took out Camps in evening. Inspection by M.O. of 3 Sections in absence.	
	20/1/17		Service at 6.30am. Inspection by M.O. of 3 Sections in morning. The whole of past week has been impossible to carry out training programme. Heavy snow and hard frosts.	
	21/1/17		Sunday Service Divine Service for 3 Sections at 11.30am at SHOQUIN. 2 otherwise proceeded on leave. Captain F.T. STAKER under Lt. WHITE. Senior Officer Came School, CAMIERS, to undergo course. Proceeded to Machine Gun School. Capt. D. J.G. DRIFT assumes command of Sqdn. Machine Gunnery from 9 to 10.15 a.m. Remainder Service. Signallers classes.	
	22/1/17		Classes for Gunners from 9 to 10.15 a.m. Remainder Service. Training & Lecture for Gunners. Lecture to Signallers on D III. Sewing for gunners. Lecture to Signallers on D III.	
	23/1/17		Hand & Foot Annual Inspection of Bks. by A.D.M.S. 1st Cavalry Division. Signallers Inoculation most Afternoon classes for Gunners. Evening lecture to Gunners. Signalling on map-reading and Bayes. Captain H. MOSS taken on strength from 16th K. E. & G Training Centre, UCKFIELD (England) and assumes command.	
	24/1/17		Continued frost during to severe cold weather. Lecture to instead of firing on range. Football match - "C" v "D" Section in afternoon. Other Sections Lectures or precautions against gas. Two other ranks proceeded on leave to U.K.	
	25/1/17		Exercise. Inoculation Classes for Gunners in morning. Afternoon Arms and kit inspection. Lecture to Gunners in evening.	
	26/1/17		Firing on Range at 9.0am. Exercise. Afternoon Gas Helmet drill. Evening Lecture to Gunners.	

Army Form C. 211.

WAR DIARY
or
INTELLIGENCE SUMMARY.
(Erase heading not required.)

Instructions regarding War Diaries and Intelligence Summaries are contained in F. S. Regs., Part II. and the Staff Manual respectively. Title pages will be prepared in manuscript.

Place	Date	Hour	Summary of Events and Information	Remarks and references to Appendices
PREURES.	27.1.17		Inspection by Medical Officer of 3 Sections Stripped Socks inspection in afternoon. Officer attended M.G. School, CAMIERS, and seemed keen on strafing Germans.	
	28.1.17		Sunday Routine. 3 Sections (Preures) on Church Parade at 11.0 a.m. PREURES. One Officer and 8 other ranks (Preures) on leave to U.K. Whole of past week snow still lying and hard frost. Very cold	
	29.1.17		Exercise. Mechanism lessons for Gunners. Afternoon stoppages for Gunners. Evening to 18.C.O.S. # Lecture on "Attacks on Villages." 10 other Rank proceeded on leave to England	
	30.1.17		Exercise. Classes for Gunners. Afternoon lecture and Evening Lecture to N.C.O.S. on map reading and use of Trench Maps. Snow	
	31.1.17		Exercise. Classes for Gunners. Afternoon. Sermon from and Vet Inspector.	

M W Strattan
Captain (St Hinans)
Commanding 22 Squadron, Machine Gun Corps.

31-1-17.

Army Form C. 2118.

WAR DIARY
or
INTELLIGENCE SUMMARY.

(Erase heading not required.)

Instructions regarding War Diaries and Intelligence Summaries are contained in F. S. Regs., Part II. and the Staff Manual respectively. Title pages will be prepared in manuscript.

Vol XI

Place	Date	Hour	Summary of Events and Information	Remarks and references to Appendices

CONFIDENTIAL

War Diary
of
2nd Squadron, Machine Gun Corps

February 1917

Volume No XIII

Army Form C. 2118.

WAR DIARY
or
INTELLIGENCE SUMMARY.
(Erase heading not required.)

Instructions regarding War Diaries and Intelligence Summaries are contained in F. S. Regs., Part II. and the Staff Manual respectively. Title pages will be prepared in manuscript.

Place	Date	Hour	Summary of Events and Information	Remarks and references to Appendices
PREUVES	1st		Morning Exercise, Sniping & Trigger Pressing for Revolver Men. — Afternoon Immediate Action for Gunners (blindfolded.) Evening lecture to B.E.F. Lecture "Indirect Fire".	
	2nd		Exercise. Sniping & Trigger Pressing for Revolver Men not on Parade yesterday. Afternoon Inspection of A.C. & D. Lecture by M.O. Evening lecture to A.C & D. Lecture "Indirect Fire".	
	3rd		Exercise. Inspection by V.O. of all horses	
	4th		Sunday Routine. No horse exercise. Still very cold & hard frost during the past week.	
	5th		Exercise. Lecture to "A" Section by M.O. Remainder GAS Helmet Drill.	
	6th		Inspection of all S.Q.D.M. Transfixit by C.O. Exercise lecture to "B" S.Q.D.M by M.O. Remainder Gas Helmet Drill. Lt. Miller & Sgt. PRATTS joined 1st Cav. Divn. School.	
	7th		Exercise & Classes for Gunners — Afternoon lecture to "C" Section by M.O. Saddle Inspection for Remainder of S.Q.D.M.	
	8th		Inspection of Trench Party. Sections assembled at ENQUIN at 10 a.m. STMSHE Sn	HM

Army Form C. 2118

WAR DIARY
or
INTELLIGENCE SUMMARY
(Erase heading not required.)

Instructions regarding War Diaries and Intelligence Summaries are contained in F.S. Regs., Part II. and the Staff Manual respectively. Title Pages will be prepared in manuscript.

Place	Date	Hour	Summary of Events and Information	Remarks and references to Appendices
PREURES	8/5		STABLES IN afternoon. Lecture to "D" Section by M.O.	
	9th		Exercise & classes for gunners. Afternoon lecture to E & F Sections by M.O.	
	10th		Exercise. Cleaning up stables. A.m. stif inspection	
	11th		Sunday. Routine. No church parade.	
	12th		Exercise. Lecture on Indirect Fire and working out calculations for same to all officers.	
			Afternoon Gun Drill etc. in his helmets. Belt filling by hand to drivers	
	13th		Exercise. Practical work in Gunnery. In due of June to range the	
			Afternoon. Gunners. Gun Drill in Gas. Helmets. Evening Lecture to Officers & NCOs by M.O. who has done Gas Course at Divnl School.	
	14th		Exercise. Inspection of Trench Pump. Dismounted Marching Order by C.O. C.2nd	
			Coy B/de at 10-30 a.m. at PREURES.	
	15th		Exercise in Small Bor respiration to all officers & NCO. Open Lecture by	
			During Gas Officer.	
	16th		Exercise. Shooting on Range (SKEPPAN) for Trench Party. Afternoon A.C.9.D	
			Lecture fitted & tested with small box respirators. Inspection of all Sections by M.O.	

HM

Army Form C. 2118

WAR DIARY
or
INTELLIGENCE SUMMARY

(Erase heading not required.)

Instructions regarding War Diaries and Intelligence Summaries are contained in F. S. Regs., Part II. and the Staff Manual respectively. Title pages will be prepared in manuscript.

Place	Date	Hour	Summary of Events and Information	Remarks and references to Appendices
PREURES	17		Exercise. Inspection of all horses by V.O.	
	18		Afternoon - B.E.F. sections fitted and tested with hot respirator. Saddles etc cleaned up and stored.	
			5 Officers, 94 O.R. despatched by motor lorry with 3 L.A.C. O.R. to be attached to 21st Ind. Div. Glass condensers ordered.	
	19		Exercise. HQ, A.C.D. Sections under 2 i/c B.E.F. under section arrangement A.D.V.S. visited Sqdn. in afternoon to see horses of A and C sections suspected of STOMATITIS.	
	20		Rain:- only B.E.F. sections exercised. Work in improving stables, reinhung arrangements & trimming up horses.	
	21		Exercise HQ, A.C. and D sections 1½ hours walking in LEROEQ and SEHEM B.E.F. under section arrangements	
	22		Exercise B.E.F. under Sqdn Leader. HQ, A.C.D under Col CHOULES. Rain.	
	23		Exercise HQ, A, C, D sections under 2-i-C to ENQUIN. B.E.F. under lectr Arrangements.	
	24		Exercise at 6-45 A.M. H.Q. A.C. & D under 2-i-C. B.E.F. under lectr.	

WAR DIARY or INTELLIGENCE SUMMARY

Army Form C. 2118

Place	Date	Hour	Summary of Events and Information	Remarks and references to Appendices
PREURES	24th/2		under took arrangements Inspection of all horses by V.O.	
	25th/2		Usual Sunday Routine. Bde troop Competition at SAMER. Pte Cullen's left in for CORPS Competition Voluntary Evening Service at 6-30 P.M.	
	26th/2		B.E. & F sections Exercise under Section Leaders. H.Q, A, C, & D under Section arrangements. Snowy weather. Spent value of punt value to eu children of horses. All "F" section horses left their teeth.	
	27th/2		Inspection of all horses outside Section billets by 6-O-C-in-C. 2nd CAV B DE. B, D & F about equal & & E section went. Command'g by 6-O-C. used of men wishing & cooked food to looker their billets.	
	28th/2		Exercise H.Q, A, C & D under 2-in-C. B, E & F under Section Arrangements. Conference at C. O's at B'de H.Q.	

H. Mey
Capt
Cm'd'g 2nd Machine Gun Sq'dn

CONFIDENTIAL.

APPENDIX
to
WAR DIARY
of
2ND SQUADRON, MACHINE GUN CORPS.

FEBRUARY 1917.

VOLUME No. XIII

1.

1917.

17th February. One Limber, 3. O.R. and 5 horses left for Trenches.

18th " . Trench Party of 5 Officers, 97 O.R. (including 3.O.R attached from 8th Light Armoured Car Batty.) proceeded to forward area from permanent Billets. Left PREVRES at 11.30 AM by Motor Lorry. Insufficient lorries (5) supplied. 2 miles from PREVRES 1 Lorry left behind for two extra lorries, the remainder of party proceeding to LABOURSE - (ref. Map sheet LENS 11, 1/100,000 Edition 2) arrived at 6.0 pm. Billeted at LABOURSE night of 18/19th. The three other Lorries arrived at 11.30 pm. Unit attached to 21st Division.

19th " . C.O. and two officers reconnoitred M.G. emplacements etc. in QUARRIES SECTOR (62nd Inf Bde.) ref. Map Sheet 36 C N.W 3 /10,000
Respirator drill, rifle drill and checking all stores and Arms inspection.

20th " . Squadron moved to Trenches. Left LABOURSE 8.45 AM and arrived VERMELLES (ref. map sheet. LENS 11, 1/100,000 Edition 3.) at 10.0 AM. Sections proceeded at once to take over in trenches, Dispositions as follows:-
C and D Sections to Left Sector under Lt. Duff.
A " B " " Right " " Lt. Dent
E " F " " Village Line " 2Lt. White.

No. 1 Section (4 guns) of 62nd M.G. Coy. to be attached for duty to the Squadron and held in Squadron Reserve at VERMELLES. Squadron HQ. at VERMELLES. Relief reported complete by 3.0 pm (1½ hours to spare.) State of Trenches very bad after the thaw - 2' of mud and water in places.
Period up to midnight 20th normal. Rain

21st February	Nothing to report from all Sections. Emplacements, Dug-outs, etc. taken over in a disgraceful condition. Day spent in cleaning these and checking and testing guns, etc. Hostile heavy T.M. active on Front & support line - Foggy. No guns fired on night 20/21st. One gun of "D" Section engaged enemy dump indirect at 5-30 pm 500 rounds - L. Roberts joined Left Sector.
22nd -"-	3 Guns searched back areas early part of night. 1500 rounds fired on night 21/22. Party of enemy about 40 strong raided and entered our trenches in Right sub-sector. At once ejected leaving several dead. One unwounded prisoner caught behind support line. Enemy placed box barrage for 30 minutes behind Support Line, Right Sector. 50/60 Shells (4.2) fired on VERMELLES at 6.0 AM - Large percentage lachrymatory - Normal during day, Enemy heavy T.M. active.
23rd -"-	During evening and night 22/23rd, 4 guns swept back areas. One gun fired on enemy party observed on fog suddenly lifting. Total 3,500 rounds expended. Day normal State of Trenches rapidly getting worse, especially in communication Trenches - Foggy
24th -"-	Night of 23/24th. 3 guns opened on enemy relief N. of CITE ST. ELIE. reported from our Front Line at 5.pm. During night Searching fire on targets in enemy's back area. Total ammunition expended 4,500 rounds. - Clear - enemy snipers, in consequence, were successful.
25th -"-	Night of 24/25th. One gun D Section opened in retaliation to enemy M.G. sweeping

WWSW

25th Febr.	VERMELLES road. Enemy gun silenced. Five guns (2 D & 1 F Section.) swept back areas and opened on enemy dumps and tramways. Total ammunition expended 5,000 rounds. Day normal. Enemy shelled occasionally, usual activity of T.Ms. and aerial darts. Fine. Relief within unit carried out as follows:- E & F Sections to Right Sector under Lt. White A & B " " Left " " Lt. Dent. C & D " VERMELLES in reserve. No. I " 62 M.G.Coy. to Village Lines under Lt. Yates (62 M.G.Coy.) Lt. Roberts to remain with Left Sector.
26th -"-	Night 25/26th. 3 Guns at O.B.1 and O.G. Carried out indirect fire on various targets and swept back areas. Total ammunition expended 7,500 rounds. Day normal. Fine.
27th -"-	Night 26/27th. 3 Guns in O.B.1 and O.G. Carried out usual indirect fire. Hostile relief reported at 6 pm. 3 Guns opened. Number rounds expended 10,000. "C" Section relieved 2 guns of No.1 Section 62 M.G.Coy. in VILLAGE LINES at 3 pm. Lieut. L.F.C. Duff evacuated to Hospital with measles.
28th -"-	Night 27/28th. Usual indirect fire during afternoon and throughout night. Total rounds expended 3,500. B.E.F. Sections and 2 Guns 62 M.G.Coy relieved by 8 guns of 71 M.G.Coy. Relief completed 6 pm. B.D.E.F. Sections billeted in VERMELLES. No.1 Section 62 M.G.Coy ceased to be attached to the Squadron.

28th February	Squadron on relief attached to 110th Infantry Brigade, 21st Division.

L.W.D. Wathen
Capt.
Commanding 2nd Machine Gun Sqdn.

Army Form C. 2118.

WAR DIARY
~~INTELLIGENCE SUMMARY~~
(Erase heading not required.)

Vol 14

CONFIDENTIAL.

WAR DIARY
of
2ND SQUADRON, MACHINE GUN CORPS

MARCH 1917

VOLUME No. XIV

Army Form C. 2118.

WAR DIARY
INTELLIGENCE SUMMARY.
(Erase heading not required.)

Instructions regarding War Diaries and Intelligence Summaries are contained in F.S. Regs., Part II. and the Staff Manual respectively. Title pages will be prepared in manuscript.

Place	Date	Hour	Summary of Events and Information	Remarks and references to Appendices
PREURES.	1/3/17		Exercise under 2nd-in-Command. Inspection of Band & L Sections by G.O.C. 1st Cavalry Division at PREURES at 10.45 a.m. Criticisms. Importance of great care in watering of horses and need of plentiful supply of Chaff.	
In the Trenches.	—"—		Inspection of Kit, clothing and all M.Gun tested and repaired. Men bathed. "A" and "C" Sections remain in trenches. Machine Gun positions etc. of 110th Infantry Brigade, reconnoitred.	
PREURES.	2/3/17		Exercise. Inspection of Squadrons Transport by Brigade Transport Officer. at PREURES 10-30 a.m. Inspection of all men and Billets by Medical Officer in afternoon.	
In the Trenches.	—"—		B, E, D and F Sections relieves 8 guns of 110 M.G.Coy in HOHENZOLLERN Sector. (ref Map Sheet 36c N.W. 3 1/10,000) Hans & Sections remained in former positions in QUARRIES SECTOR, whole under 110 Inf Bde. No 1 Section 110 M.G. Coy attached to squadron for Duty. Guns disposed as follows:- 5 Guns Left Sector under 2/Lt. White 3 " Right " -"- Lt. Dent 6 " (Inf.Coy) to VILLAGE LINE under 2/Lt. Fanning 2 " QUARRIES SECTOR under 2/Lt Roberts.	

WSW

WAR DIARY
INTELLIGENCE SUMMARY.
(Erase heading not required.)

Army Form C. 2118.

Place	Date	Hour	Summary of Events and Information	Remarks and references to Appendices
PREURES	3/17		Exercise. Lieut. C. E. Miller rejoins from 1st bar. Divisional School. Lieut. A. L. Roy-Lewis proceeds to 1st Signal Sqdn. for Signalling Course.	
Trenches.	-"-		Whole sectors now occupied by 16 Guns known as ZOLLERN Left and Right. Day and night normal. Guns fires 7,000 rounds during night on back areas. Trenches in better condition in this sector - daily improving. Fine in evening - wind changes to N.E. Gas Alert.	
PREURES.	4/17		Usual Sunday routine. Arms inspection after Sates.	
Trenches.	-"-		During night Gas alarm at 11.50 p.m. 1.10 a.m. and 2 a.m. lasting 1/2 hour each. All ranks stood-to. Shrapnell & Gas noticed near REDOUBT CRATER. Enemy used Gas Stella & Gas Bombs. 3 Gas Stella fell near Gun R.53 at 12.10 a.m. Day and night Normal. Guns fired 13,750 rounds during 24 hours. "C" Section from VILLAGE LINE relieved "A" Section at O.B.1. and FARMERS LANE at 8.30 a.m. Lieut. Dent took over command of "C" Section in addition to his other 3 Guns. Lieut. Roberts to H.Q. and 1/2 of VILLAGE LINE Guns.	
Preures.	5/17		Snow. Exercise.	
Trenches	-"-		Day and night normal. 5,000 rounds fires during previous 24 hours	

Army Form C. 2118.

WAR DIARY
or
INTELLIGENCE SUMMARY.
(Erase heading not required.)

Instructions regarding War Diaries and Intelligence Summaries are contained in F. S. Regs., Part II. and the Staff Manual respectively. Title pages will be prepared in manuscript.

Place	Date	Hour	Summary of Events and Information	Remarks and references to Appendices
Trenches	5/3/17		One of our aeroplanes brought down at 11.0 A.m. at G.6.a. 93.07. behind enemy front line. 3 Guns fired on it at intervals during evening and night. Snowing. Wind N.E.	
PREURES. Trenches	6/3/17		Exercise. Day and night normal. 15,600 rounds fires during previous 24 hours. Number of Gas Shells fell near Gun Position in FARMERS LANE during night. – 2 men of Gun Team slightly affected by the Gas. Condition of trenches not improved after fall of snow.	
PREURES. Trenches	7/3/17		Exercise. Very cold wind. Lieut. D.J.G. Duff rejoined from Hospital. Day & night normal. 14,000 rounds fires during 24 hours – Harassing Back areas, Cross Tracks, Knick train tracks etc. Strong N.E. Wind. Cold. French Hard and clean. Work carried on on Trench maintenance. Vermelles slightly shelled about 4 p.m.	
PREURES. Trenches	8/3/17		Snow. Shells all morning. Exercise in afternoon when weather improved. Day and night normal. 23,750 rounds fires on various targets. Reconnaissance carried out of positions for new guns in front	WW?W

Army Form C. 2118.

WAR DIARY
INTELLIGENCE SUMMARY.
(Erase heading not required.)

Instructions regarding War Diaries and Intelligence Summaries are contained in F.S. Regs., Part II. and the Staff Manual respectively. Title pages will be prepared in manuscript.

Place	Date	Hour	Summary of Events and Information	Remarks and references to Appendices
Trenches	8/3/17		Line S. of Southern Crater in connection with Raid. # 3 Gas Shells fell at Gun position V.35 about 6.10 p.m.	# See Appendix I
PREURES.	9/3/17		Exercise. Inspection of all N.C.O.s and Men by Med Officer in afternoon.	
Trenches	"		Day and night normal - 23,800 rounds expended on various targets. Tramways, tracks, etc. Parties of enemy crossing open ground various times and reported to Brigade and Battalion H.Q. Further reconnaisance as on 8th inst. carried out with No. 18 Gun Teams. G.O.C. 1st Cavalry Division inspected billets of Squadron H.Q. in VERMELLES at 12 noon.	
PREURES.	10/3/17		Exercise. Inspection of all horses by Veterinary Officer	
Trenches	"		Day and night normal. Hostile Machine Guns showing more activity on our ration Dumps. 22,500 rounds expended in 24 hours. Fire.	
PREURES.	11/3/17		Naval Sunday routine	
Trenches	"		Quiet. Enemy Machine Guns active on Ration Dumps and HULLUCH ROAD. 24,000 rounds expended in 24 hours on back areas. On two occasions guns dispersed working parties by direct fire. Hostile Machine Guns etc. observed. Fire. State of Trenches good. Clean & dry.	[initials]

Army Form C. 2118.

WAR DIARY
~~INTELLIGENCE SUMMARY.~~
(Erase heading not required.)

Place	Date	Hour	Summary of Events and Information	Remarks and references to Appendices
PREURES Trenches	12/3/17	—	Exercise. Situation Normal. Enemy Heavy Medium T.M.s active in front of Reserve Trench and on FARMERS LANE. 19,500 rounds expended during 24 hours. Heavy rain during night. Trenches (particularly C.T.s) bad. A lot of work required on all emplacements.	
PREURES Trenches	13/3/17	—	Exercise. 12 horses and 6 men returned from Pioneer Battalion. Situation Normal. 15,000 rounds expended during 24 hours on visual targets. One other rank evacuated Wounded, accidentally self-inflicted.	
PREURES Trenches	14/3/17	—	Exercise. Inspection of Bizets by 2nd in command. Situation Normal. 19,250 rounds expended during 24 hours on selected targets, chiefly by day. Rain.	
PREURES Trenches	15/3/17	—	Exercise. Situation Normal. FARMERS LANE and GORDON ALLEY (Rear Gun Positions) Slightly Shelled at 4 pm. One Gun "A" section in VILLAGE LINE and one Gun "C" section at position R.53, relieves by 2 guns 110 M.G. Coy. On relief these guns moves up to mining tunnel near SOUTHERN CRATER and	M07W.

Army Form C. 2118.

WAR DIARY
INTELLIGENCE SUMMARY.
(Erase heading not required.)

Instructions regarding War Diaries and Intelligence Summaries are contained in F. S. Regs., Part II. and the Staff Manual respectively. Title pages will be prepared in manuscript.

Place	Date	Hour	Summary of Events and Information	Remarks and references to Appendices
Treuxles.	15/3/17		Placed under orders of Lieut. Roberts ready to take up positions for raid. The extra two guns of 110 M.G.Coy. attached to Squadron during raid.	Appendix I
PREURES.	16/3/17		Exercise.	
Treuxles	-"-		Raid carried out. Zero hour 5 a.m. The 2 guns (under Lieut. G. Roberts) in front line trench covered Right Party of raiders, on whom enemy M.G's never got into action, though the raiders were held up at the hostile wire. Remainder of guns fires on normal targets during night and barrage fire on enemy front line and C.T's on flanks of raid. Total number of rounds expended :- 57,000. During the day, all remaining gun positions occupied by guns of the Squadron were relieved by guns of 110 M.G.Coy. Squadron relieves by 110 M.G.Coy. Relief complete at 1.30 p.m. On relief, all ranks bathed, later marching to NOYELLES and billets there for the night.	* Appendix II. Appendix 3
PREURES.	17/3/17		Exercise. Horse-Quoting parade at ENQUIN.	
NOYELLES.	-"-		Seven motor-lorries arrived at 7.50 A.M. for return of Squadron to billets. Three of these lorries were despatched to VERMELLES for guns.	Pur XW.

T2134. Wt. W708—776. 500000. 4/15. Sir J. C. & S.

Army Form C. 2118

WAR DIARY
~~INTELLIGENCE SUMMARY.~~
(Erase heading not required.)

Place	Date	Hour	Summary of Events and Information	Remarks and references to Appendices
NOYELLES.	17/3/17		Stores etc. Whole party left Noyelles at 9.0 a.m. Halted 40 minutes at ESTRE BLANCHE, and arrived at PREURES 3.50 p.m.	
PREURES.	18/3/17		Sunday Routine. Church Parade 11.45 am PREURES. Lt. Roberts to Div. Gas Warfare School.	
	19/3/17		Exercise. Cleaning up for dismounted Parly, and Arms Inspection. Shoes and gun parts checked and cleaned. Rain.	
	20/3/17		Exercise. Mtd. French Party on parade. Inspection of all Kit. Fitting of Clothing. All horses inspected by Veterinary Officer. Lt. Roberts returned from Warfare Div Gas School.	
	21/3/17		Exercise. Trimming up of horses. Saddles and equipment cleaned. Rain at intervals.	
	22/3/17		Section Drill at 9 a.m. New Cavalry Machine Gun Drill. Ammo inspection. Orders received at 9.50 p.m. to stand-to ready to move at 8 hours' notice. Show.	
	23/3/17		Early Exercise. Morning. Limbers packed. Surplus Stores and Kits handed in etc. Afternoon all ranks fitted with new Small Box Respirators and those already in use returned to Store.	
	24/3/17		Exercise and Section Drill or Squadron Parade grounds at 9 am.	WSW

Army Form C. 2118.

WAR DIARY
or
INTELLIGENCE SUMMARY.
(Erase heading not required.)

Instructions regarding War Diaries and Intelligence Summaries are contained in F.S. Regs., Part II. and the Staff Manual respectively. Title pages will be prepared in manuscript.

Place	Date	Hour	Summary of Events and Information	Remarks and references to Appendices
PREUDES.	24/3/17		Box Respirators checked and marked.	
	25/3/17		Sunday Routine Church Parade at ENQUIN at 10.45 am. for Free Sections stripped saddle inspection at Noon	
	26/3/17		Inspection by Commanding Officer of all Sections in marching Order, complete with Transport, etc. Free Sections in morning and Free in afternoon. Exercise accordingly. Snow at intervals.	
	27/3/17		Exercise and Drill on Squadron Parade Grounds at 9 am Ammunition checked and cleaned. Rain at intervals.	
	28/3/17		Section Drill on Blankets at 9 am in Squadron Drill grounds. Afternoon arms inspection and preparation for Brigade Marching Order Route March.	
	29/3/17		Route March for all units of 22 Cav. Bde. in marching order. Echelon "A" Packed. Squadron Parade 6.30 Am. Starting Point (T of HUBERSENT) reached at 9.45 am. Returned to Billets at 12.30 pm. Stables in afternoon. Heavy rain.	RWB[?]
	30/3/17		Musketry practice for all men armed with rifle at 8.30 am.	

Army Form C. 2118.

WAR DIARY
INTELLIGENCE SUMMARY.
(Erase heading not required.)

Place	Date	Hour	Summary of Events and Information	Remarks and references to Appendices
PREVRES.	30/3/17		Remainder exercise. Visual work for Signallers. Inspection of all N.C.O.s and men by Medical Officer.	
	31/3/17		Exercise and Inspection of all horses by Veterinary Officer commencing at 10.30 a.m. All horses have slightly improved since return of Trench Party. "E" Section in worst condition. Squadron has been standing-to on 6 hours' notice all past week. Stormy and rain at intervals.	

31-3-17.

W.S. Mather Captain (8th Hussars)
Comdg. 2nd Squadron, Machine Gun Corps.

SECRET   APPENDIX I

                                                C.T.39.

H.Q.
   110th Infantry Brigade.
   ─────────────────────

                In accordance with your orders to move up two
                Machine Guns of the 2nd. Machine Gun Squadron
                to assist in the forthcoming raid, I put forward
                the following proposals:-

No.1 Gun.   Gun mounted behind parados in ALEXANDER TRENCH at
                G.11.b.30.83. The position is about 3 yards from
                Sniper's exit of FARMER'S LANE — RAT CREEK TUNNEL,
                affording an easy exit for gun and men, also cover,
                in the event of a retaliatory bombardment. This
                position commands the whole of the enemy parapet
                from G.5.d.50.31 to G.11.b.69.60.

No.2 Gun.   At junction of ALEXANDER TRENCH and MOUSE RUN
                G.11.b.48.69. There is a small dugout close by
                which would afford cover as for other gun.
                This gun also covers the whole of the enemy
                parapet in the same area as No.1 Gun.

                        I propose that Gun No.2 should traverse
                enemy parapet from G.5.d.40.43 to G.5.d.75.00.
                Not to sweep enemy's parapet from to to G.5.d.70.10 to
Note.   This gun will be given very definite orders as to *G.11.b.72.38*
                limitation of traverse so as to no-wise endanger
                the raiding party.
                Both guns to maintain their fire until return of
                raiding party.

                I suggest that two Lewis guns in ALEXANDER TRENCH
                be detailed to take on the two hostile M.G.s
                located at   , and that they fire
                on no other target, — sweeping the enemy parapet
                being left to the two M.G.s.

                These two M.G.s to be relieved in VILLAGE LINE
                by two guns of 110th M.G.Coy. by arrangement
                direct between O's. C. concerned.

                Copy of my operation orders for above will be
                forwarded later.

                The remaining guns in the sector to maintain
                barrage fire on enemy communication trenches.

                                           [signature]
                                                 Captain,
10.3.17.   Commanding 2nd. Machine Gun Squadron.

APPENDIX II

S E C R E T.

OPERATION ORDERS.
BY
Captain L.W.S.WATHEN,
Commanding 2nd Machine Gun Squadron.

1. The following will be the dispositions of the guns of this Squadron in connection with the raid to be carried out on the 16th instant.
   1 gun "A" Section, and 1 gun C Section will take up positions in front line trench under orders issued direct. The remainder of the guns of the Squadron will carry out barrage fire as under:-

2. Attached memo shows targets and calculations for guns of your sector. All guns will open on these targets at ZERO minus two minutes, and maintain rapid fire until ZERO plus 35 minutes. Gun at R.66 will open barrage fire at ZERO minus 10, continuing until ZERO plus 35.

3. At ZERO plus 35 all Machine Gun fire will cease, and guns will be immediately laid on their S.O.S. lines. Teams will <u>stand to</u> in dugouts - double sentries at posts as usual.

4. The following is time-table:-

    a. Trench Assembly   Before Zero 10 mins.
    b. Feint "A" Artillery & Smoke starts   "   "   10 "
       Called "X"
    c. Mine exploded and mine Artillery
       and Mine smoke start. Called "Y"   "   "   5 "
    d. Raid smoke starts.   "   "   2 "
    e. 1. Raid Artillery starts   )
       2. Infantry leave our trenches)   (Z E R O .
    f. Infantry begin to leave
       enemy trenches.   (After "   25 "
    g. Infantry reach our lines   "   "   (35) "
    h. Smoke ceases.   "   "   35 "

5. Time of ZERO will be notified by me to Os. C. left and Right Sectors at gun position R.66 about 5 p.m.; and to O.C. VILLAGE LINE. Lala.

                                          [signature]
                                                        Captain,
16.3.17.   Commanding 2nd Machine Gun Squadron.

SECRET. APPENDIX III Copy No. 6.

OPERATION ORDERS
by
Captain L.W.D.WATHEN,
Commanding 2nd. Machine Gun Squadron.

Relief.

1. The 2nd. Machine Gun Squadron (less 2 guns) will be relieved in the line by 110th Machine Gun Company on 16th instant.

2. The above two guns, at positions V.37 in VILLAGE LINE and E.58a in O.B.1. will be relieved by 2 guns of 110th Machine Gun Company on evening 15th inst. under separate orders.

3. No.1 Section, 110th Machine Gun Company, will remain in present positions, coming under orders of O.C. 110th Machine Gun Company from 16th instant.

4. Relief will commence from Squadron H.Q. at 11.0 a.m. Guides from each gun team will report at H.Q. at 10.45 a.m.

5. In addition to usual Trench and M.G. emplacement stores, the following will be handed over:-

   10 Belt boxes per gun.
   Gun Boots.
   List of Targets.
   All Maps.

   Order Boards and Range Cards.

6. Os.C.Sectors will make out, in duplicate, lists of Trench Stores etc. handed over, 1 copy to be handed to Officer taking over, and 1 copy to be returned to H.Q. immediately relief complete.

7. Rations will be sent up tonight for breakfast on 16th only.

8. On relief, teams will proceed independently to Sqdn. H.Q. All men will bathe at VERMELLES from 12 noon to 1.0 p.m. and from 2 to 3.0 p.m.

9. After baths, all sections will proceed to NOYELLES, where the Squadron will be billeted on night 16/17th. All guns, Ammunition, stores, etc. will be left in Squadron store at VERMELLES.

10. Lorries will arrive at NOYELLES billets at 8.0 a.m. on 17th inst. for return of Squadron to 1st Cavalry Division. Three lorries will then be despatched to VERMELLES for above stores, etc. with two men per section. These lorries will pick up the others at NOYELLES on return journey.

                                    L.W.D.Wathen.
                                              Captain,
15.3.17.   Commanding 2nd. Machine Gun Squadron.

          Copy No.1 To 110th Infantry Brigade.
            "   " 2   O.C. Left Sector.
            "   " 3   O.C. Right Sector.
            "   " 4   O.C. VILLAGE LINE.
            "   " 5   O.C. 110th Machine Gun Company.
            "   " 6   Office Copy and Diary.

Army Form C. 2118.

WAR DIARY
or
INTELLIGENCE SUMMARY.
(Erase heading not required.)

Instructions regarding War Diaries and Intelligence Summaries are contained in F. S. Regs., Part II. and the Staff Manual respectively. Title pages will be prepared in manuscript.

Vol 15

Place	Date	Hour	Summary of Events and Information	Remarks and references to Appendices
			CONFIDENTIAL WAR DIARY of 2nd SQUADRON, MACHINE GUN CORPS. APRIL 1917. VOLUME No. XV	

WAR DIARY

INTELLIGENCE SUMMARY
(Erase heading not required.)

Army Form C. 2118.

Place	Date	Hour	Summary of Events and Information	Remarks and references to Appendices
PREURES.	1/7/17		Sunday routine. Voluntary Service for R.C's at 9-30 A.M.	
	2/7/17		Musketry for all crews to Remainder exercise. Heavy snow in afternoon. Outdoor work cancelled.	
	3/7/17		Snow in morning renders training impossible. Afternoon revolver shooting. Orders at 9 P.M. that Brigade will march from present area Eastwards on 5th inst.	
	4/7/17		Exercise and preparation to march.	
	5/7/17		Brigade concentrates in FRUGES area. Squadron left PREURES at 10.15 A.M. and marches via HUCQUELIERS to MANINGHEM. Six miles. Arrives 11.30 A.M. All men and horses of all Sections, less F Section, in billets.	
MANINGHEM.	6/7/17		No move. Orders for march postponed 24 hours. Exercise. Remainder of horses placed in billets.	
	7/7/17		Brigade concentrates at FRUGES and march continues to NAVRANS area. ref Map. LENS Sheet II. 1/100,000 and HAZEBROUCK Sheet 5A 1/100,000. Squadron left MANINGHEM at 7.0 A.M. arrives the concentration point at 8.0 A.M. Marches via FRUGES to ANVIN, where Squadron billets for the night.	

Army Form C. 2118

WAR DIARY
INTELLIGENCE SUMMARY.
(Erase heading not required.)

Place	Date	Hour	Summary of Events and Information	Remarks and references to Appendices
ANVIN	7/4/17		All horses in field. Men in billets. Echelon "B" Brigaded "Gap Organization" begun.	
	8/4/17		March continued eastwards. Squadron left ANVIN at 11.20 A.M. Brigade starting point CONTEVILLE thence via HUCLIERS - LA THIEULOYE - FREVILLERS - BETHONSART - MINGOVAL to bivouac about FREVIN CAPELLE. Arrives at 5 p.m. Squadron schools on high ground - only 2 tents and 3 trench covers drawn. Tents to be at 1 hour's notice.	
FREVIN CAPELLE	9/4/17		No move. Very bad weather. Snow and rain with high wind.	
	10/4/17		Orders received at 2.10 p.m. to march at 2.30 p.m. Squadron saddles-up and all sections reported ready to move in 33 minutes. Brigade marches via MONT ST. ELOI to ANZIN ST. AUBIN. Immediately on arrival orders received that march will be continued at once eastwards. Marches via ST CATHERINE - ST NICOLAS to a position on road just E of ST LAURENT BLANGEY. Frequent blocks and halts owing to traffic and difficulty in crossing where road crossed old Front Line trench. Bivouaced on road-side about 1.30 A.M. Squadron horses off-saddles and tied to trees, railings.	
ST LAURENT BLANGEY	11/4/17		was able to water and feed.	RW&D

Army Form C. 2118.

WAR DIARY
or
INTELLIGENCE SUMMARY.
(Erase heading not required.)

Instructions regarding War Diaries and Intelligence Summaries are contained in F.S. Regs, Part II. and the Staff Manual respectively. Title pages will be prepared in manuscript.

Place	Date	Hour	Summary of Events and Information	Remarks and references to Appendices
ST LAURENT BLANGY	11/4/17		etc. in a wood. 500x E. of T. in ST LAURENT BLANGY. 9100 horses (L.D.) of "B" Section with Echelon "A" died - either of Yew poisoning or hard work and exposure. Brigade Saddles up ready to move to co-operate in the successful attack of 9th Division as per Brigade Operation Orders. 1 Section (B) attached to 4th Dragoon Guards and latter moves to ATHIES on 1st Cav Bde. moving forward.	
		12.30pm		
		4pm	Orders received to turn into bivouac. Horses watered, off-saddles and fed. Heavy Snow.	
	12/4/17	7.45am	All units of Brigade ready to march westward. S. Horse 10.30 AM are Squadron moves owing to heavy traffic. Bad going on track across old trench lines. Large number of horses of Brigade stuck in mud. Only 4 horses of Squadron dropped out - all soon caught up, halted in ST NICOLAS for Squadron to close up, but troop and half in rear entered town by different route thus getting ahead of Squadron. All Sections reached old Bivouac S of FREVIN CAPELLE by 3.0 pm. Extra tents drawn.	UNXW

T134. Wt. W708-776. 500000. 4/15. Sir J. C. & S.

Army Form C. 2118.

WAR DIARY
or
INTELLIGENCE SUMMARY.
(Erase heading not required.)

Instructions regarding War Diaries and Intelligence Summaries are contained in F. S. Regs., Part II. and the Staff Manual respectively. Title pages will be prepared in manuscript.

Place	Date	Hour	Summary of Events and Information	Remarks and references to Appendices
FREVIN CAPELLE.	13/1/17		No move. Horses groomed and cleaning up attempted. Most of remainder of Brigade in huts with horses under cover. Standing-to at 2 hours' notice. Fine but very cold.	
	14/1/17.		No move. Horses suffered in last few days by exposure and lack of hay. Forage increased to 12 lbs oats 12 lbs hay, and 2 lbs bran # horse evacuated. Fine. Voluntary C. of E. Service in evening.	
	15/1/17		No move. Rain and very stormy.	
	16/1/17		No move. 140 O.R. of Squadron bathed at HQ and FREVIN CAPELLE.	
	17/1/17.		Brigade marched from FREVIN CAPELLE area to FILLIEVRES area. Head of Brigade passed Starting point at 7.0 Am. route SAVY - St POL - CROISETTE - LINZEUX - FILLIEVRES. Squadron billeted at ROUGEFAY, arriving at 2 pm. Every horse under cover. Very good billets for horses and men and not scattered. Owing to the very heavy wind and consequent difficulty in saddling up, whole squadron turned out late this morning. Weather worst possible conditions. Heavy wind snow and rain	

Army Form C. 2118.

WAR DIARY
INTELLIGENCE SUMMARY.
(Erase heading not required.)

Instructions regarding War Diaries and Intelligence Summaries are contained in F.S. Regs., Part II. and the Staff Manual respectively. Title pages will be prepared in manuscript.

Place	Date	Hour	Summary of Events and Information	Remarks and references to Appendices
ROUGEFAY	18/1/17		Walking exercise in morning. General Cleaning up. Horses out (attached to 18th Hussars) by A.D.V.S. to BnDn. for debility. On the whole condition of horses has not suffered greatly although horses Much as horses. had during recent weather and hard work as was expected. G.O.C. Cavalry Corps inspected the unit on line of march on 17th and was very pleased with condition of horses and congratulates the unit. Orders received that Brigade area to be changed.	
	19/1/17		Brigade moves to an area about FRESSIN. Squadron billets in area MENAGE – CONTES – ST. VAAST (N of river) ref map ABBEVILLE Sht 14 1/100,000 Squadron left ROUGEFAY at 8.0 AM arrives CONTES at 12.30 PM. HQ, Transport and 2 Troops (1st and 3rd) billeted in CONTES. 2nd Troop at ST. VAAST. Billets for men and horses good but scattered. Fine. Slight rain later.	
CONTES.	20/1/17		Walking exercise in morning. All officers, Sergeants and full Corpals Lectures by C.O. on punctuality, general discipline etc.	
	21/1/17		General cleaning up. Fine	
	22/1/17		Walking Exercise. Weekly inspection of all kit and equipment. Sunday Routine. Holy Communion Service – C.of E. at 8.0 am	

Army Form C. 2118.

WAR DIARY
~~INTELLIGENCE SUMMARY.~~
(Erase heading not required.)

Place	Date	Hour	Summary of Events and Information	Remarks and references to Appendices
CONTES.	28/4/17		Walking exercise and grazing for all horses at 8.30 am daily. Grazing in afternoon from 3.30 to 4.0 pm	
	28/4/17		Brigadier inspected all horses of the unit on Tuesday, 24th inst, at 6.0 pm at CONTES. Three riding horses cast. O.C. A.S.C. 1st Can.Div. inspected all transport of the unit on Wednesday 25th at 5 pm at CONTES. Divisional Gas Officer inspected all Small Box Respirators on 24th inst. During the week training of Signallers and reserve signallers was continued. During grazing, instruction given in (1) Fire Orders (2) Judging Distance, (3) Map Reading and (4) Range finding. Weather fine during week. 4 O.R. arrived as reinforcement from Base on 24th inst. Two horses transferred from 18th Hussars (to remain with Lumber attacks (6 letter).	
	29/4/17		Sunday Routine. Voluntary Service C.of E. at CONTES at 6.30 pm.	[signature]

Army Form C. 2118.

WAR DIARY
INTELLIGENCE SUMMARY.
(Erase heading not required.)

Place	Date	Hour	Summary of Events and Information	Remarks and references to Appendices
CANTES	30/7		Walking Exercise and grazing in morning. Conferred with individual instruction in Fire Orders, etc. Conference of Unit Commanders at Brigade H.Q. at 11.0 am. Subject: "Economy in food". Afternoon Gun Drill and "immediate action".	

M. S. Mathew Captain (8th Hussars)
Commanding 2nd Squadron, Machine Gun Corps.

Army Form C. 2118.

WAR DIARY
~~INTELLIGENCE SUMMARY.~~
(Erase heading not required.)

Vol 16

War Diary
of
2ND Squadron, Machine Gun Corps

May 1917.

Volume Nº XVI

CONFIDENTIAL

Place	Date	Hour	Summary of Events and Information	Remarks and references to Appendices

Army Form C. 2118.

WAR DIARY
INTELLIGENCE SUMMARY.
(Erase heading not required.)

Instructions regarding War Diaries and Intelligence Summaries are contained in F.S. Regs., Part II. and the Staff Manual respectively. Title pages will be prepared in manuscript.

Place	Date	Hour	Summary of Events and Information	Remarks and references to Appendices
CONTES.	1917 MAY. 1st		Range Practice Vickers for 1st and 3rd Sections. Sub-section Drill at 7.0.A.M for 2nd Section. Afternoon S.B.R. Drill and Gun Drill. Following changes made in the organisation of the Cavalry Branch of M.G.C. 4 Guns with personnel = 1 Section 2 Guns with personnel = 1 Sub-section 1 Gun with personnel = 1 Detachment. In consequence, troops from today's date, became Sections, and are numbered No 1, 2 and 3. (= 2 original Sections from 4th Dpk., 9th Lancers and 18th Hussars respectively.) Sections become Sub-sections and are lettered A.B.C. etc. as heretofore.	
	2nd		Section Drill and "Mounted Action" for Nos 1 and 3 Sections. Range Practice - Vickers for No 2 Section. In afternoon, all Sections had baths at HESDIN from 3 to 6 p.m. 42 other ranks arrived from Base, as reinforcements, and taken on strength. Dismounted Party completed to 53 O.R.	MWM
	3rd		Range Practice - Vickers, for all Sections in morning. Afternoon, Grazing	

WAR DIARY
INTELLIGENCE SUMMARY.
(Erase heading not required.)

Army Form C. 2118.

Place	Date	Hour	Summary of Events and Information	Remarks and references to Appendices
CORTES	1917 May 3rd		and checking all ammunition in belts. 14 remounts (7 pack and 7 riding horses) joined from Base.	
	4th		Section Drill for all sections in morning. In afternoon digging M.G. emplacements. Grazing for all horses.	
	5th		Walking Exercise and Grazing in morning. All Officers inspected and discussed the different emplacements dug on previous afternoon. Inspection of Fish-tailed remounts by E.O.C. 2nd Cav. Bde. at Gradon. H.Q. at 12 noon. Weekly inspection of all kit and equipment.	
	6th		Sunday Routine. Church Parade at 10 a.m. CORTES.	
	7th		Grazing and Exercise at 8.0 a.m. Action with new Gun pack practise (iews 4.5-7 1/2 gun with cross lead and tripod and 1 box of ammunition on same pack) Afternoon, Gun Drill and Clearing Saddles.	
	8th		Physical Drill to Nos 1 and 3 Sections at 6.15 a.m. Exercise & Grazing at 8.30 a.m. Afternoon 1 detachment from each Sub-Section helps for Divisional Horse Show. 1 Detachment from each of 1st and 2nd Sections left in charge of Cpl. Moore & Richardson and Brigade Major, 2nd Cav Bde.	Pushill

Army Form C. 2118.

WAR DIARY
— of —
INTELLIGENCE SUMMARY.
(Erase heading not required.)

Instructions regarding War Diaries and Intelligence Summaries are contained in F. S. Regs., Part II. and the Staff Manual respectively. Title pages will be prepared in manuscript.

Place	Date	Hour	Summary of Events and Information	Remarks and references to Appendices
CONTES.	1917 May 9th	8.0 a.m.	Grazing and Exercise at 8.0 a.m. Afternoon Gun Drill and S.B.R. Drill.	
	10th		Physical Drill for H.Q. and No 2 Section at 5.15 a.m. Exercise and Grazing at 8.0 a.m. All Scouts paraded at 8.30 a.m. for Map Reading etc. Those attending School by S.B.R. Cavalry Corps. at CONTES at 12 noon. 5 horses died. Afternoon Semaphore Drill.	
	11th		Exercise at 8.0 a.m. in Drill order. Gonder Rests New Gun-pack tubes Hund inspection. Orders received that Division will leave present area on 13th inst.	
	12th		Exercise and Grazing as Yesterday at 8.0 a.m. Afternoon employed in packing Synbure Saddles etc.	
CUHEM	13th		Sunday — Brigade lookd to an area about BOMY. Squadron left CONTES at 7.15 a.m. and marched via FRUGES to CUHEM arriving at 2.30 p.m. where Squadron billeted for the night. Dismounted Party marched on foot about 17 miles. (Ref. Map HAZEBROUCK 1/100,000.)	Posted
ECQUEDECQUES	14th		Brigade March to an area about St HILAIRE arts-proceeding under yesterday. Squadron paraded at 7.45 a.m. and Marched via	

Army Form C. 2118.

WAR DIARY
—of—
INTELLIGENCE SUMMARY.
(Erase heading not required.)

Instructions regarding War Diaries and Intelligence Summaries are contained in F.S. Regs., Part II. and the Staff Manual respectively. Title pages will be prepared in manuscript.

Place	Date	Hour	Summary of Events and Information	Remarks and references to Appendices
ECQUEDECQUES	1917 May 14th		LIGNY-LEZ-AIRES to ECQUEDECQUES arriving at 11.0 am. (about six miles.) where Squadron billeted for the night.	
LES AMUSOIRES	15th		Brigade marched to an area about ROBECQ, units proceeding independently. Squadron paraded at 7.45 am. and marched via LILLERS – BUSNES to billets at LES AMUSOIRES arriving at 10.0 am. (about 6 miles.) Made 3 days march done at a walk.	
	16th		Preparation to proceeding to the trenches. Afternoon S.B.R. drill. Officers limbers packed. All saddlery packed up.	
ROELINCOURT	17th		5 Officers and 104 O.R. (under command of C.O.) proceeded by motor-bus to encampment in area 1800x N of ROELINCOURT (Ref. map sheet 51B N.W. 1/20,000 Squadron in Reserve next to camp of 1st Cavalry Division. Digging party Squadron attached to 5th Division XIII Corps.	
	18th		Orders received to take over 12 gun positions in 13th and 15th Brigade areas. This order cancelled later, and squadron detailed to be in Divisional Reserve until relief of 5th Division by 2nd Division about 24th inst. D.M.G.O. 5th Division interviewed by C.O. re the line	RW W

WAR DIARY
INTELLIGENCE SUMMARY

Army Form C. 2118.

Place	Date	Hour	Summary of Events and Information	Remarks and references to Appendices
ROCLINCOURT.	1917 May 19th		Camp arrangements improved – Bivouacs built etc.	
	20th	9.30 AM	Hostile shelling of areas about the camp. One shell falling in camp of 1st Cavalry Division. Digging Party causing casualties. All ranks at once ordered to vacate camp and remain in surrounding trenches and short holes. Inspection of camps by G.O.C. 1st Cavalry Division during this time. In evening 1st Cav. Div. Digging Party moved encampment to LOURIE. Obtained permission for Squadron to remain in present camp owing to forthcoming move and small area of camp.	
	21st		Orders received to take up gun positions in areas of 13th and 15th Brigades. Relief to be completed by 5.30 AM 22nd inst. Relief postponed 24 hours. Two other Lewis proceeded to England on Leave.	
	22nd		Preliminary reconnaissance of positions carried out by C.O. and Section Officers in afternoon. During night of 22/23rd relief carried out as follows. (Ref. map sheet GAVRELLE, 1/20,000.) No. 1 Section relieved 4 guns of 205th M.G. Coy. at B11a 9.7. No. 2 Section relieved 4 guns of 15th M.G. Coy. at B11a 5.5. No. 3 Section relieved 4 guns of 96th M.G. Coy.	RWSW

Army Form C. 2118.

WAR DIARY
—or—
INTELLIGENCE SUMMARY.
(Erase heading not required.)

Instructions regarding War Diaries and Intelligence Summaries are contained in F.S. Regs., Part II. and the Staff Manual respectively. Title pages will be prepared in manuscript.

Place	Date	Hour	Summary of Events and Information	Remarks and references to Appendices
	1917 May			
	22nd		at B.11a 3.5. All guns to fire on S.O.S on barrage lines as follows:-	
			No 1 Section on OPPY Wood and Village.	
			No 2 " Southern half of FRESNOY and FRESNOY WOOD.	
			No 3 " Northern half of same.	
B.15 Central	23rd		Relief reported complete by 11.45 p.m. H.Q. of Squadron in Sunken Road (ARLEUX — MAISON COTE) at B.15 Central. Transport in camp of 1st Cavalry Division. Digging, Carrying and E. of L. OURIS.	
			Situation all quiet. Lines are in shell holes, and positions nothing to report. Camouflaged as much as possible. Remainder of gun teams of Nos. 2 and 3 Sections in shelter trench (M.G. Bank) in rear of positions.	
			No 1 Section commenced splinter-proof shelters on a railway bank.	
	24th		Relief of Brigade by 5th Division by 2nd Division commenced. O.C. Proceeded to England on leave. the O.C. evacuated sick.	
	25th		Situation quiet. Relief of 5th Division by 2nd Division completed night 24/25th. Situation quiet. 1 o.r. evacuated to Hospital. Enemy Shelled area behind ARLEUX intermittently. GAS ALERT ON	PMSW

T2134. Wt. W708—776. 500000. 4/15. Sir J. C. & S.

Army Form C. 2118.

WAR DIARY
INTELLIGENCE SUMMARY.
(Erase heading not required.)

Place	Date	Hour	Summary of Events and Information	Remarks and references to Appendices
B.15 Central	1917 May 26th	7.45 am	Hostile shelling of areas between ARLEUX and Railway embankment increased. Cross roads at Squadron H.Q. heavily shelled with 5.9"s for 40 minutes.	
	27th		Nothing of importance occurred. Our artillery carried out intense bombardment of hostile ration dumps. Transport and ration party orders to parade at H.Q. at Midnight instead of 10pm as usual. Weather fine - very hot.	
	28th	10.15 pm	Enemy shewed back areas intermittently throughout the day. O.C. proceeded to England on leave. Received orders to select fresh gun positions.	
	29th		Above positions selected.	
	30th		New Gun positions taken up as follows:- No 2 Section - in rear of front line to cover OPPY and Round in front of Same. No 1 Section - in old positions, barrage fire on OPPY and OPPY Wood and in the event of ARLEUX Loop falling, to cover ground S.W. of ARLEUX	Appendix I.

Army Form C. 2118.

WAR DIARY
or
INTELLIGENCE SUMMARY.
(Erase heading not required.)

Instructions regarding War Diaries and Intelligence Summaries are contained in F. S. Regs., Part II. and the Staff Manual respectively. Title pages will be prepared in manuscript.

Place	Date	Hour	Summary of Events and Information	Remarks and references to Appendices
B.15 Central	1917 May 30th		No. 3 Section crossfire by subsections from high ground N and S. of WILLERVAL – ARLEUX Road, holding ground N. and N.W. of ARLEUX. Heavy rain.	
	31st		Situation quiet. Orders received at 3.0 p.m. for 2nd M.G. Sqdn to be relieved by 5th and 27th M.G. Coys during night 31st/1st.	

W. W. Strathcon, Capt (Bt Major)
Commanding 2nd Machine Gun Squadron.

SECRET.   Ref. Map. GAVRELLE 1/20,000.

Disposition of the Squadron is as follows:-

1. One gun at   B.11.d.85.60
   "   "   "   B.11.d.15.45
   "   "   "   B.11.c.80.80
   "   "   "   B.11.c.5.1.

   These guns cover from C.7.c.0.4. to B.18.b.6.4..
   enemy frot line. and ground behind our front line.
   They have no lines for barrage fire, as the positions
   are under direct observation from enemy front line.

2. Four guns at B.11.a.9.5.

   These guns only fire on S.O.S. signal on their barrage
   lines as follows: OPPY and OPPY Wood, i.e.. C.7.c.3.0.
   to B.18.b.6.4., searching to a line from C.13.9.0. to
   C.19.a.6.8. (Should enemy gain ARLEUX Loop, these guns
   to command ground to W. and S.W. of ARLEUX).

3. Two guns at B.4.d.7.6.   and
                B.4.d.6.6.

   These guns cover the ground to N.W. and N. of ARLEUX.
   They can also fire at high ground about 9.a.9.5.

4. Two guns at T.28.d.5.4.   and
                T.28.d.65.60.

   These guns cross with above guns (para 3) covering
   the ground to S.W. and S. of ARLEUX.

5. Guns in paras 3 and 4 will fire on barrage lines on
   FRESNOY and FRESNOY Wood on an S.O.S. signal. (Same
   areas as from last positions. These to be worked out
   as soon as possible.)

30.5.17.

APPENDIX 1.

SECRET.

Army Form C. 2118.

Vol 17

WAR DIARY
INTELLIGENCE SUMMARY
(Erase heading not required.)

CONFIDENTIAL

WAR DIARY

OF

2nd SQUADRON, MACHINE GUN CORPS.

JUNE 1917.

VOLUME XVII

Army Form C. 2118

WAR DIARY
or
INTELLIGENCE SUMMARY.
(Erase heading not required.)

Instructions regarding War Diaries and Intelligence Summaries are contained in F. S. Regs., Part II. and the Staff Manual respectively. Title pages will be prepared in manuscript.

Place	Date	Hour	Summary of Events and Information	Remarks and references to Appendices
B.15 Central	1/6/17	12:30 AM	Relief of Squadron complete. Section on relief proceeded independently to Transport lines N.E. of ECURIE. Men to rest during morning, baths in afternoon.	
ECURIE	2/6/17		Squadron returned to Billets at LES AMUSOIRES by trues, together with 1st Cavalry Division Digging Party. Embused at G.9.c.3.8 (ref Map Sht 51B 1/20,000. at noon. Reached billets at 5.30 p.m. 4 pack horses joined unit.	
LES AMUSOIRES.	3/6/17		Sunday routine. Cleaning up for French Party. Baths at ROBECQ in afternoon.	
	4/6/17		Exercise from 6 to 8.30 A.M. Arms inspection. Inspected of S.B.R.'s Belt ammunition checked and cleaned. G.O.C. 2nd Cavalry Brigade visited horse lines at 11.0 a.m. and inspected all horses during stables. Following extract from Honours and Rewards. "French Decoration – CROIX-DE-GUERRE, awarded to No. 41235 Lance-Corporal LEO JAMES BURGESS, 2nd Machine Gun Squadron."	
	5/6/17		Exercise from 6 to 8.30 A.m. Kit inspection of French Party.	[signature]

Army Form C. 21

WAR DIARY
INTELLIGENCE SUMMARY
(Erase heading not required.)

Instructions regarding War Diaries and Intelligence Summaries are contained in F.S. Regs., Part II. and the Staff Manual respectively. Title pages will be prepared in manuscript.

Place	Date	Hour	Summary of Events and Information	Remarks and references to Appendices
Les Amusoires	6/6/17		Physical Training for No. 1 Section at 6.15 Am and Exercise at 8.15 Am. Remainder exercise and grazing at 8.0 Am. Afternoon saddle Inspection. 1 horse evacuated for Veterinary reasons. 2 O.R. Granted leave to U.K.	
	7/6/17		Physical Training for No. 2 Section at 6.15 am and Exercise at 8.15 Am. Remainder Exercise and grazing at 8.0 A.m. Inspection of all other Ranks by M.O.	
	8/6/17		Physical Training for No. 3 Section at 6.15 Am and Exercise @ 8.15 Am. Remainder Exercise at 8.0 am.	
	9/6/17		Exercise at 8.0 Am. Afternoon Aquatic Sports in the Canal.	
	10/6/17		Sunday Routine. Church Parade at 12 noon. Orders received for French Party to proceed following day for attachment to XIII Corps. Later orders cancelled	
	11/6/17		Exercise at 8.0 Am. Inspection of Cook-houses and Latrines by G.O.C. 2nd Cavalry Brigade. Several horses of "B" Subsection suspected of Skin disease. Veterinary Officer informed. Gun Drill in S.B.Rs.	[illegible]

T2134. Wt. W708—776. 500000. 4/15. Sir J. C. & S.

WAR DIARY
INTELLIGENCE SUMMARY.
(Erase heading not required.)

Army Form C. 2118

Place	Date	Hour	Summary of Events and Information	Remarks and references to Appendices
Les Amusoires	11/6/17		in afternoon.	
	12/6/17		Exercise at 8.0.A.m. Preparation & Equipment for trenches. All horses of N.o.1 Section isolated in Separate field, with suspected skin disease.	
	13/6/17		5 Officers and 102 O.R. (under Capt. L.K.J. Kraken) proceeded by bus to XIII Corps area. Embus at Les Amusoires at 9.0.A.m. Proceeded independently and arrived at Ecurie X Roads at 12.30 p.m. Party in Nissen Huts about A.32.c.4.3. (Ref.Map Sh. 51B N.W. 1/20,000). Reported to XIII Corps in evening. Squadron attached to 31st Division	
Ecurie	14/6/17		C.O. went round the line of the Right Brigade, 31st Division with the Divisional Machine Gun Officer. Orders received that Squadron will go into the line about 19th inst.	
	15/6/17		Physical training from 7 to 7.30 A.m. Squadron Parade for Arms Inspection and Gun Drill (advanced) at 9.a.m.	
	16/6/17		As for 15th inst.	
	17/6/17		Sunday Routine. C.O. and 2 Officers visited the positions to be taken over. Orders received that Squadron will take over	[initials]

Army Form C. 2118

WAR DIARY
or
INTELLIGENCE SUMMARY.
(Erase heading not required.)

Place	Date	Hour	Summary of Events and Information	Remarks and references to Appendices
ECURIE.	17/6/17		positions in the line in GAVRELLE Sector from 18th to 28th inst. Very hot weather for several days.	
	18/6/17		2nd M.G. Squadron relieves the 93rd M.G. Coy in the line on night 18th/19th as follows :—	
			No. 1. Section H Guns (Nos 1 to 4) in front line in WILLIE TRENCH.	
			" 2 Section 4 " (Nos 5 to 9) in Support line	
			" 3 " {2 " (- 9 to 10) " DITCH POST and RED LINE	
			{2 " in reserve. (The gun teams of these guns to be used for making emplacements and carrying ammunition for ab operation on 28th inst.)	
In the line 19/6/17 (GAVRELLE Sector)			H.Q.rs at B.28.c.7.2 in old German Gun-pit. Relief reported complete by 3.15 A.M. 19th inst. Work carried out improving all emplacements and digging alternative emplacements, etc. Quiet in front line. Support line shelled intermittently with 9.2" and 5.9"s. Enemy shelled round about Sqdn HQrs from 11 a.m to 1.30 p.m with 5.9"s and again in evening. Weather fine and hot.	[initials]

WAR DIARY
or
INTELLIGENCE SUMMARY.
(Erase heading not required.)

Army Form C. 2118

Place	Date	Hour	Summary of Events and Information	Remarks and references to Appendices
In the Line (GAVRELLE SECTOR)	20/7		No. 8 gun fires 200 rounds on hostile aeroplane flying low over our front line at 5.15 am. Work on improving emplacements continued. Emplacements for Nos. 9 and 10 guns completed. Hostile artillery quieter. Our Artillery carried out wire-cutting and trench destroying shoots on enemy front line, during which our front line cleared and M.Gs moved to emplacements in rear of parados. Also frequent "hurricane bombardments" of two minutes' duration. During night large number of our own 18" shells fell behind parados immediately in rear of No. 4 Gun - all "duds". Heavy rain and thunderstorms.	
	21/7		Situation normal. Hostile artillery more quiet. Our own carried out usual programme of intense bombardments of 2 minutes' duration at irregular intervals throughout the day. Rain.	
	22/7		Situation Normal during the day. Rain. The Brigade on our left carried out a successful raid on CADORNA TRENCH. 16 prisoners reported taken by 31st Division (only 1 reaching our lines through hostile barrage.) 93rd Brigade co-operated with M.G. and Rifle fire on ~~~~~~~~	[signature]

WAR DIARY

INTELLIGENCE SUMMARY.

Place	Date	Hour	Summary of Events and Information	Remarks and references to Appendices
In the line (GAVRELLE Sector)	22/6/17		R. flank of raid. Zero hour 10.20 p.m. 4 Guns of the Squadron in front line were ordered to open fire on enemy front and support lines from Zero plus 3 to Zero plus 45. 4 Guns in Support line were ordered to carry out searching fire on area East of GAVRELLE Support Trench from Zero plus 3 to Zero plus 45. Total number of rounds fired = 17,250. Both Guns of "B" Subsection were heavily shelled very soon after opening fire, hostile barrage falling on our front line at that point. (Both Guns were twice knocked over and put out of action and each time both Guns were got into action again at once. These Guns were commanded by Lance-Corporals MAXWELL and HALL who, with their respective detachments succeeded in carrying out orders under difficult circumstances, the portion of the trench having been blown down during the hostile barrage). Casualties = 3 O.R. wounded. (Cpl. Bull, L/Cpl. Hall, Pte. Bosker).	Initial
	23/6/17		After this, 4 Guns in front line (No.1 Section) were relieved by No.2 Section from Support line. Relief complete by 1.45 a.m. (23rd.)	Initial

Army Form C. 2118.

WAR DIARY
INTELLIGENCE SUMMARY
(Erase heading not required.)

Place	Date	Hour	Summary of Events and Information	Remarks and references to Appendices
In the line (GAVRELLE Sector)	23/6/17		Situation normal. Maintenance work carried out in front line trench. Enemy shelled back areas throughout the day. Also front line near No.4 gun position with 77 mm. shells. Rain at intervals.	
	24/6/17		Situation normal. During night of 23/24th hostile raiding party - about 20 strong - approached our line in right sub-sector and was driven off by Lewis gun fire. He then approached the next M.G. position on our right (No. from No.4 Gun) and succeeded in capturing the gun. Enemy shelled the RO line in front of Saplin HQ heavily during afternoon blowing in two M.G. shafts. He shelled the ridge behind HQ with 5.9's and shrapnel for an hour at 1.0AM	
	25/6/17		Day and night normal and quiet. Our artillery carried out normal programme of wire-cutting and "hurricane" bombardments. Hostile artillery less active. Work carried out, new emplacements for special enterprise completed and others begun.	
	26/6/17		Situation fairly quiet. All new special emplacements completed. Formation of Ammunition Dumps commenced. Hostile artillery	[illegible]

WAR DIARY

INTELLIGENCE SUMMARY

Army Form C. 2118

Place	Date	Hour	Summary of Events and Information	Remarks and references to Appendices
In the field (GAVRELLE Sector)	26/6/17		active with 5.9's, 4.2 and 77 m.m. Shells, on Front and Support Lines and in rear of latter during afternoon and evening.	
	27/6/17		During night of 26/27th Squadron was relieved by 93rd M.G. Coy. Relief reported complete by 4.30 a.m. On completion of Relief all guns took up new positions as under for co-operation in an attack by XIII Corps on hostile French system. During relief hostile artillery very active. One emplacement (new) badly damaged. One Vickers Gun permanently put out of action. Casualties :- 1 O.R. wounded. New positions occupied :- No.3 Section near junction of TYNE ALLEY and N. TYNE ALLEY. Positions dug in the open. No.1 Section in Support Line, about B.30.c. No.2 " -- do -- " B.30.a	
	28/6/17		Situation during day normal. All guns in Squadron co-operated as follows in an attack launched by 5th and 31st Division on enemy front line N. of OPPY WOOD until	

WAR DIARY or INTELLIGENCE SUMMARY

Army Form C. 2118

Place	Date	Hour	Summary of Events and Information	Remarks and references to Appendices
In the line (GAVRELLE Sector)	28/6/17		to S. end of CADORNA TRENCH, 400ˣ N of GAVRELLE. Zero hour 7.10 p.m. An hour before Zero, one gun of No 2 section received direct hit from enemy shell and was completely destroyed with tripod. This left 10 guns in action. (Gun put out of action on 27th not yet replaced.) From Zero to Zero plus 40, all guns opened rapid fire on targets — indirect covering fire on R. flank of attack. Zero plus 40 to noon 29th inst. All guns ordered to fire on targets at irregular intervals with bursts of 125 rounds. Guns in 2 alternate groups were arranged to fire simultaneously. At Zero plus 25, one gun of 121 section was temporarily out of action (had been previously hit by shell fire and heat of firing caused puncture in barrel-casing to open). Gun in action again by Zero plus 80. Fire was sustained throughout night until 10 a.m. (29th inst) when cease-fire was ordered owing to attraction by enemy shell fire on guns and adjacent infantry. Heavy Hostile Artillery retaliation on support line around the gun positions between 8 and 9 p.m. No hostile	Appendix I ←

Army Form C. 2118.

WAR DIARY
INTELLIGENCE SUMMARY.
(Erase heading not required.)

Instructions regarding War Diaries and Intelligence Summaries are contained in F.S. Regs., Part II. and the Staff Manual respectively. Title pages will be prepared in manuscript.

Place	Date	Hour	Summary of Events and Information	Remarks and references to Appendices
In the Field (Gavrelle Sector)	28/6/17		activity after 1.0 A.m. Attack was successful - all objectives taken with loss of few casualties. large numbers of prisoners taken. Conflicting reports as to exact numbers that eventually reached our cages. Enemy counter-attack during night which was driven off. At 3.15 A.m. all guns laid on a target S.W. of OPPY WOOD from which position it was reported a counter-attack was to be expected. The latter did not develop. Casualties:- Lieut C.H. MILLER and 1 OR. wounded. 2 OR. unfit for duty owing to shell fire (suffering from severe shock after being buried).	15-8 prisoners
	29/6/17		4 Guns in Group "F" (No3 Section) relieved 4 guns of 92nd M.G. Coy. and took up new positions in Left Brigade Sector. Relief complete by 11.30 p.m. Situation quiet during day. Rain. No hostile counter-attacks	
	30/6/17		Situation very quiet. No S.O.S. signal observed on front covered by guns, which did not open fire. Heavy rain. Orders received at 5.p.m. that the 4 guns of No 3 Section will be relieved by 4 guns	Russell

Army Form C. 2118.

WAR DIARY
or
INTELLIGENCE SUMMARY.
(Erase heading not required.)

Instructions regarding War Diaries and Intelligence Summaries are contained in F. S. Regs., Part II. and the Staff Manual respectively. Title pages will be prepared in manuscript.

Place	Date	Hour	Summary of Events and Information	Remarks and references to Appendices
In the Line (GAVRELLE Sector)	30/6/17		of the 9th M.G. Coy and that the remaining guns would be withdrawn during the night of 30th June/1st July. WMcArthur. Captain (8th Hussars) Commanding 2nd Machine Gun Squadron. 30-6-17.	

APPENDIX 1.

2nd. Machine Gun Squadron.

FIRE PROGRAMME.

1. **Distribution.**

    No.1 Section known as "H" Group.
    No.2   "   "   " "G"   " .
    No.3   "   "   " "F"   " .

2. **Time Table.**

    All Guns will open rapid fire from Zero to Zero plus 40 minutes. Subsequently fire will be opened in rapid bursts of 125 rounds as follows:- (Each time denotes 11.0 am until mid-day, or Zero plus 1 day - 29th).

Time	Guns	Time	Guns
8.0 p.m.	(2 guns "H" Group. / (2 " "F" "	5.15 a.m.	(2 Guns 'H' Group. / (2 " 'F' "
8.50 "	(2 Guns "F" Group. / (2 " "G" "	5.55 "	(2 " 'H' " / (2 " 'G' "
9.15 "	(2 " "H" " / (2 " "G" "	6.35 "	(2 " 'F' " / (2 " 'G' "
9.45 "	(2 " 'H' " / (2 " 'F' "	6.50 "	(2 " 'H' " / (2 " 'G' "
10.25 "	(2 " 'G' " / (2 " 'H' "	7.10 "	(2 " 'F' " / (2 " 'G' "
11.10 "	(2 " 'F' " / (2 " 'G' "	7.45 "	(2 " 'H' " / (2 " 'F' "
11.35 "	(2 " 'H' " / (2 " 'F' "	8.10 "	(2 " 'H' " / (2 " 'G' "
12.30 a.m.	(2 " 'H' " / (2 " 'G' "	8.55 "	(2 " 'F' " / (2 " 'G' "
12.50 "	(2 " 'F' " / (2 " 'G' "	10.0 "	(2 " 'H' " / (2 " 'F' "
1.40 "	(2 " 'H' " / (2 " 'G' "	10.15 "	(2 " 'H' " / (2 " 'G' "
2.20 "	(2 " 'H' " / (2 " 'F' "	10.35 "	(2 " 'F' " / (2 " 'G' "
2.55 "	(2 " 'G' " / (2 " 'H' "	11.5 "	(2 " 'H' " / (2 " 'F' "
3.15 "	(2 " 'F' " / (2 " 'G' "	11.35 "	(2 " 'G' " / (2 " 'F' "
3.25 "	(2 " 'H' " / (2 " 'F' "	11.45 "	(2 " 'H' " / (2 " 'G' "
4.5 "	(2 " 'H' " / (2 " 'G' "	12 noon.	(2 " 'H' " / (2 " 'F' "
4.40 "	(2 " 'F' " / (2 " 'G' "		

3. On S.O.S., all guns to open on targets. S.O.S. = RED - GREEN - RED.

/4. In the event of

Sheet 2.

4. In the event of a Counter-attack from OPPY, 'H' Group will fire with same Q.E. but 20° North of original target. 'G' Group will fire with same Q.E. but 40° North of original target.
   Target will not be changed except on order from me. Order will be in code thus:- G. LEFT or H. LEFT, or G and H LEFT. When Counter-attack has been dealt with, guns will relay on order thus:- G. RELAY, or H. RELAY, or G. and H. RELAY.

5. Elevation to be constantly checked, and sandbags placed to prevent depressing of muzzle.

6. Runners from each group will be at B.17.c.60.1.

7. I shall be at junction of TYNE and N. TYNE ALLEY. This may be changed and will be notified to you.

8. All Section Officers will syncronise watches at nearest Battalion Headquarters at 3.30 p.m. to-day.

9. I (or representative) will be at Squadron Headquarters until 5.0 p.m. to-day.

                 (Sgd)   L. W. D. WATHEN,   Captain,
28.6.17.   Commanding 2nd. Machine Gun Squadron.

Army Form C. 2118

WAR DIARY
INTELLIGENCE SUMMARY.
(Erase heading not required.)

Instructions regarding War Diaries and Intelligence Summaries are contained in F. S. Regs., Part II. and the Staff Manual respectively. Title pages will be prepared in manuscript.

Place	Date	Hour	Summary of Events and Information	Remarks and references to Appendices
			CONFIDENTIAL. WAR DIARY of 2ND SQUADRON, MACHINE GUN CORPS. JULY 1917. VOLUME No. XVIII	

WAR DIARY

INTELLIGENCE SUMMARY.
(Erase heading not required.)

Army Form C. 2118

Place	Date	Hour	Summary of Events and Information	Remarks and references to Appendices
GAVRELLE Sector.	1/7/17		Nos 1 and 2 Sections withdrawn from positions in the line. No 3 Section relieved by one Section of 94th M.G. Coy. Relief completed by 1-30 a.m. H.Q. and all Sections proceeded to ROCLINCOURT, billeted in Nissen Huts. At 1.0 p.m. orders received verbally from 31st Division for one Section to return to the line at once and to remain in reserve under G.O.C. 94th Inf. Bde, owing to expected hostile counter-attacks. Remainder of Squadron remained at ROCLINCOURT ready to move at a moment's notice.	
	2/7/17		Hostile counter-attacks not having developed, No 3 Section was withdrawn at 11.0 p.m. returning to ROCLINCOURT.	
	3/7/17		2nd M.G. Squadron left XIII Corps area, returning to 1st Cav. Div. Embussed at ECURIE X roads at 8.30 a.m. and arrived at LES AMUSOIRES at 12.15 p.m.	
LES AMUSOIRES	4/7/17		Exercise as usual. Cleaning up of Trench party. Orders received to arrange relief with a M.G. Coy. on the following day at a rendezvous S.E. of LOCON. This order cancelled same evening. One free cadre of Mange in Squadron on return from trenches.	
	5/7/17		Exercise at 7.30 a.m. Cleaning of Saddlery and checking same in afternoon.	initials

WAR DIARY
INTELLIGENCE SUMMARY
(Erase heading not required.)

Army Form C. 2118.

Instructions regarding War Diaries and Intelligence Summaries are contained in F. S. Regs., Part II. and the Staff Manual respectively. Title pages will be prepared in manuscript.

Place	Date	Hour	Summary of Events and Information	Remarks and references to Appendices
LES AMUSOIRES	6/7/17		Exercise at 7.30 am. Inspection of Cook-houses by Inspector of Catering.	
	7/7/17		Exercise at 7.30 am. All horses saddled.	
	8/7/17		Sunday Routine. Saddle inspection by C.O.	
	9/7/17		Exercise at 7.30 am. All horses saddles. Machine Gun Classes in afternoon.	
	10/7/17		Exercise at 7.30 to 10.0 am. Inspection of all S.B. Respirators by Divisional Gas Officer at 10.30 am, who reported condition of all S.B.Rs very satisfactory. Exercise from 7.30 to 9.30 am. Inspection of all horses by A.D.V.S., 1st Cavy. Division at 11.30 am who stated that he considered the horses in the Squadron to be in good condition. Machine Gun Classes in afternoon.	
	11/7/17			
	12/7/17		Exercise as usual. Arms inspection.	
	13/7/17		Exercise at 7.30 am. Preliminary heats of Squadron Sports. Mounted and Dismounted Events.	
	14/7/17		Exercise at 7.30 am. Final of Sports postponed owing to weather.	
	15/7/17		Sunday Routine.	
	16/7/17		Exercise at 10.30 am. Owing to 10th and 9th Cavalry Brigades passing through area before this hour. Lieut. DENT attended as member of a Court-Martial	

Army Form C. 2118

WAR DIARY
INTELLIGENCE SUMMARY.
(Erase heading not required.)

Instructions regarding War Diaries and Intelligence Summaries are contained in F.S. Regs, Part II. and the Staff Manual respectively. Title pages will be prepared in manuscript.

Place	Date	Hour	Summary of Events and Information	Remarks and references to Appendices
LES AMUSOIRES.	16/7/17.		at B.S. Amusoires. In afternoon, Final of Squadron Sports which were successful. "B" Subsection winning the prize for greatest aggregate points.	
	17/7/17		Exercise at 7.30 a.m. All horses saddled and packs loaded.	
	18/7/17.		Exercise and Machine Gun Classes. Orders received for 2nd and 9th Squadrons Power Battalions together with 2nd and 9th Machine Gun Squadrons (whole under command of G.O.C. 2nd Cavalry Brigade) to hold themselves in readiness to reinforce the 1st PORTUGUESE Division in the line about NEUVE CHAPELLE. C.O. reconnoitred the line together with G.O.C. and other officers concerned.	WD29.
	19/7/17		Conference of C.O's of Regiments and Squadrons at Brigade H.Q. in afternoon. Exercise as usual. Ammunition cleaned and preparations for proceeding to the line. C.O. reconnoitres M.G. positions in the line held by PORTUGUESE Division.	
	20/7/17		Exercise at 7.0 a.m. on blankets. Inspection of all horses by G.O.C. 2nd Cavalry Brigade at 11.0 a.m. G.O.C. stated he considered the horses fall inspections in good condition and well turned out. The horses of the transport requiring improvement. Afternoon, Machine Gun Classes.	WD30.

WAR DIARY
INTELLIGENCE SUMMARY.
(Erase heading not required.)

Army Form C. 2118

Place	Date	Hour	Summary of Events and Information	Remarks and references to Appendices
Les Amusoires	20/7/17		Capt. H. Misa attended as a Member of Court-Martial at Headquarters. D"H" Battery, R.H.A.	
	21/7/17		Exercise at 7.30 a.m. Packs loaded. Concert by Pierrot Troupe in the evening.	
	22/7/17		Sunday Routine C of E. Service at 12 noon.	
	23/7/17		Inspection of all sections in Marching Order, two sections in morning and one in afternoon.	
	24/7/17		Inspection by C.O. of Transport in Marching Order.	
	25/7/17		Exercise and arms Inspection	
	26/7/17		Exercise at 7.30 a.m. Machine Gun Classes in afternoon.	
	27/7/17		Exercise at 7.30 a.m. Machine Gun Classes in afternoon.	
	28/7/17		Lieuts. I.M. Le Roy-Lewis and R.E. Roberts with H Squadron Squadron took part in a Divisional Scheme for co-operation with aeroplanes near ROBECQ. Exercise 7.30 a.m. Kit and equipment inspection. Capt. H. MISA and Sgt. H. BAKER proceeded to G.H.Q. Small Arms School to attend a course of instruction at the Machine Gun Branch, Bourre.	

Army Form C. 2118

WAR DIARY
INTELLIGENCE SUMMARY
(Erase heading not required.)

Place	Date	Hour	Summary of Events and Information	Remarks and references to Appendices
LES AMUSOIRES	28/7/17		Commencing 29th July and dispersing on 21st August 1917.	
	29/7/17		Sunday Routine. Church Parade for C. of E. cancelled owing to weather. Non Conformist Service at 12.0 noon.	
	30/7/17	7.30 am	Exercise at 7.30 am. Rain interfered with outdoor work. Mechanism classes held indoors.	
	31/7/17	7.30 am	Exercise at 7.30 am. Gun Drill Parades and Fire Control and passing of Orders.	
			N.B. LEAVE. During the month 2 officers and 38 other ranks proceeded to United Kingdom on Leave.	
			Honours & Rewards.	
			41231 Sgt L. BULL. Awarded Bar to Military Medal.	
			41264 L/Cpl MAXWELL G Awarded Military Medal.	
			Both awards by Corps Commander, XIII Corps, for "Gallantry in the Field"	
			4/11-7-17	

31/7/17

W.N.Nathan Captain
Commanding 2nd Squadron, Machine Gun Corps.

Army Form C. 2118.

WAR DIARY
~~INTELLIGENCE SUMMARY~~
(Erase heading not required.)

Place	Date	Hour	Summary of Events and Information	Remarks and references to Appendices

Instructions regarding War Diaries and Intelligence Summaries are contained in F.S. Regs., Part II. and the Staff Manual respectively. Title pages will be prepared in manuscript.

CONFIDENTIAL

WAR DIARY
of
2ND SQUADRON, MACHINE GUN CORPS. (CAVALRY).

AUGUST 1917.

VOLUME No XIX.

WAR DIARY
INTELLIGENCE SUMMARY.
(Erase heading not required.)

Army Form C. 2118

Instructions regarding War Diaries and Intelligence Summaries are contained in F. S. Regs., Part II. and the Staff Manual respectively. Title pages will be prepared in manuscript.

Place	Date	Hour	Summary of Events and Information	Remarks and references to Appendices
LES AMUSOIRES.	1/6/17		Exercise and Mounted Action at 7.30 a.m. Gun Classes in afternoon. Rain.	
	2/6/17		Exercise and Mounted Action. Gun Classes. Heavy Rain.	
	3/6/17		Exercise at 7.30 a.m. Bathing Parade at ROBECQ (30 men per Section) from 11 a.m. to 1 p.m. Afternoon Stables.	
	4/6/17		Exercise and Mounted Action at 7.30 a.m. Arms and Kit inspection. Gas Officer and N.C.O.'s attended Gas Lecture by D.G.O. at ROBECQ at 10.0 a.m.	
	5/6/17		Sunday Routine. Brigade Church Parade at 11.0 a.m. at "B" Squadron, 9th Lancers. After the parade service, the G.O.C. 2nd Cav. Bde. presented medal ribbons to recipients to 2nd Cav. Bde. Undermentioned N.C.O.'s of this unit were decorated as follows:— 41231. Sergeant L.S. BULL – Bar to Military Medal. 41235. Lance Corporal L.J. BURGESS. - Croix-de-Guerre.	
	6/6/17		Exercise at 7.30 a.m. Afternoon Gas Drill for all Sections and Transport. Visual test for Spendue (Bonfront the week). Owing to recent heavy rains horse lines of N°1 and N°2 Sections moved from Squadron field to some standing in farm yards. Also Transport.	

Army Form C. 2118

WAR DIARY
— of —
INTELLIGENCE SUMMARY.
(Erase heading not required.)

Instructions regarding War Diaries and Intelligence Summaries are contained in F.S. Regs., Part II. and the Staff Manual respectively. Title pages will be prepared in manuscript.

Place	Date	Hour	Summary of Events and Information	Remarks and references to Appendices
LES AMUSOIRES	7/8/17		Exercise at 7.30 am. Afternoon Saddle Inspection. Course for N.C.O. per Detachment on Mechanism and Gun Drill commenced under S.S.M. (Continued Daily).	
	8/8/17		Exercise 7.30 am in Drill Order. Mounted Action.	
	9/8/17		Inspection by the A.M.G.O. of all Subsections in rotation in Marching Order at Les Amusoires, commences at 9.0 am.	
	10/8/17		Exercise at 7.30 am. Arms and Kit inspection. N.C.O.s Course in Gun Drill and Mechanism carried on daily throughout the week.	
	11/8/17		Exercise at 7.30 am in Drill order. New Bathing Parade at Robecq at 11.0 am till 1.0 pm. Afternoon Free.	
	12/8/17		Sunday routine. Voluntary Church Service to R.C.s and Presbyterians.	
	13/8/17		Squadron parade in Marching order for inspection by C.O. at 6.0 am at Les Amusoires, followed by Route March to Calonne — Robecq — to billets. Afternoon, Gun Pit Site filled. Range prepared.	
	14/8/17		Exercise. Range prepared. C.O. (Capt. L.W.D. Walker) having proceeded to	

WAR DIARY
or
INTELLIGENCE SUMMARY.
(Erase heading not required.)

Army Form C. 2118

Place	Date	Hour	Summary of Events and Information	Remarks and references to Appendices
LES AMUSOIRES.	14/7/17		England on leave. Lieut. D.F.G. DUFF assumed command of the Squadron.	
	15/6/17		All Dismounted men on strength of Squadron (44 other Ranks) proceeded to M.G.C. Base Depôt for transfer to M.G.C. INFANTRY, duty conducted to Base by Lieut. E.F. ROBERTS, who returned unit on completion of duty. One section range practice. Remainder Exercise. Firing to be discontinued until range made safe.	
	16/6/17		Exercise. Gun Drill and Grazing. Afternoon Mechanism classes.	
	17/6/17		Exercise. Blankets Saddle inspection.	
	18/6/17		Stables 7.0 a.m. Inspection of Billets at midday. Voluntary Church Service (C. of E.) at 6.30 p.m.	
	19/6/17		F & log-gn's completed range in morning. Exercise.	
	20/6/17		No. 3 Section at Range Practice. Remainder Exercise.	
	21/6/17		Exercise as usual.	
	22/6/17		No. 1 Section at Range Practice. Remainder Exercise.	
	23/6/17		Mores of the Squadron paraded at 11.0 a.m. for inspection. One horn Transport chosen for breeding purposes. Exercise as usual.	D.F.D.

WAR DIARY
— or —
INTELLIGENCE SUMMARY.
(Erase heading not required.)

Army Form C. 2118.

Place	Date	Hour	Summary of Events and Information	Remarks and references to Appendices
LES AMUSOIRES	24/8/17		Exercise. Capt. H. Hicks returned from H.E. School and assumed Command of the Squadron.	
	25/8/17		Exercise and Bathing Parade.	
	26/8/17		Sunday Routine. Capt. L.W.D. NATHEN assumed command of the Squadron on return from leave to U.K.	
	27/8/17		Brigade marched to an area near MANDONNE (Ref. map. HAZEBROUCK Sht. 5A. 1/100,000.) Squadron paraded at LES AMUSOIRES at 7.0 a.m. and arrived at HEZECQUES at 1.0 p.m. where Squadron billeted the night.	
HEZECQUES	28/8/17		Heavy wind, fine but heavy rain after arrival at billets. March resumed to an area about SAMER (ref. map CALAIS 1/100,000.) Squadron left HEZECQUES at 7.15 a.m. and arrived at ENQUIN at 12.30 p.m. Horse lines in field above village. Men's billets bad owing to lack of accommodation. Heavy rain throughout the day.	
ENQUIN	29/8/17		Exercise and arrangement of billets.	
	30/8/17		Exercise under Section arrangements. Nos. 1 and 2 Sections moved men's billets also horses of former. All remain in ENQUIN.	S.S.

WAR DIARY

~~INTELLIGENCE~~ SUMMARY.

(Erase heading not required.)

Army Form C. 2118

Place	Date	Hour	Summary of Events and Information	Remarks and references to Appendices
ENQUIN	30/6/17		Exercise. Stripped Saddle Inspection in afternoon. One horse of transport destroyed owing to broken leg.	
			Capt. Ulsia proceed to U.K. on leave.	
			Capt. L.H.D. Mather proceed to M.G. School to attend advance course of instruction.	
			Lieut. D.F.G. Duff assumed command of the Squadron.	
			During the month establishment of M.G. Squadrons increased as follows.	
			1 Extra Sergeant per Subsection = 6.	
			1 " Corporal " " = 6.	
			Decreased as follows.	
			Riding horses reduced from 184 to 182. Draught horses from 78 to 66. L.G.S. horses reduced from 18 to 15. 3 L.G.S. wagons transferred to Regt. 1 cart to H.Q. Mob. 9 G.S. and 16 F. Horses repatched, with two L.D. horses per limber but no drivers.	
			Strong of month. 3 Off. and 50 O.R. proceed to U.K. on leave.	Lieut. W.R.
			D.F.G. Duff [signature]	
			31/8/17 Commanding 22 Machine Gun Squadron.	

Army Form C. 2118.

WAR DIARY
or
INTELLIGENCE SUMMARY.
(Erase heading not required.)

Vol 20

CONFIDENTIAL

War Diary.
of
2nd Squadron, Machine Gun Corps (Cavalry)

September 1917.

Volume No. XX.

WAR DIARY
INTELLIGENCE SUMMARY.
(Erase heading not required.)

Army Form C. 2118

Instructions regarding War Diaries and Intelligence Summaries are contained in F.S. Regs., Part II. and the Staff Manual respectively. Title pages will be prepared in manuscript.

Place	Date	Hour	Summary of Events and Information	Remarks and references to Appendices
ENQUIN	1/7		Exercise.	
	2/7		Sunday routine. Divine Service (C of E) at 11:15 a.m.	
	3/7		Range Practice for N.C.O. section at 10 a.m. Remainder Sub-Section Drill. Afternoon GAS drill. Respirators worn for one hour continuously.	
	4/7		No. 2 Section rifle pattern remainder Subsection drill. Afternoon, instructor class for N.C.O's and Gun pit Drill.	
	5/7		No. 3 Section Range Practice. Remainder Subsection drill. Afternoon Instructors Class. Revolver practice for officers so armed.	
	6/7		Riflemen practised in rapid loading. Section Drill. Afternoon. Cartridgeless Revolver practice for men so armed. Riflemen practised in rapid loading.	
	7/7		Section Drill. Instructors Class. Rapid loading practice.	
	8/7		Exercise on Blankets. Arms and overcoat inspection.	
	9/7		Sunday routine. Holy Communion. 30 other ranks transferred to M.G.C. Base Depot no surplus establishment.	WRW

WAR DIARY
INTELLIGENCE SUMMARY

Army Form C. 2118.

Place	Date	Hour	Summary of Events and Information	Remarks and references to Appendices
ENQUIN	10/2/17		Subsection training. Grazing Instructors Class	
	11/2/17		Subsection training. Gun S. Instructor's Class	
	12/2/17		No.1 Section Range Practice. Remainder Subsection training. Revolver Practice. Repeating service too Riflemen.	
	13/2/17		No.2 Section Range Practice. Gas Drill and Grazing.	
	14/2/17		No.3 Section Range Practice. Remainder Subsection drill.	
			Instructors Class. Bayonets.	
	15/2/17		Section Drill. Capt. N. Mice assumed command of the Squadron on return from leave. Hose Captain Parade by D.D.R. Car Corps at 3AM.R.	Shinecastle
	16/2/17		Sunday Service (hon-compulsory) at 9.15am	
	17/2/17		Subsection training. Instructors Class. Grazing.	
	18/2/17		Subsection training. Instructors Class. Grazing. Instructors in use of Clinometer. Elevation and direction dials.	
	19/2/17		Subsection drill and Range Practice. Instructor Class.	
	20/2/17		Gas Drill followed with Foot Drill. Revolver Practice. Subsection Drill and Range Practice. Instructor Class.	CNTR

WAR DIARY
INTELLIGENCE SUMMARY
(Erase heading not required.)

Army Form C. 2118.

Place	Date	Hour	Summary of Events and Information	Remarks and references to Appendices
ENQUIN	21/9/17		Exercise. Divisional Athletic Sports. Lt. Williams succeeded in winning High Jump. Squadron's Tent Pegging Team placed 3rd.	
	22/9/17		Exercise. Saddle Inspection.	
	23/9/17		S.B.R. Inspection. Squadron proceeded to S.M.E.R. in afternoon to be put through "GAS" by D.G.O.	
	24/9/17		Demonstration of M.G. Barrage at G.H.Q. School Arms School. 12 O.R. under Lieut. J. Duff and Lt. E. Roberts attended. Remainder Arms Inspection.	
	25/9/17		Exercise. Divisional Field Day Reveille 4.30 am. The 2nd Car Reg (WHITE Force) and 9th Car Reg (KHAKI force) took part. The Squadron, less 1½ Sections, reported to Gt. Givers at 7.30 am. The remainder (1½ Sections) remained in reserve. Points noted — That Troop Officers kept machine guns hidden out of action for themselves, instead of allowing men protection for doing so.	
	26/9/17		Walking Exercise.	
	27/9/17		Exercise at T.O. Am. Gregory. 2 N.C.Os proceeded to S.M.E.R.	MNTC

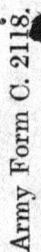

WAR DIARY
INTELLIGENCE SUMMARY
(Erase heading not required.)

Army Form C. 2118.

Place	Date	Hour	Summary of Events and Information	Remarks and references to Appendices
ENQUIN	27/7		to attend Divisional Gas School. Course of 4 days duration	
	28/7		Squadron took part in a Divisional Field Day, area about HUBERSENT (Ref: Map CALAIS 1/100,000. 1st and 2nd Cavalry Brigades took part. 3rd Cavalry Brigade covering the march of an Infantry Div. from CAMIERS to ENQUIN = KHAKI D.V. 1st Cavalry Brigade (WHITE Force) expected to hinder march from a Northerly direction. No 1 section attached to 4th Supp: Park. No 2 " " " " " " 18th Hussars. No 3 " " " in Brigade Reserve. "Enemy" drove in our outpost line over night when operations ceased, no special points brought out. Captain L.D.D. WATHEN assumed command of the Squadron on return from Machine Gun School.	
	29/7		Walking Exercise on Roads at 7.0 am Saddle inspection.	
	30/7		Sunday Routine. Church Parade (Cof E) at 9.30 am.	AWAL

Army Form C. 2118

WAR DIARY
INTELLIGENCE SUMMARY.
(Erase heading not required.)

Place	Date	Hour	Summary of Events and Information	Remarks and references to Appendices
ENQUIN	Sept.		Weather fine throughout the month. During the month, 2 Officers and 47 other Ranks proceeded on Leave to the United Kingdom.	

W.R.Arthur
Captain (A.H.S)
Commanding 2nd Squadron, Machine Gun Corps (Cavalry).

Army Form C. 2118.

WAR DIARY
INTELLIGENCE SUMMARY.
(Erase heading not required.)

CONFIDENTIAL

WAR DIARY
of
2nd SQUADRON, MACHINE GUN CORPS. (CAVALRY).

OCTOBER 1917.

VOLUME Nº 21.

Army Form C. 2118.

WAR DIARY
INTELLIGENCE SUMMARY.
(Erase heading not required.)

Place	Date	Hour	Summary of Events and Information	Remarks and references to Appendices
ENQUIN	1/10/17		Service on Blankets at 8.30 a.m.	
	2/10/17		Section Drill at 8.30 to 9.0 a.m. Squadron Drill from 9.0 a.m. Afternoon. Lecture to all N.C.O.s by Commanding Officer on "Recent changes in Machine Gun Practice".	
	3/10/17		Nos. 2 and 3 Sections at Section Parade at 6.30 a.m. No. 1 Section Tactical Scheme under Coml. Officer. Rendezvous, BEAURIEZ at 9.0 a.m. Afternoon. Lecture to all N.C.O.S. by C.O. on "Barrage Fire".	
	4/10/17		Nos. 1 and 3 Sections at Section Parade at 6.30 a.m. No. 2 Section Tactical Scheme under C.O. Same as previous day. Lecture to all N.C.O.s in afternoon on "Barrage Fire".	
	5/10/17		Exercise on Blankets at 8.30 a.m. All Saddles (packs) and Limbers loaded. Afternoon Arms inspection. Orders received that Brigade would probably move on 6th inst.	
	6/10/17		No move. Exercise cleaning up billets, etc.	
	7/10/17		Brigade moved to WATTEN area. Squadron paraded at ENQUIN at 8.15 a.m. Starting point, DESVRES STATION, Reached WATTEN at 6.30 p.m. where [illegible]	

Army Form C. 2118.

WAR DIARY
INTELLIGENCE SUMMARY.
(Erase heading not required.)

Instructions regarding War Diaries and Intelligence Summaries are contained in F.S. Regs., Part II. and the Staff Manual respectively. Title pages will be prepared in manuscript.

Place	Date	Hour	Summary of Events and Information	Remarks and references to Appendices
WATTEN	7/10/17		Squadron billeted the night. Horses on lines 2 miles from the billets. Ref. CALAIS and HAZEBROUCK Maps 1/100,000.	
	8/10/17		Brigade marched to HOUTKERQUE (Ref. HAZEBROUCK 1/100,000) area, via WORMHOUDT. Squadron paraded 8.0am reached HOUTKERQUE at 3.30pm. Horse lines in a field, cover for about 80 men. Tents for remainder. Later all men got under cover.	
HOUTKERQUE	9/10/17		No move. Exercise on blankets at 8.30 a.m. Horses lost little in condition. 9 cases of lameness, and 3 bad ~~stiffer~~ sore backs.	
	10/10/17		⎫ No move. Exercise and cleaning saddles. Arms inspection.	
	11/10/17		⎬ Constant rain.	
	12/10/17		⎭ Brigade marched back to WATTEN area - Squadron parade at 7.15 a.m. Marched via WORMHOUDT - BOLLEZEELE - WATTEN - FORET D'EPERLECQUES to LA CALIFORNIA Farm where Squadron billeted the night. Reached billets at 3.15 p.m.	
	13/10/17		Brigade marched to billets in SAMER area. (Map CALAIS 1/100,000) Squadron paraded at 8.0 a.m. Marched via NORDAUSQUE -	Rushld

Army Form C. 2118.

WAR DIARY
INTELLIGENCE SUMMARY.
(Erase heading not required.)

Instructions regarding War Diaries and Intelligence Summaries are contained in F.S. Regs., Part II. and the Staff Manual respectively. Title pages will be prepared in manuscript.

Place	Date	Hour	Summary of Events and Information	Remarks and references to Appendices
ENQUIN	13/10/17		BONNINGUES - DESVRES to ENQUIN, where Squadron re-occupied former billets. Arrived at 4.30 p.m. Heavy rain all day.	
	14/10/17		Sunday. Cleaning up. Voluntary Church at Noon. Horses stood the marches well, few cases of lameness etc. Orders received to get all horses under cover. Village of PREVRES, LE FAYEL and BOIS RATEL to be used if necessary.	
	15/10/17		Exercise on Blankets at 6.30 a.m. Arrangements made for moving into new billets.	
	16/10/17		Exercise on Blankets at 8.30 a.m. Squadron now billeted as follows:- H.Q. No.1. Section and Transport, at ENQUIN. Nos 2 and 3 Sections, at PREVRES.	
	17/10/17		Exercise at 8.30 a.m. Work carried out on Stables and billets.	
	18/10/17		Exercise. Saddle Inspection.	
	19/10/17		Exercise. Arms, Kit and Equipment Inspections.	
	20/10/17		Exercise at 6.30 a.m.	

WAR DIARY
INTELLIGENCE SUMMARY

(Erase heading not required.)

Army Form C. 2118

Place	Date	Hour	Summary of Events and Information	Remarks and references to Appendices
ENQUIN	21/7		Sunday Routine. Celebration of Holy Communion at ENQUIN at 8.0 A.m.	
	22/7		Section Parades in Stable Order at 8.30 A.m.	
	23/7		G.O.C. 2nd Cav: Bde. and A.D.V.S. 1st Cavalry Division inspected all horses of the Squadron as follows:— ENQUIN at 11-30 A.m. PREURES at 12 noon. G.O.C. states that the horses were throughout in very good condition. Exercise in afternoon.	
	24/7		Section parades at 8.30 A.m. Section N.C.O.s under C.O. in Tactical Ride. Afternoon, saddle inspection.	
	25/7		Nos 1 and 2 Sections at Section fire or Squadron Parade ground. No. 3 Section Range Practice (Vickers Guns) with Small Box Respirators.	
	26/7		Section Parade for all Sections at 8.30 A.m. Exercise and Map reading. Afternoon, Anno inspection.	
	27/7		Section Parade for all subsections at 8.30 A.m. Inspection of all.	WW20

Army Form C. 2118.

WAR DIARY
INTELLIGENCE SUMMARY.
(Erase heading not required.)

Instructions regarding War Diaries and Intelligence Summaries are contained in F.S. Regs., Part II. and the Staff Manual respectively. Title pages will be prepared in manuscript.

Place	Date	Hour	Summary of Events and Information	Remarks and references to Appendices
ENQUIN	27/10		Clothing and Equipment.	
	28/10		Sunday. Divine Parade Service (C. of E.) at HUCQUELIERS at noon for Nos 1, 2 and 3 Sections	
	29/10		Subsection Parades at 8.30 a.m. Medical Inspection at PREURES at 10.30 a.m. and at ENQUIN at 4.0 p.m.	
	30/10		Subsection parades at 8.30 a.m. on Parade Ground. All Sections by Equitation. Afternoon, Lecture to N.C.O.s of No. 1 Section by C.O. on "Barrage Fire" at 2.15 p.m.	
	31/10		Parade arranged for Baths at RECQUES from 4 to 6 p.m. cancelled owing to weather. Afternoon 1st Round of Inter-Subsection Football Competition played off. During the Month 10 Officers and 27 Other Ranks proceeded to U.K. on Ordinary Leave.	

[signature]
Captain & Lt. Colonel
Commanding 2nd Squadron, M.G.C. Cavalry.

Army Form C. 2118.

WAR DIARY
or
INTELLIGENCE SUMMARY.
(Erase heading not required.)

Wt 22

CONFIDENTIAL.

War Diary
of
2ⁿᵈ Squadron, Machine Gun Corps, (Cavalry.)

November 1914.

Volume No. 22

WAR DIARY
INTELLIGENCE SUMMARY.
(Erase heading not required.)

Army Form C. 2118.

Place	Date	Hour	Summary of Events and Information	Remarks and references to Appendices
ENQUIN	1/7		Squadron Drill at 8.30 am. Afternoon Arms inspection.	
	2/7		Section Drill at 8.30 am (cancelled for exercise owing to weather). Afternoon - Stripped Saddle inspection.	
	3/7		Exercise at 7.30 am. Parade of all N.C.O.S at ENQUIN at 9.30 am on Blankets. Afternoon - Football tie played.	
	4/7		Sunday Routine.	
	5/7		Brigade Route March. Squadron Parade at ENQUIN X roads at 9.35 am.	
	6/7		Range Practice (Vickers) for all Sections at 8.30 am. Afternoon Barrage Drill under Section arrangements.	
	7/7		As for 6th instant. Brigade Route March for Cyclists in Marching Order paraded at 7.30 am.	
	8/7		As for 6th instant. Medical inspection at ENQUIN at 10 am at PREURES at 10.15 am.	
	9/7		Exercise on Blankets at 8.30 Am under Section arrangements.	

WAR DIARY
INTELLIGENCE SUMMARY.
(Erase heading not required.)

Army Form C. 21

Place	Date	Hour	Summary of Events and Information	Remarks and references to Appendices
ENQUIN	10/4/17		Brigade marched to FRUGES area (ref: HAZEBROUCK 1/100,000) Squadron arrived at PREVRES at 9.30 am. Squadron reached CAPELLE NEUVE at 3 pm. Were it billeted for the night.	
	11/4/17		March resumed to BAILY area (Ref map LENS 1/100,000) Squadron parade on FRUGES - HESDIN road at 9 am squadron reached LONGUEVILLETTE at 6 pm. Nos. 1 and 3 Sections under cover, No 2 Section and Transport in open. Impossible to deliver rations etc by lorry owing to bad roads. 30 limbers despatched to the HEM-CANDAS road at 7 pm. Distance of march 46 miles. Rained during the day. Captain H. M¢La. rejoining in evening from M.G.C. T.C. GRANTHAM, England	
	12/4/17		March resumed in afternoon to CONTAY area (Ref Map. AMIENS 1/100,000). Squadron paraded at LONGUEVILLETTE at 1.30 pm. and proceeded independently to BEAUCOURT-SUR-HALLUE and billeted the night. Reached billets at 5 pm. Good billets	MNS[?]
	13/4/17		March continued to BRAY area (Ref Map AMIENS 1/100,000)	

Army Form C. 2118

WAR DIARY
INTELLIGENCE SUMMARY
(Erase heading not required.)

Instructions regarding War Diaries and Intelligence Summaries are contained in F. S. Regs., Part II. and the Staff Manual respectively. Title pages will be prepared in manuscript.

Place	Date	Hour	Summary of Events and Information	Remarks and references to Appendices
BRAY area	13/11		Squadron paraded at 3 pm and joined Brigade at Starting Point at FRANVILLERS at 4.30 p.m. Squadron reached SUZANNE at 9.30 p.m. and billeted there. Horses made cover in ruined houses.	
	14/11		March continued to PERONNE area. Squadron paraded at 4 p.m. Arrived at DOINGT at 9 p.m. Horses in the open. Men in Nissen Huts.	
DOINGT	15/11		Majority of Horses placed under cover in ruined houses. Remainder scattered amongst latter to screen them from aeroplane observation. Gun gear checked and cleaned.	
	16/11		Exercise on Blankets and general cleaning up. As for 16th inst. 6.O. attended conference at Brigade H.Q.	
	17/11		on following operations. Baths for 60 men at BOISLE.	
	18/11		As for 16th inst. 6.O. attended conference at Divisional H.Q.	
	19/11		on following operations. Surplus gear stored. General preparations for limbers packed.	MWSh

WAR DIARY
INTELLIGENCE SUMMARY

Army Form C. 2118

Place	Date	Hour	Summary of Events and Information	Remarks and references to Appendices
DOINGT.	1917		March. Baths for 90 men at BUIRE. Squadron parade at Midnight at Brigade starting point (outside billets) to proceed to advance concentration area at FINS	
FINS.	28/11		Squadron arrived at E.14.B.3. N.W. of FINS about 4 p.m. Off-Saddled. Stood to at 7.30 a.m. No. 1 Section (Lieut DENT) reported to O.C. 4th Dragoon Guards at 9.35 a.m. 4th Dragoon Guards moved forward at 9.30 a.m. followed by remainder of Brigade "A" Subsection (Lt. ROBERTS) attached to Leading Squadron of 4th Dragoon Guards, moving via TRESCAULT - RIBECOURT to BOIS-de-NEUF. Giving up Infantry attack being held up at FLESQUIERES, 4th Dragoon Guards did not reach BOIS-de-NEUF before 3.15 p.m. At 3.15 p.m. "A" Sqdn, 4th B.Gds. with "A" Subsection of this unit pushed on through NOYELLES. At about 3.45 p.m. one gun of "A" Subsection (Sergeant BERRY) was attached to leading troop advancing on LA VALLEE WOOD. This gun came into action against enemy convoy at 300 yds range; about 30 Germans and all the horses	✗ Ref Special Map Sheet 11 Enemy has organization

MWSQ

WAR DIARY
or
INTELLIGENCE SUMMARY
(Erase heading not required.)

Army Form C. 2118

Place	Date	Hour	Summary of Events and Information	Remarks and references to Appendices
	20/4		being killed. About 40 prisoners were taken at the same time. Also fired into stables in LA FOLIE. Position counter-attacked. The gun was surrounded, but was man-handled back all the losses of the detachment having been killed or stampeded. No 2 Gun of A Subsection opened with opening fire from NOYELLES. Target:- Germans advancing from CANTAING at 700 yds range. Simultaneously both guns of A Subsection came into action on Sunken road E of BOIS-de-NEUF producing searching fire on CANTAING. All guns recalled to H.Q. at Dragoon Guards about 4.30 p.m. and dug-in between BOIS-de-NEUF and NOYELLES. Squadron (less 1 Section) moved with remainder of Brigade on TRESCAULT - MARCOING road. At 6.30pm turned S to RIBECOURT - MARCOING - RIBECOURT. Went into bivouac. (Did not off-saddle all night.) Casualties: (Lpl. FISHER wounded.)	
	21/4		At 4 a.m. "F" Subsection (Lt. White) despatched to report to O.C. 18th Hussars. This Subsection took up position with 15th Hussars	MWThL

WAR DIARY
INTELLIGENCE SUMMARY

Place	Date	Hour	Summary of Events and Information	Remarks and references to Appendices
	21/11/17		Continuing the right of 4 D.Gds. to the CANAL-de-L'ESCAUT at 8 am "E" Subsection (4 p. know) despatched to report to 86th Infantry Brigade. This Subsection took up position on N. side of BOIS-de-NEUF. At 11.30 am the Squadron (less 2 Sections) moved to MARCOING. At 12 noon No 2 Section was despatched to report to O.C. 9th Lancers, this section came into action on right flank of the occupied by the Brigade about CHATEAU TALMA (one gun East of Canal). A system of Machine Gun defence was then organized for the right and guns arranged accordingly. One gun (E Subsection) withdrawn into close support on the gun "A" Subsection out of action. Brigade relieved by 9th Cav Bde. Relief of 7th M.G. Squadron complete by 11.45 pm. On relief squadron marched to RIBECOURT and off saddled. Casualties NIL. 7 Horses Killed. 2 Wounded.	
	22/11/17		Then reached at 9 am that Brigade would concentrate about METZ-en-COUTRE. Squadron marked independently and went	PWX19

Army Form C. 2118

WAR DIARY
—or—
INTELLIGENCE SUMMARY.
(Erase heading not required.)

Instructions regarding War Diaries and Intelligence Summaries are contained in F. S. Regs., Part II. and the Staff Manual respectively. Title pages will be prepared in manuscript.

Place	Date	Hour	Summary of Events and Information	Remarks and references to Appendices
METZ-en-COUTRE	22/7		into bivouac 1/2 mile S of METZ. All men and horses in the open.	
	23/7 to 27/7		No move took place. Squadron ordered to go into action dismounted on 25/7. Others subsequently cancelled.	
	28/7		Brigade marched to BRAY area. Squadron paraded at 10.15 am. marches via CERY - MARICOURT - SUZANNE to BRAY and arrived at 5.30 pm. Men Squadron went into billets. (Ref. Map. AMIENS 1/100,000	
	29/7		Exercise and cleaning up.	
	30/7		Orders received about 11 am. that front of VII Corps was broken and that the Brigade would move East as soon as concentrated at BRAY. Left BRAY at 2.30 pm. and went into billets occupied by the Squadron up to 19th inst at DOINGT. (Ref. Map AMIENS 1/100,000)	

W.B. Matthews Captain [?]
2nd Squadron Machine Gun Corps (Cav.)
Commanding 2nd Squadron Machine Gun Corps (Cav.)

T2134. Wt. W708—776. 500000. 4/15. Sir J. C. & S.

Army Form C. 2118

Vol 23

WAR DIARY
or
~~INTELLIGENCE SUMMARY.~~
(Erase heading not required.)

CONFIDENTIAL.

WAR DIARY
of
2ND SQUADRON, MACHINE GUN CORPS, (CAVALRY).

DECEMBER 1914.

VOLUME No. 23.

Place	Date	Hour	Summary of Events and Information	Remarks and references to Appendices

Instructions regarding War Diaries and Intelligence Summaries are contained in F. S. Regs., Part II. and the Staff Manual respectively. Title pages will be prepared in manuscript.

Place	Date	Hour	Summary of Events and Information	Remarks and references to Appendices
DOINGT.	1917 Dec 1st		Brigade Marched to E.14.b. near LONGAVESNES (Ref. map Sheet 62.C 1/40,000) Squadron parade 7.30 am. marched via BUSSU to above and went into bivouac. Weather extremely cold	
	2nd		Orders received about 3pm for all guns to proceed to the line dismounted with the 2nd Cavalry Dismounted Brigade. Dismounted party (Capt L.W.D. Warthen Strength 5 Officers 96 O.R.) left at 6 pm. and went into the line at BOIS GAUCHE (Ref. map ENEMY REAR ORGANIZATION Sheet 2) as follows:- "F" Subsection (Lt White) in Front Line in GAUCHE Wood "C" and "D" Subsections (Lt Duff) in close support in GAUCHE WOOD, fire direct on positions in rear R German line. "L" Subsection (Lt Johnson) near Railway Embankment 200 x N of Wood	Initial

E.14.b.

WAR DIARY
INTELLIGENCE SUMMARY.
(Erase heading not required.)

Army Form C. 2118.

Place	Date	Hour	Summary of Events and Information	Remarks and references to Appendices
E.H.C.	21st	3.30	"A" and "B" Subsections (of Dent) in Barrage positions in Sunken Road 500± W of GAUCHE WOOD. Squadron relieved positions of 13th and 14th Machine Gun Squadrons. Four Guns of 13th M.G. Squadron remained in Barrage positions in Sunken Road coming under orders of 2nd M.G. Squadron. Relief complete by 10 p.m. Positions of "C" and "D" Subsections incorrectly taken over owing to positions being inaccurately prematurely "out-going" detachment before of all positions properly organized during the night.	
	3.30		Forward positions constantly shelled throughout the day, particularly those of "C" and "D" Subsections. Lieut Johnson and 2. O.R. (E Subsection) were wounded about 8 am. Guns of this Subsection later withdrawn to positions 100± in rear with	PTO

WAR DIARY
INTELLIGENCE SUMMARY
(Erase heading not required.)

Army Form C. 21

Instructions regarding War Diaries and Intelligence Summaries are contained in F.S. Regs., Part II. and the Staff Manual respectively. Title pages will be prepared in manuscript.

Place	Date	Hour	Summary of Events and Information	Remarks and references to Appendices
F.14.C.	3rd		unsaved fields of fire. Nothing of importance occurred during the day. Horses of the Brigade less M.G. Sqdn. marched back to BRAY area, those of latter moved to LONGAVESNES. (Ref. map 62.C. 1/40,000.)	
LONGAVESNES	4th		Nothing of importance occurred during the day. "C" and "D" Subsections' positions shelled intermittently. 2L Humphries posted as missing since midnight 2-3/3/17. The Squadron was relieved in the evening by the 4th M.G. Squadron. Relief complete by 8 p.m. On relief the dismounted party marched to LONGAVESNES and rejoined remainder of Squadron.	
	5th		Cleaning up of Trench Party and organisation of Ammunition Stores etc. Horse lines here very muddy and work beginning to lose condition.	
	6th to 10th		No event took place. Squadron "Stood-to" at one hour's notice from 6 to 9 h.m. and from 3 p.m. till dark daily. In	WWhl

WAR DIARY
INTELLIGENCE SUMMARY
(Erase heading not required.)

Army Form C. 2118.

Place	Date	Hour	Summary of Events and Information	Remarks and references to Appendices
LONGAVESNES	6/12		The event of a hostile Counter-attack, Squadron ordered to move up and immediately take up positions in accordance with instructions received direct from 2/ Division.	
	to 10/12			
	11/12		The Colonel & the Squadron (less 25 remaining with Dismounted party) & 6 officers and 95 O.R.) marched to BRAY under Capt. L. MySA.	
	12/12 to 15/12		No more took place. Squadron "Stood-to" daily as above. All positions which would be occupied in the event of hostile Counter-attack thoroughly reconnoitred. Dismounted parades held daily.	
	16/12		The Dismounted party returned to BRAY by rail. Squadron left LONGAVESNES at 3 p.m. and marched to ROISEL, entrained there at 5 p.m. and arrived at BRAY at 8.50 p.m.	
BRAY	17/12		Cleaning up. Heavy snow. Squadron in same billets in BRAY.	

WAR DIARY
INTELLIGENCE SUMMARY.
(Erase heading not required.)

Army Form C. 2118.

Place	Date	Hour	Summary of Events and Information	Remarks and references to Appendices
BRAY	17th 18th to 22nd		BRAY as before.	
	23rd		No move took place. Heavy frost and snow.	
			The Brigade Marched to DOINGT area (less HQP AMIENS 1/100,000) Squadron paraded at BRAY at 8.30 a.m. reached COURCELLES at Noon. Marched at a walk owing to roads frozen. All horses in built up stables all of which are finished with roofs, but walls and standings not begun.	
COURCELLES	24th 25th		Exercise backbones and evens built and Mess tables put up. Squadron "Stood-to" at one hours notice from midnight to midnight.	
	26th		Christmas Day observed in 2nd Cavalry Brigade.	
	27th		Exercise at 8.30 a.m. Work begun on improving stables and building standings. 17 Remounts (11 Riding	MTLO

WAR DIARY
—or—
INTELLIGENCE SUMMARY.
(Erase heading not required.)

Army Form C. 2118

Place	Date	Hour	Summary of Events and Information	Remarks and references to Appendices
COURCELLES	27th		and 6 baok mules) arrived for Base, and taken on he Strength. He though died suddenly.	
	28th		Exercise Stable building etc continued. Conference for C.O.s at H.Q. 1st Can. Div. at 10 am.	
	29th to 31st		Normal Exercise daily at 8.30 am. Work carried out on Stables, huments, &c.	
			During the month 2 O.R. proceeded on Leave to U.K.	
			__Honours & Awards.__	
			__MILITARY MEDAL.__	
			For the Action on 20th November 1917.	
			No. 41246 L/Cpl Giles. J	
			No. 41032 Sgt. Renzie A	
			(Sgd) W. Mather. Captain (E. Hussars)	
			Commanding 2nd Squadron M.G.C. (Cavalry).	

T2134. Wt. W708—776. 500000. 4/15. Sir J. C. & S.

Army Form C. 2118.

2 Cav Bde

WD 24

WAR DIARY
or
INTELLIGENCE SUMMARY.
(Erase heading not required.)

Instructions regarding War Diaries and Intelligence Summaries are contained in F. S. Regs., Part II. and the Staff Manual respectively. Title pages will be prepared in manuscript.

Place	Date	Hour	Summary of Events and Information	Remarks and references to Appendices
			CONFIDENTIAL. WAR DIARY. of 2nd SQUADRON, MACHINE GUN CORPS (CAVALRY). JANUARY 1918. VOLUME Nº 24.	

Army Form C. 2118.

WAR DIARY
INTELLIGENCE SUMMARY
(Erase heading not required.)

Place	Date	Hour	Summary of Events and Information	Remarks and references to Appendices
COURCELLES	1918 JAN. 1st		Exercise. Building of standing, Stables &c.	
	2nd		Exercise 8.30 a.m. Afternoon, Veterinary Officer's inspection of Nos 1 and 2 Sections and Headquarters at 2.30 p.m. for mange. Two cases of this sent to No 1 Mobile Veterinary Section. Court of Enquiry assembled at Headquarters at 10 a.m. to enquire into the circumstances of the death of No 4/321 Private P. Hough. Machine Gun Corps. (c.)	
	3rd		Exercise at 8.30 a.m. Building of standings, and trenches round huts for aerial protection continued. 3 Other Ranks arrived as reinforcements from M.G.C. Base Depot, and taken on the strength.	
	4th		Exercise at 8.30 a.m. Medical Inspection of all Other Ranks at 10.30 a.m. Horses of No 3 Section inspected by V.O. for mange. One doubtful case. Cleaning of Saddlery and Harness in afternoon. 2nd Lieut. D.R.CHEADLE arrived this day from M.G.C. Base Depot for duty with the Squadron and taken on the strength.	
	5th		Exercise at 8.30 a.m. Weekly inspection of all O.R., Huts, Cookhouses &c. by C.O. at 10.30 a.m. Kit inspection for all Sections, Transport and H.Q.	MUSH?

Army Form C. 2118.

WAR DIARY
INTELLIGENCE SUMMARY.
(Erase heading not required.)

Place	Date	Hour	Summary of Events and Information	Remarks and references to Appendices
COURCELLES	5th		At same time, usual fatigues on stable buildings etc in afternoon. 18 Other Ranks admitted to Temporary Hospital during the past week.	
	6th		Weather cold. Frost and snow.	
	7th		Sunday Routine. Church Parade (Church of England) at 11:15 a.m. Exercise 8:30 a.m. Afternoon Gas Drill and S.R.R. inspection. Fatigues on diggings, etc.	
	8th		Exercise and fatigues on stables, huts etc.	
	9th		Exercise at 6:30 a.m. Arms inspection of whole Squadron in afternoon.	
	10th		Exercise 8:30 a.m. Stable buildings. Orders received at 9 p.m. that 1st Dismounted Division would relieve 3rd Dismounted Division in the Right Sector of the line – Relief to be completed by 15th inst.	
	11th		Exercise at 8:30 a.m. Baths for French party from 12 noon to 10 p.m. at DOINGT. Cleaning belt ammunition and checking gun parts etc in afternoon. C.O. reconnoitred the line held by 2nd and 3rd Dismounted Divisions with a view to assuming duties of D.M.G.O. to	Initial

Army Form C. 2118.

WAR DIARY
INTELLIGENCE SUMMARY.
(Erase heading not required.)

Instructions regarding War Diaries and Intelligence Summaries are contained in F. S. Regs., Part II. and the Staff Manual respectively. Title pages will be prepared in manuscript.

Place	Date	Hour	Summary of Events and Information	Remarks and references to Appendices
COURCELLES	11th		Dismounted Divisions.	
	12th		Lecture 8.30 am. Parade of Direct Party. Conference of C.O.s of Machine Gun squadrons at Squadron H.Q. at 10. a.m.	
	13th		Under Routine. Advance Party proceeded to H.Q. 3rd Dismounted Division en Retire and hence to LE VERGUIER. C.O.s parade for French Party at 2 p.m. Lieut. S.H. de Roy-Lewis ordered to report and proceeded to O.C. M.G.C. (Cav.) Training Centre, UCKFIELD, England, and struck off the strength.	
	14th		Exercise in morning. Dismounted Party of 6 Officers and 83 O.R. under Capt. Duff proceeded to LE VERGUIER by lorry to relieve the 6th Machine Gun Squadron. Left COURCELLES at 3.30 p.m. Captain H. M'ISA assumed Command of the Squadron in the absence of Capt. C.N.D. MATHEN (to Dublin of D.M.G.O.) Captain G. DENT 1/c of Rear Party. Party dismounted from horses at VENDELLES and proceeded to LE VERGUIER. Guns equipment re brought up to gun emplacements in limbers. Relief complete at	

WAR DIARY
INTELLIGENCE SUMMARY.
(Erase heading not required.)

Army Form C. 2118.

Place	Date	Hour	Summary of Events and Information	Remarks and references to Appendices
COURCELLES	14th	7.30 p.m.	Details of shot. Ref map Sheet 62.C. 1/40000. Barrage took over from 6th M.G.Squadron in A.2 Subsector. Right Sector of CAVALRY CORPS FRONT. Guns were disposed as under:- 1 Subsection (A. Roberts) in FAGGOT WOOD. L.35.c. to fire on S.O.S. lines. 6 Guns in LE VERGUIER FORTS, FORT GREATHEAD 2 guns (Lt. Chinnock) (Lt. Cheadle) FORT DYCE 2 guns (Lt. Loverall). FORT BELL 2 guns (Lt. Loverall).	
	15th		All gun teams had good new shaft dug outs to live in, but not named positions very body sites. Nothing to report. No shelling. Work continued in Anti-Aircraft defences, communication trenches etc.	
	16th		Rest of work to be done in revetting communication trenches, dug-outs etc. All guns inspected by D.M.G.O. 1 O.R. admitted Hospital Sick. 1 Reinforcement from Rear H.q. [signature]	

Army Form C. 2118.

WAR DIARY
INTELLIGENCE SUMMARY.
(Erase heading not required.)

Instructions regarding War Diaries and Intelligence Summaries are contained in F.S. Regs., Part II. and the Staff Manual respectively. Title pages will be prepared in manuscript.

Place	Date	Hour	Summary of Events and Information	Remarks and references to Appendices
COURCELLES	17th		Rain. Situation quiet. Position at FORT GREATHEAD visited by the Major-General commanding.	
	18th		Positions in forts inspected by R.E. Work continued in trenches. Routine from B.H.Qrs. been as under. Stand-to 6.15 to 7.30 a.m. Fatigues and work in trenches from 9 am to 12.30 pm. Men sleep from 1 to 4.30 pm. Stand-to 4.30 to 5.30 pm.	
	19th		Nothing to report. Slight shelling of LE VERGUIER by enemy artillery.	
	20th		M.G. emplacements in LE VERGUIER inspected by G.O.C. Dismounted Vickers M.G. mounting improved for Anti-aircraft mounting for Anti-aircraft defence. Guns not already mounted	
	21st		Weather normal. 2 O.R. admitted hospital.	
	22nd		Guns under L/Limoth. in FORT DYCE relieved guns under L/Roberts in FAGGOT WOOD. Relief completed by 7.30 pm.	
	23rd		Situation normal. Lieut. Roberts proceeded to Rear party and Capt.	MMRhl

T2134. Wt. W708—776. 500000. 4/15. Sir J. C. & S.

WAR DIARY or INTELLIGENCE SUMMARY

Army Form C. 2118.

Place	Date	Hour	Summary of Events and Information	Remarks and references to Appendices
COURCELLES	23rd		Staff took command of his guns, 21 and 22 in FORT DYCE.	
	24th		Situation Normal. Advance officer of 13th M.G. Squadron reported and two Stern gun positions in the afternoon.	
	25th		Situation Normal. Squadron was relieved by 13th M.G. Squadron under Capt. Lisson-Mays. Relieving Squadron reached H.Q. at 6.30pm. Relief completed at 7.30pm. Where the trucks met them. Squadron proceeded under their officers to JEANCOURT where they embussed. Arrived at COURCELLES at 10 pm.	
	26th		Exercise and cleaning up. Good work has been done during the absence of Trevor party on the "Standing" etc.	
	27th		Sunday Routine. Church parade (C.of.E.) at COURCELLES at 9.45 am. Capt. Miller and Lieut. Cage reconnoitred BROWN LINE.	
	28th		Exercise 8.30 am. 2nd in Command assumed duties of Duty Officer in Cavalry Corps reserve from noon 27-1-18. All Numbers kept loaded until further orders. C.O. and Capt. Dent reconnoitred	W.S.L.

WAR DIARY or INTELLIGENCE SUMMARY.

(Erase heading not required.)

Army Form C. 2118.

Place	Date	Hour	Summary of Events and Information	Remarks and references to Appendices
COURCELLES	28th		BROWN LINE and Selected firepositions to defence of same. Lt Roberts proceeded to England on 14 days leave. Capt and Q.M. Duff proceeded to 124 Machine Gun Squadron on promotion to 2nd in Command of that Squadron, and struck off the Strength.	
	29th		Exercise at 8.30 am. Working parties on digging round huts. Baths at DOINGT from 10.45 am to 12 noon for 100 O.R. Stables at 3 pm. E.O. accompanied H.O.C. round defence of BROWN LINE.	
	30th		Exercise at 7 am. Working parties on digging round huts (Anti-Aircraft defence) and cleaning limbers etc at 9.30 am till 11 am. Dismounted parade for inspection by the Corps Commander at 1.50 pm. Stables 3.30 pm. G.O.C. 5th Cav. Div. held above inspection and complimented he unit on its smart and soldierlike appearance on parade and the good turn out of the men.	WSG.

Army Form C. 2118.

WAR DIARY
INTELLIGENCE SUMMARY.
(Erase heading not required.)

Place	Date	Hour	Summary of Events and Information	Remarks and references to Appendices
COURCELLES	3rd		Paraded at 7am. Officers fatigue of 4 limbers and 20 men at 8.30 am. Squadron fatigues at 9.30 am. Stables 3pm.	

W.H.S. Mather,
Captain (8th Hussars),
Commanding 2nd Squadron Machine Gun Corps (Cav.)

Army Form C. 2118.

WAR DIARY
or
INTELLIGENCE SUMMARY.
(Erase heading not required.)

JM 25

CONFIDENTIAL.

War Diary
of
2nd Squadron, Machine Gun Corps. (Cavalry).

February 1918.

Volume No. 25.

Place	Date	Hour	Summary of Events and Information	Remarks and references to Appendices

Army Form C. 2118.

WAR DIARY
or
INTELLIGENCE SUMMARY.
(Erase heading not required.)

Instructions regarding War Diaries and Intelligence Summaries are contained in F. S. Regs., Part II. and the Staff Manual respectively. Title pages will be prepared in manuscript.

Place	Date	Hour	Summary of Events and Information	Remarks and references to Appendices
COURCELLES	1918 Feb. 1st.		Exercise and took continued on digging AA defences around huts and improving billets	
	2nd.		Exercise. Baths for 120 men at DOINGT in morning. 10 OR under Gas NCO proceeded to FLAMICOURT to fit SBRs.	
	3rd.		Usual Sunday routine	
	4th.		Exercise at 8.30 am. under Section arrangement. Afternoon Arms inspection.	
	5th.		Exercise for Nos 1 and 3 Sections. All horses of No 2 Section and 70 horses of Transport proceeded to BEAUMETZ for dipping as a precaution against mange.	
	6th.		Exercise all horses saddled. Inspection of Squadron Cook horses and Billets by G.O.C. 2nd Cavalry Brigade. Capt. [?] Walsh proceeded on leave to MENTONE.	
	7th.		Exercise. Medical Inspection at 10.30 am. Afternoon Cleaning of Belts Ammunition and Gun Parts. Sanitation work continued.	

WAR DIARY
INTELLIGENCE SUMMARY
(Erase heading not required.)

Army Form C. 2118.

Place	Date	Hour	Summary of Events and Information	Remarks and references to Appendices
COURCELLES	8th		Stables 8.30 a.m. All Horses inspected by G.O.C. Int[er]. Br[igade]. at 10.30 a.m. Afternoon: Work continues on Stables and A.A. defences	
	9th		Exercise 8.30 a.m. Baths at DORNET allotted for 100 men. A. Bty. proceeded to H.Q. 1st Cav. Bde. to furnish A.A. Defence.	
	10th		Usual Sunday Routine.	
	11th		Exercise. Arms inspection at 10.45 a.m. Cleaning of Saddlery and harness for inspection by C.O. at 4 p.m.	
	12th		Exercise at 8.30 a.m. Fatigues in afternoon.	
	13th		Exercise at 8 a.m. Gas Drill at 10 a.m.	
	14th		Squadron proceeded to BUIRE for disinfection at the baths here. Exercise and Stables under Section arrangements to fit in with Bath programme.	
	15th		Exercise at 8 a.m. Work on A.A. Defences continued.	
	16th		8 Guns and 63 O.R. under Lieut. N. WHITE, with Lt. H.W. JOHNSON and 2 Lt. W.H. PAGE proceeded to JEANCOURT mounted arriving here about 2 p.m. On arrival at JEANCOURT, this party went	MW2/c

WAR DIARY
INTELLIGENCE SUMMARY
(Erase heading not required.)

Army Form C. 2118.

Place	Date	Hour	Summary of Events and Information	Remarks and references to Appendices
COURCELLES	16th		into Tents in reserve to H.Q.S. of 1st Dismounted Division.	
JEANCOURT			Capt. C. Dent proceeded with the party and brought back Battle Horses	
	17th		Capt. L.W.D. Hatton (C.O.) assumed duties of D.M.G.O. 1st Dismounted Division	
			Capt. C. Dent proceeded on leave to U.K. Capt. J. Mison rejoined from leave to MENTONE, and assumed command of Rear Party.	
			Inspection of Guns, Belts, S.A.A. etc. at 10 a.m.	
	18th		Stand to 5 a.m. to 6.30 a.m. and 5.30 p.m. to 6.30 p.m. dismounted	
			Drill in the morning. Barrage Drill in afternoon	
	19th		Parades as for 18th. Corrected Clinometers and Compasses with "K" Battery R.H.A. Went round Proposed Positions on left with D.D.M.G.O. Dismounted Divisions and D.M.G.O. 1st Dismtd. Division	
	20th		Went round forts in LE VERGUIER (preparatory to relief) with O.C. Canadian M.G. Squadron. Barrage Drill in morning	
	21st		Relieved Canadian M.G. Squadron in LE VERGUIER. Relief complete by 12 noon. Slight shelling by Enemy Artillery in afternoon	LWDH

WAR DIARY
INTELLIGENCE SUMMARY
(Erase heading not required.)

Army Form C. 2118.

Instructions regarding War Diaries and Intelligence Summaries are contained in F.S. Regs., Part II. and the Staff Manual respectively. Title pages will be prepared in manuscript.

Place	Date	Hour	Summary of Events and Information	Remarks and references to Appendices
COURCELLES	22nd		LE VERGUIER intermittently shelled all day.	
	23rd		1 Ok. joined from Rear Party to replace 10k. Evacuated Sick. Four guns carried out Indirect Overhead fire on G.14.c.4.4 to G.20.a.82 from position L.29.c.4.2, from 8pm. till 12 midnight. Totals rounds fired 15,500 rounds. LE VERGUIER Shelled Rather heavily during day. Capt. H. M'SA admitted to Hospital, Sick.	
	24th		Situation normal. Hostile artillery quiet.	
	25th		Situation normal.	
	26th		Little shelling in the morning. Visited Right Subsector with DINGO. 1st Diamond Divn preparatory to relief on 27/28th. Four guns carried out Indirect Overhead fire from L.29. & A.2. on Target from G.20.a.9.2. to G.14.c.8.0. Total rounds fired 8,000. "E" Infantrie's Guns at FORT DYCE damaged by piece of enemy H.E. 2/Lt. D.R.CHEADLE and 110 R. joined from Rear Party.	
	27th		Relieved 1st M.G.Squadron in Right Subsector. Relief complete	M.W.D.

Army Form C. 2118.

WAR DIARY
INTELLIGENCE SUMMARY
(Erase heading not required.)

Place	Date	Hour	Summary of Events and Information	Remarks and references to Appendices
COURCELLES	27th		at 9.45 p.m. During relief, received orders to "Stand to and Man Battle Stations". Orders received to stand down at 11.15 p.m.	
	28th		Situation normal. Orders received at 3.15 p.m. to prepare to "Mobile Attack" and to remain so until further notice. A further 2 guns and teams were sent up to "Forward Area". Here they remained in a position of readiness at SPOIL FOOT WOOD R.8.b.Central (ref map. Sheet 62.c 1/40,000). Battle Casualties from 16th to 28th Lt. Nil. During the month 25 O.R. proceeded on leave to U.K. Honours & Rewards. 41256 Serjt S. HARGREAVES A.T. 22nd M.G. Sqdn. Awarded the Belgian Decoration CROIX-DE-GUERRE, by his Majesty the King of the Belgians.	

W.V.S.Luther, Captain (Secretary)
Commanding 22nd Squadron Machine Gun Corps (Cav.)

Vol 26

CONFIDENTIAL

War Diary
of
2ⁿᵈ Squadron, Machine Gun Corps, (Cavalry.)

March 1918.

Volume No. 26.

Army Form C. 2118.

WAR DIARY
INTELLIGENCE SUMMARY.
(Erase heading not required.)

Instructions regarding War Diaries and Intelligence Summaries are contained in F. S. Regs., Part II. and the Staff Manual respectively. Title pages will be prepared in manuscript.

Place	Date	Hour	Summary of Events and Information	Remarks and references to Appendices
COOKERS QUARRY (Sh. 62c 1/40,000) (Right Subsector)	Mar 1918 1st		Situation Normal.	
	2nd		Enemy attempted raid on INTERNATIONAL POST but were prevented by our M.G. covering it. S.O.S. signal sent up by Corps on left at 11.50 pm. Nothing developed.	
	3rd		Situation Normal.	
	4th		Orders received on Feb. 28th to "Prepare for Hostile Attack and remain so until further notice" cancelled. Situation normal.	
	5th		Slight Shelling at irregular intervals of PARKER COPSE and between PONTRU and BERTHAUCOURT. Eight men (one per detachment) Returned to Details at COURCELLES and were relieved by a similar number from the Details.	
	6th		Situation normal.	
	7th		Normal.	
	8th		Reference 1/10,000 Special Sheet. Two guns fired from RED HOUSE L.36.c.7.3. on target from G.33.A.99.90 to G.27.c.85.90. Time 7 pm to 10 pm. 7,000 rounds fired.	
	9th		Raid by 1st. Dismounted Division. Zero Hour 12 midnight 9/10th March.	

WAR DIARY

INTELLIGENCE SUMMARY

Army Form C. 2118.

Place	Date	Hour	Summary of Events and Information	Remarks and references to Appendices
COKERS QUARRY	9th	M.N	36 M.Gs. assisted divided into 3 batteries of 10 and one of 6 guns. 2nd M.G. Squadron. One battery of 10 guns at M.7.a. 65.20. Target from M.4.a. 57.80 to G.33.d 80.70. Total rounds fired 51,250. Firing from Zero to Zero + 50. German barrage fell some 200+ in front of Battery position.	
	10th		Officers of 72nd and 191st M.G. Coys visited gun positions when tasks etc were explained to them preparatory to relief by 72nd Coy South of WATLING STREET and 91st by North of WATLING STREET. Relief by 72nd Coy complete at 11.15 p.m. Men returned to COURCELLES by Motor Lorry from BIHECOURT at 10 p.m.	
	11th		Relieved by 191st Coy North of WATLING STREET. Relief Complete by 10 p.m. Returned to COURCELLES at 12.15 a.m. 11/12th March.	
COURCELLES.	12th		Usual routine. Cleaning up of French huts. Orders received that a dismounted party with 8 guns would proceed to ROISEL on the 14th not in reserve to 66th Division.	
	13th		Exercise. Cleaning and checking gun parts, ammunition etc.	

WAR DIARY
INTELLIGENCE SUMMARY

Army Form C. 2118.

Place	Date	Hour	Summary of Events and Information	Remarks and references to Appendices
COURCELLES	14th		Dismounted party of 3 Officers and 52 O.R. with 6 guns under Lieut. H.O. Johnson proceeded to ROISEL and relieved 8th M.G. Squadron (as reserve Coy to 66th M.G. Battalion). Capt. Mahon and Lt. Johnson arrived at ROISEL about 12 noon to reconnoitre for positions. Dismounted party arrived at ROISEL at 4 p.m. At 11.55 p.m. Order was received to "man Battle Stations". All positions reported occupied by 2.10 a.m. 15th inst. Further order received instructing 32 M.G. Coy. to resume normal condition at 7 a.m. unless otherwise ordered.	
ROISEL	15th		French party returned to ROISEL about 8 a.m. Cleaning guns, repairing limbers etc. Lt. Johnson visited left positions with Lt. Christie.	
	16th		French party moved from Adrian Hut to Ellars in the vicinity of Bn.H.Q. Lt. Johnson met R.E. Officers and arranged for dug-out for guns Nos. 1 and 2. Lt. Johnson reported to 199th Inf. Bde. S.O. Lt. Johnson reported to Bn.J.D. re dug-outs and gun positions in Light loose enemy shelling about midnight 16/17th about 6 shells.	

WAR DIARY
INTELLIGENCE SUMMARY.
(Erase heading not required.)

Army Form C. 2118.

Place	Date	Hour	Summary of Events and Information	Remarks and references to Appendices
ROISEL	17th		Morning Drill. Brew parade. Improvement to Billets, construction of Mess Room and Cook House began. Afternoon Gas Drill. G. Johnson reported to 196th Bde. H.Q. Evening: Local reserves S.A.A. established for Guns 2, 6, 7 and 8. 6 p.m. Enemy shelled vicinity of Roisel Station with 5.9's. About 10 shells arrived. 10 p.m. Further enemy shelling with 5.9's in vicinity of Roisel Station. About 20 shells. Midnight 17/18 Enemy shelling with H.V guns of light calibre. Some shells falling in the vicinity of Transport Billets.	
	18th	3am	Gas Alarm received. Action taken. All ranks warned. Morning parade Gun Drill. Work continued on Mess room and Cook House. Afternoon Gas Drill. Evening: Local reserve S.A.A. established for Nos. 1, 2, 3 & 4 Guns. Two emplacements dug for Nos 1 and 2 Guns. (7 O.R. under L/Sgt.)	
	19th		Morning. 45 O.R. bathed at ROISEL. Afternoon Gun drill. Evening. 7 O.R. under L/Sgt. dug new emplacements for Guns Nos. 3 and 4, the existing emplacements being useless as targets was not visible from them.	

Army Form C. 2118.

WAR DIARY
INTELLIGENCE SUMMARY.
(Erase heading not required.)

Instructions regarding War Diaries and Intelligence Summaries are contained in F.S. Regs., Part II. and the Staff Manual respectively. Title pages will be prepared in manuscript.

Place	Date	Hour	Summary of Events and Information	Remarks and references to Appendices
ROISEL	20th		Morning Drill order Parade. Mechanism Classes. Afternoon Gas Drill and Route March.	
	21st	5.35 a.m.	Order received "Man Battle Positions". Trench Party moved off at 6 a.m. All Positions reported occupied at 7.20 a.m.	
		8/9 a.m.	One fun destroyed by shell fire. Casualties 1 O.R. killed 10 R. wounded. Thick Mist. Gas Masks on 2 hours. ROISEL shelled all day with H.E. and shrapnel. Very conflicting reports re situation, but it now (6 p.m.) seems certain that enemy has advanced beyond TEMPLEUX QUARRIES on left of Sector and has advanced as far as and into PRIEUL WOOD on Right of Sector. 197th Bde. HQ. moved to rear about 4 p.m.	
		10 p.m.	Lt. Johnson reported at 197th Inf. Bde. HQ and was told enemy held TEMPLEUX. Comparative quiet for rest of night. Remainder of Squadron (at EVREUILLY) moved to LE MESNIL.	
	22nd	2.30 a.m.	2 O.R. fired from Back area to replace Casualties. One fine and one limbered G.S. wagon arrived from rear.	
		3 a.m.	Transport sent to HAMELET in anticipation of enemy shelling	

T2134. Wt. W708—776. 500000. 4/15. Sir J.C. & S.

Army Form C. 2118.

WAR DIARY
INTELLIGENCE SUMMARY.
(Erase heading not required.)

Place	Date	Hour	Summary of Events and Information	Remarks and references to Appendices
ROISEL	22.2		ROISEL at dawn. Very thick mist. enemy German attacks continued. 4 Lft guns came into action about 10 a.m. and fired on numerous targets. 2 guns under Lt Bull fired five times repelled enemy attacks. Owing to retirement of Infantry all four guns were eventually surrounded. They then fought their way out with a small party of Infantry. L/Cpl Fisher got his gun out, L/Cpl Moseley who was carrying his gun was shot and the other two had to be abandoned after being rendered useless. 4 Light guns came into action about same time as the Lft guns and had many good targets. Col Westley's fire caught enemy in sunken road in column inflicting very heavy casualties. Lft four guns withdrew with Infantry to "Been line" about to m. after which they were relieved. Lieut Johnson collected right guns at BERNES and went to LEMESNIL where Left Gun team joined up. Owing to lack of transport guns had to be left at BOVEN COURT. There were fetched by Johnson next morning on a hand cart. Casualties were:	

WAR DIARY or INTELLIGENCE SUMMARY

Army Form C. 2118.

Place	Date	Hour	Summary of Events and Information	Remarks and references to Appendices
	22nd		1 O.R. killed. 1 O.R. wounded. Missing. 2 O.R. Missing and 1 O.R. wounded. The Squadron moved to DEVISE in afternoon. About midnight again moved to PRUSLE X Roads and dug in out post line.	
	23rd		About 6 a.m. horses came for out post party and Squadron moved to MORCHAIN where they remained all day. Here the French party joined up. Horses shelled, but no casualties. Moved to CURCHY. Three remaining Mobile Guns moved at 6 a.m. to go to CARNOY. From here they went up ao French party under Lt. Roberts with Dismounted Colo. Remainder moved to CERISY to Bivouac.	
	24th		Directed to CAPPY.	
	25th		Guns under Lt. Roberts were in line with Ismds Bde between MONTAUBAN and BONAFAY HOOD. Came into action about 8 a.m. and fired on numerous targets all day. 3 enemy machine guns were seen to be knocked out by our fire and numerous other casualties inflicted. Two German attacks were broken up. Squadron moved to bivouac at BUSSY-LES-DAOURS. Casualties 1 O.R. killed.	

WAR DIARY of INTELLIGENCE SUMMARY.

Army Form C. 2118.

Place	Date	Hour	Summary of Events and Information	Remarks and references to Appendices
BUSSY-LES-DAOURS	26th		Dismounted Bde and the 3 m/guns with it, relieved.	
	27th	1	4 guns went up with Genl. Beale-Browne's Column to cover right flank of Infantry retirement from BRAY. 2nd Cavalry Brigade was in reserve. Two guns with Capt Dent attached to General Greenwood's Composite Bde to hold line of river ANCRE at HEILLY. Remained there until 6 p.m. when owing to change in plan they returned to the column. Meanwhile the remaining two guns under 2/Lt. Stonewall were attached to 1st Hussars. General Beale-Browne's force took up line from MARICOURT to SAILLY-LE-SEC before nightfall. Capt Dent's 2 guns were with 9th Lancers on right. 2/Lt Grievall's guns on right with 18th Hussars. About 12 mn. 3 more guns came up with Colonel Sewell's column. Two under Lt Johnson were attached to 1st Hussars sector. 2/Lt Cheadle had the remaining guns near the Ancre opposite HEILLY. Echelon B bivouaced overnight. All guns relieved by 1st Cav Bde and returned to Column H.Q. except 2 guns under Lt Cheadle attached to 4th Dragoon Guards. These	

Army Form C. 2118.

WAR DIARY
INTELLIGENCE SUMMARY.
(Erase heading not required.)

Instructions regarding War Diaries and Intelligence Summaries are contained in F. S. Regs., Part II. and the Staff Manual respectively. Title pages will be prepared in manuscript.

Place	Date	Hour	Summary of Events and Information	Remarks and references to Appendices
Bussy-Les-Daours	27th		The A.G. Bde. advanced along river through SAILLY LAURETTE and towards CHIPILLY, where enemy were encountered in force. One Gun came into action on the SAILLY LAURETTE - MORLANCOURT Road and fired on enemy in wood for two hours. 4th Dragoon Guards then took up line by SAILLY LAURETTE Cemetery where this Gun again came into action firing on enemy retreating from village after counter-attack by the 11th Hussars. Also fired on large masses of enemy on South Bank of SOMME West of CERISY, with good results. Three Guns were meanwhile with Brigade HQ in SAILLY-LE-SEC. 2 Hrs. 2 moved up in support of 4th Dragoon Guards under Capt. Bent and Lieut. Johnson and came into action on left flank of 4th Dragoon Guards, firing on small bodies of Germans advancing and inflicting casualties. Meanwhile the Hird Sam under C Roberts covered the Bridge at SAILLY-LE-SEC. This line was withdrawn in the evening to SAILLY-LE-SEC line. Squadron returned to HAMELET. Casualties 1 OR wounded.	

WAR DIARY
INTELLIGENCE SUMMARY

Army Form C. 2118.

Place	Date	Hour	Summary of Events and Information	Remarks and references to Appendices
HAMELET.	28/6		Moved up at 7am to Bois-de-VAIRE and remained there in support until the evening. After dark sent up 4 guns with 18th Hussars to support Americans in front of NARFUSÉE as they had left their trenches. All four guns in front line under Lieut Johnson and 2/Lt Cheadle.	
	29/6		Remained in neighbourhood of Bois-de-VAIRE until evening when Squadron returned to HAMELET, leaving 4 guns still in line. One gun (under Cpl Balls) fired on small parties of Germans advancing and on a battery advancing at 18 hundred yards. Horse were killed and 2 of the guns retired at the gallop. Spr Watkins 1 O.R. were killed and 2 of the guns retired at the gallop. Spr Watkins 1 O.R. wounded.	
	30/6		Squadron moved up to a point in support North of VILLERS BRETTONEUX. Remained there all day. In evening returned to FOUILLOY to bivouac. 4 guns in line relieved by four teams of 9th M.G. Squadron. Sent in two teams under Lt Davenall in addition to the 4 relieved.	
Bussy-le-Daours	3rd		Moved back at 7am to BUSSY-LES-DAOURS and bivouaced there	

WAR DIARY

INTELLIGENCE SUMMARY

(Erase heading not required.)

Army Form C. 2118.

Instructions regarding War Diaries and Intelligence Summaries are contained in F. S. Regs., Part II. and the Staff Manual respectively. Title pages will be prepared in manuscript.

Place	Date	Hour	Summary of Events and Information	Remarks and references to Appendices
			During the month 2 Officers and 16 O.R. proceeded on ordinary leave to U.K. Strength of unit on 1st inst. was 10 officers 219 O.R. " " " " 31st " 10 " 200 " A.W. Johnson, Lieutenant. 2nd Squadron Machine Gun Corps (Cavalry)	

WAR DIARY
or
INTELLIGENCE SUMMARY

Army Form C. 2118

CONFIDENTIAL.

WAR DIARY.
of
2ND SQUADRON. MACHINE GUN CORPS. (Cavalry.)

APRIL 1918.

VOLUME No. 27.

Army Form C. 2118.

WAR DIARY
INTELLIGENCE SUMMARY.
(Erase heading not required.)

Place	Date	Hour	Summary of Events and Information	Remarks and references to Appendices
BUSSY-LES-DAOURS.	1918. April 1st		Two guns in action under Lt. Loverall at BOIS-de-TAILLAUX (Ref. Map Sheet 62.D 1/40,000) attached 9th M.G. Squadron. Situation quiet.	
	2nd		Remaining 10 guns of the Squadron proceeded to the line at BOIS-de-TAILLAUX, relieving the 9th M.G. Sqdn. The two guns already in line came under Capt. Dent. Relief complete at 10 p.m. 6 guns in front line, 2 in support, and 4 in Barrage positions, on Eastern edge of BOIS-de-VAIRE.	
	3rd		Situation quiet all day. 1st Dismounted Division relieved by 4th Aus. Inf. Bde. Horses at BUSSY-les-DAOURS. Capt. L.W.D. Walken assumed Command from leave. (Capt. Dent i/c French Posts).	
	4th		At 5.30 a.m. enemy put down heavy barrage lasting 1½ hours on our front line and BOIS-de-VAIRE. Enemy attacks developed at 7 a.m. West of MARFUSEE. No 2 Gun (Lce Foster) on the MARFUSEE - FOUILLOY road repelled two attacks on enemy attacking third time, fired all remaining ammunition and withdrew. No 1 Gun, missing (Sgt Hopkins) with detachment, probably destroyed by hostile bombardment. Nos 3.4.7.5 guns, no enemy attack developing to their front, opened fire about 8 a.m. to their right	MWS70

WAR DIARY
INTELLIGENCE SUMMARY
(Erase heading not required.)

Army Form C. 2118.

Place	Date	Hour	Summary of Events and Information	Remarks and references to Appendices
	4th		and right rear where enemy had gained on front line, causing him heavy losses. Were ordered to withdraw by Infantry Commander. No.6 Gun (Sgt Eldridge) did not open fire owing to no target, gun also out of action from shellfire. Were ordered to withdraw, and on way back encountered enemy at close quarters, whom they held up with rifle fire. All M.G. Guns reported to 14th M.G. Battalion, were ordered to AUBIGNY being out of action, later receiving orders to rejoin 1st Can. Div. The Support Guns were picked up by L/Cpl on his withdrawal with Nos 3, 4, & 5 Guns, and came into action later. Reserve Guns opened on Barrage lines at 7 a.m. but after 1/2 hour owing to mist causing situation to be obscure, were ordered to man "Battle Stations". These Guns came into action about 9 a.m. on advancing enemy causing him heavy casualties. One Gun blown up, was replaced by No.2 Gun on withdrawal from first position. All Guns remained in action until enemy had gained wood to their rear, when G.O.C. 41st Inf. Bde. ordered them to withdraw to a line W. of	MNW20

WAR DIARY or INTELLIGENCE SUMMARY

Army Form C. 2118.

Place	Date	Hour	Summary of Events and Information	Remarks and references to Appendices
BOIS-de-VAIRE	4th		Owing to lack of belts and guns being clogged with mud, two had to be sent to FOUILLOY for cleaning and to collect belts. Remaining 2 guns under Capt. Dent took up a position to cover right flank of our infantry, and opened fire on enemy advancing on high ground S. of BOIS-de-VAIRE. Line was now withdrawn to conform with remainder and guns placed to cover valley N. of BOIS-de-VAIRE. Later another gun was sent to FOUILLOY to be cleaned and for more belts. Remaining gun withdrawn about 7 p.m. Meanwhile 3 guns sent to FOUILLOY came into action again with 1st M.G. Squadron, remaining with them until morning of 6th April when relieved. Casualties:- Killed. 2 O.R. Wounded: Lt. E.E. Roberts and 10 O.R. Missing. 4 O.R. Wounded + Missing. 2 O.R. Horses moved from BUSSY-LES-DAOURS to DAOURS in morning. Returned to near BUSSY-LES-DAOURS owing to enemy shelling, and in afternoon marched to AMIENS. Remainder of trench party marched to	MOSLO

WAR DIARY

INTELLIGENCE SUMMARY.

Army Form C. 2118.

Place: BOSSY-LES-DAOURS.
Date: 4th

Honours & Awards

The Military Cross.

T/Captain. G. Dent. 2nd M.G. Squadron.
Lieut. L.F. Roberts. Welsh Horse Yeo (T.F.) Attached 2nd M.G. Squadron.

The Distinguished Conduct Medal.

41231 Sgt. L.S. Bell. (M.M) 2nd M.G. Squadron.
41356 Pte. A. Atterbury. 2nd M.G. Squadron.

The Military Medal.

51811. L/Cpl. J. McFeat. 2nd M.G. Squadron.
41334 Pte. W. Palmer. 2nd M.G. Squadron.

Bar to Military Medal.

41246 L/Cpl. S. Ficken (M.M). 2nd M.G. Squadron.

Army Form C. 2118.

WAR DIARY
INTELLIGENCE SUMMARY.
(Erase heading not required.)

Instructions regarding War Diaries and Intelligence Summaries are contained in F.S. Regs., Part II. and the Staff Manual respectively. Title pages will be prepared in manuscript.

Place	Date	Hour	Summary of Events and Information	Remarks and references to Appendices.
AMIENS.	5th.		Remainder of French party rejoined Squadron at AMIENS. Squadron billeted in large farm S.W. edge of town, men in barns.	
	6th.		Cleaning up and checking gun parts, etc.	
	7th.		Exercise. 8 new Vickers guns received from Ordnance, replacing those lost in action. Ammunition drawn up and preparations made for further action.	
	8th.		Exercise and cleaning up. Baths.	
	9th.		Exercise. Arms inspection. Baths. Saddle cleaning.	
	10th.		Morning Exercise and Stables. Orders received to move to billets at MONTIERES. In process of moving orders received to move to OCOCHE (Lens 1/100,000) Left AMIENS at 3 p.m. On arrival at FIENVILLERS (at 8pm) found Brigade had gone on to AUXI-LE-CHATEAU, march to RACHIMONT (Lens 1/100,000). Billeted there the night	
RACHIMONT.	11th.		Arrived 12.30 a.m. (11th). Distance of 45 miles; very hard march on the horses. Stood to at 1 hour's notice from 7 a.m. Later ordered to saddle	MM819

Army Form C. 2118.

WAR DIARY
INTELLIGENCE SUMMARY.
(Erase heading not required.)

Place	Date	Hour	Summary of Events and Information	Remarks and references to Appendices
	11th		To saddle up by noon. Concentrated at ROUGEFAY at 1.30 p.m. and marched to GALAMETZ and went into billets - 7 miles.	
GALAMETZ	12th		Stables during morning. At 12.15 p.m. orders received to saddle up later to concentrate at FILLIÈVRES at once. Moved out of Billets at 2.10 p.m. and marched to HEUCHIN area. Squadron Billets at PRÉDEFIN (Ref. HAZEBROUCK 1/100,000). Arrived 7.30 p.m. Marched very fast.	
PRÉDEFIN	13th		No move. Stood to at 1 hour's notice from 7am. At 10.40 am. ordered to stand to at 3 hours notice.	
	14th		Sunday Routine. Walking Exercise. Standing to at 3 hours' notice. At 4.45 p.m. orders received to vacate PRÉDEFIN by 6.30 p.m. to 41st Infantry Brigade. Marched out at 6.10 p.m. to BOYAVAL (LENS 1/100,000) On arrival found billeting arrangements changed and Squadron proceeded to FIEFS (HAZEBROUCK 1/100,000) Arrived at 8 p.m.	
	15th		Walking Exercise and Stables. Following remounts issued to the Squadron. 13 Rdg. 9 Bk.	WW529

Army Form C. 2118.

WAR DIARY
INTELLIGENCE SUMMARY.
(Erase heading not required.)

Place	Date	Hour	Summary of Events and Information	Remarks and references to Appendices
FIEFS.	16th		Moved billets from FIEFS to BEAUMETZ-LEZ-AIRES. Marched at 12.30 p.m. arrived at 2 p.m. Brig-General L. Beale-Browne D.S.O. addressed all officers and Sergeants at FIEFS in the morning on his relinquishing Command of the 2nd Cavalry Brigade.	
BEAUMETZ-LEZ-AIRE.	17th		No move. Exercise and cleaning up.	
	18th		No move. Saddle and Kit inspection.	
	19th		Stand to at 2½ hours' notice until further orders.	
	20th			
	21st		Sunday routine. Church Parade 30 all ranks (O.R.'s) at BOMY at 11.15 a.m. after which the Divisional Commander presented decorations awarded for recent operations. Following were decorated:- No.41546 F/c L. Fisher (M.M.) Bar to Military Medal. 41334 Pte N. Palmer (---) Military Medal	
	22nd		G.O.C. 1st Cav. Div. inspected the Squadron in Field Service Marching Order. All transport on parade, at BEAUMETZ-LEZ-AIRE at 2.15 p.m. G.O.C. inspected throughout the Squadron, but G.O.C. stated large deficiencies in equipment.	WW519

WAR DIARY
INTELLIGENCE SUMMARY.
(Erase heading not required.)

Army Form C. 2118.

Instructions regarding War Diaries and Intelligence Summaries are contained in F. S. Regs., Part II. and the Staff Manual respectively. Title pages will be prepared in manuscript.

Place	Date	Hour	Summary of Events and Information	Remarks and references to Appendices
	22nd		Re considered condition of horses very good, and turnout satisfactory.	
	23rd		Exercise at 8.30 a.m. Afternoon Gun Drill for Last joined reinforcements.	
	24th		— to —	
	25th		Section parades at 8.30 a.m. Afternoon Gun Drill and Mechanism Classes with S.B.Rs.	
	26th		Tactical Ride under C.O. for all officers and 1 Sergeant per Subsection. Afternoon Saddle Inspection	
	27th		Exercise at 8.30 a.m. Baths at Tactical ride cancelled owing to fog.	
	28th		LISBOURG during morning. Sunday routine. All horses watered at GREUPPE. Church parade at BEAUMETZ-LEZ-AIRE at 11.30 a.m.	
	29th		Exercise at 8.30 a.m. Gun Tactical ride cancelled owing to rain. Drill in afternoon.	
	30th		Section Parades at 8.30 a.m. Afternoon Preparation for inspection in Field Service Marching Order following day. 10 O.R. reinforcement arrived from the Base.	

Strength of unit on 1st inst. was 10 Officers & 200 o.r.
" " " " " 30th " " 9 " - 220 "

W.S. Mather, Captain
Commanding 2nd Cavalry Machine Gun Squadron

CONFIDENTIAL.

Vol 28

WAR DIARY.
of
2ⁿᵈ Squadron. Machine Gun Corps. (Cavalry).

May. 1918.

Volume No. 28.

Army Form C. 2118.

WAR DIARY
or
INTELLIGENCE SUMMARY.
(Erase heading not required.)

Instructions regarding War Diaries and Intelligence Summaries are contained in F.S. Regs., Part II. and the Staff Manual respectively. Title pages will be prepared in manuscript.

Place	Date	Hour	Summary of Events and Information	Remarks and references to Appendices
Beaumetz-les-Aire (Hazebrouck 1/100,000)	1918 May 1st		Inspection of Transport by G.O.C. 2nd Cav Bde at BEAUMETZ-LEZ-AIRE at 11 am. Inspection of H.Q. and all sections in Field Service Marching Order by the Commanding Officer at BEAUMETZ at 8.30 am.	
	2nd		Tactical Ride for all officers. Rendezvous 1 mile N. of BOMY at 9.15 am. G.O.C. 2nd Cav Bde. was present and later he inspected certain billets and Cookhouses of the Squadron. Arms Inspection in afternoon.	
	3rd		Inspection parade 8.30 am. Equitation and Grazing Afternoon. Arms inspection and Medical Inspection.	
	4th		Subsection Brades at 8.30 am. Baths for 63 men at BOMY.	
	5th		Sunday Routine. Rain	
	6th		2nd Cav Bde moved to COYECQUE area. Squadron marched to DENNEBROEUCQ (5 miles) Billets very scattered	
Dennebroeucq	7th		E'Service at 8.30 am on Blankets Cleaning up for inspection. Heavy rain. G.O.C. 2nd Cav Bde inspected the Squadron, the Transport in Delivrir.	
	8th		Marching Order at GLEM at 10 am. General Turnout good	WW710

T2134. Wt. W708—776. 500000. 4/15. Sir J. C. & S.

Army Form C. 2118.

WAR DIARY
INTELLIGENCE SUMMARY.
(Erase heading not required.)

Instructions regarding War Diaries and Intelligence Summaries are contained in F. S. Regs., Part II. and the Staff Manual respectively. Title pages will be prepared in manuscript.

Place	Date 1918 May	Hour	Summary of Events and Information	Remarks and references to Appendices
DENNEBRŒUCQ	8th		and clean. L.S.R. Drill in afternoon.	
	9th		Orders received for Exercise and parades until further orders in close vicinity to Billets. Subsection parades at 8.30 a.m. Equitation. Afternoon Pack horse Drill.	
	10th		Subsection parades at 8.30 a.m. Mounted Action. Afternoon Pack-Horse Drill.	
	11th		All Subsections carried out M.G. Range Practices – 300 x yards range. 6 men per fire.	
	12th		Sunday. Whole squadron bathed and clothes disinfected at Bomy. Second Change of clothing issued.	
	13th		2nd Can. Cav. Bde. took part in a Divisional scheme in the "Bomy Manœuvre Area". Enemy represented by 1st Can. Bde. Squadron paraded 8.15 a.m. Returned to Billets at noon. Rain.	
	14th		Exercise and grazing on blankets at 8.30 a.m. Afternoon Inspection of Arms and Equipment of whole Squadron.	MWW

Army Form C. 2118.

WAR DIARY
of
INTELLIGENCE SUMMARY.
(Erase heading not required.)

Place	Date	Hour	Summary of Events and Information	Remarks and references to Appendices
DENNEBROEUCQ	May 1916 15th		Subsection Sports at 8.30 am. Drill	
	16th		All Subsections carried out M.G. Range Practice - 300 x 8 arif. Pack horse drill in afternoon. Weather warm. Sharpen knives fire.	
	17th		Squadron took part in attack scheme against the 9th Lancers. No 2 Section reported to 9th Lancers at OYECQUE at 8.15am. Remainder paraded at GLEM at 8.15am. Returned to billets by 1 pm. Weather hot.	
	18th		Whole Squadron bathed at BRISE Lake in morning. C.O. attended a conference at Divisional HQrs at 5.30 pm.	
	19th		Sunday Routine. Church of England Parade Service at DENNEBROEUCQ at 11.30 am.	
	20th		Subsection Parades at 8 am. Drill. Gas Parade and Medical Inspection. Packing of saddles and Limbers etc. All Officers attended a lecture by Divisional Gas Officer at OYECQUE at 6 pm.	
	21st		2nd Can. Bde. marched to Emery area (ABBEVILLE (1100,000) Squadron.	MR 10

Army Form C. 2118.

WAR DIARY
or
INTELLIGENCE SUMMARY.
(Erase heading not required.)

Place	Date	Hour	Summary of Events and Information	Remarks and references to Appendices
	1918 May			
BOUBERS	21st		Paraded at 8.30 a.m. and marched via MARDONNE and HENOVILLE to BOUBERS (Ref. Maps, HAZEBROUCK, CALAIS and ABBEVILLE 1/100,000). About 17 miles.	
	22nd		March continued. Units marched independently, operation frustrated at 7.15 a.m. and marched via CAMPAGNE and REMY to SAULCHOY (Abbeville 1/100,000). Arrived at 11.15 a.m. About 12 miles. Best day weather dry.	
SAULCHOY	23rd		Exercise and grazed at 8 a.m. Afternoon cleaning saddles and washing underclothing.	
	24th		Exercise and grazing at 8 a.m. Tactical Ride under C.O. for all officers at 8.30 a.m. Inspection of arms and ammunition in afternoon.	
	25th		Exercise and grazing at 8 a.m. Weekly Kit inspection 10.15 a.m.	
	26th		Sunday Routine. Grazing at 8 a.m.	
	27th		Inspection parade 8 a.m. Equitation for officers and N.C.O.s. Inspection in afternoon. 3 Reg. horses arrived from base.	

Army Form C. 2118.

WAR DIARY
INTELLIGENCE SUMMARY
(Erase heading not required.)

Place	Date	Hour	Summary of Events and Information	Remarks and references to Appendices
SAULCHOY	1916 May 28th		Exercise and Grazing at 8 am. Tactical Ride under C.O. for all officers at 8.30 am. L.L's of all troops tested in Lachrymatory Gas in afternoon. Gun Drill classes.	
	29th		Subsection parades at 8 am. Equitation. Gun classes at 2 pm. Also instruction on German Machine Gun.	
	30th		Subsection parades at 11 am. Equitation. Gun classes 2 pm.	
	31st		Exercise and Grazing at 8 am. Tactical Ride under C.O. for all officers and 1st Sergeants at 8.30 am. Harness inspection in afternoon.	

Strength of unit on 1st May. 9 Officers 220 O.R.
" " " 31st " 11 " 214 "

W.P. Llatten
Captain (8th Hr.)
Commanding 2nd Cavalry Machine Gun Squadron

Vol 29.

CONFIDENTIAL

WAR DIARY
of
2ND SQUADRON, MACHINE GUN CORPS, (CAVALRY).

JUNE 1918.

VOLUME No. 29.

Army Form C. 2118.

WAR DIARY
~~INTELLIGENCE SUMMARY.~~
(Erase heading not required.)

Instructions regarding War Diaries and Intelligence Summaries are contained in F.S. Regs, Part II. and the Staff Manual respectively. Title pages will be prepared in manuscript.

Place	Date 1918	Hour	Summary of Events and Information	Remarks and references to Appendices
SAUCHOY. (Abbeville 1/100,000).	June 1st		Exercise and grazing at 8 a.m. on blankets. Kit inspection 10.30 a.m.	
	2nd		Sunday Routine. Voluntary Service R.C.s at SAUCHOY at 10 a.m.	
	3rd		Inspection parade at 8 a.m. 'A' 'B' and 'C' Subsections Equitation on Squadron ground from 8.15 to 9.15 a.m. 'D' 'E' and 'F' Subsections from 9.15 to 10.15 a.m. Range practice for all riflemen in No.2 Section at 2 p.m. Instruction on the Machine Gun.	
	4th		Tactical rides under Section arrangements, all N.C.O.s taking part. Range practice (Rifle) for No.3 Section at 2 p.m. Remainder instruction on the Machine Gun.	
	5th		Exercise and grazing on blankets at 8 a.m. Ground too hard to carry out any further equitation, also horses slightly losing condition. Tent pegging for all officers at 9.15 a.m. Range Practice (Rifle) for No.1 Section at 2 p.m. Instruction on German M.G. for No.2 Section. Arms inspection by Armourer for No.3 Section. Squadron Parade at 10 p.m. for Gas Drill.	MNW

Army Form C. 2118.

WAR DIARY
or
INTELLIGENCE SUMMARY.
(Erase heading not required.)

Instructions regarding War Diaries and Intelligence Summaries are contained in F. S. Regs., Part II. and the Staff Manual respectively. Title pages will be prepared in manuscript.

Place	Date	Hour	Summary of Events and Information	Remarks and references to Appendices
SAUCHOY	1918 June 6th		Tactical rides under Section arrangements. All N.C.O.s on parade. Remainder exercise and grazing. Signallers tests at Bde HQ.	
	7th		Rifle Practice for HQrs and Transport at 2 p.m. Tactical Ride under C.O. for all Officers and as many N.C.Os as possible. Rendezvous near No.1 W Section's billets at 8.15 a.m. Remainder Exercise and Grazing on blankets. D.G.O. delivered a lecture on German Gas Shells to all ranks at 3 p.m.	
	8th		Early Exercise. Baths and Foden lorry used at SAUCHOY during the morning.	
	9th		Sunday Routine. Parade Service (C. of E.) at SAUCHOY at 10 a.m.	
	10th		Subsection Parade at 8 a.m. Exercise and instruction in I.D. No.1 Section Revolver shooting 2 p.m. Remainder instruction on the Machine Gun. Squadron parade at 10 p.m. for Gas Drill.	MW310

WAR DIARY or INTELLIGENCE SUMMARY

Army Form C. 2118.

Place	Date 1918 June	Hour	Summary of Events and Information	Remarks and references to Appendices
SAULCHOY	11th		All officers attended a tactical ride held by the Brigadier (G.H. Bruce also out) rendezvous at VALLOIR ABBAYE at 9 am. Remainder Exercise at 8 am. Revolver Shooting for N°3 Section at 2 pm.	
	12th		Remainder instruction on the M.G. One case of MUMPS - Squadron isolated for 3 weeks. Subsection parades at 8 am. Revolver Shooting for N°2 Section at 2 pm. Arms inspection. Capt. L.W.D. NATHEN. } Mentioned in Despatches by Field-Lieut. E.E. ROBERTS. M.C. } Marshal Sir D. Haig, 7.20.5.18.	
	13th		N°1 Section used Training Ground (Jumping and Tent pegging) at Douries. Remainder Subsection parades at 8 am. Afternoon, Stripped Saddle inspection.	
	14th		Squadron (Transport without limbers) inspected by C.O. in Field Service Marching Order at SAULCHOY at 8.15 am. Afternoon, instruction on the Machine Gun.	
	15th		Exercise on Blankets. Baths at SAULCHOY from 9 am to 3 p.m.	WWS19.

WAR DIARY or INTELLIGENCE SUMMARY.

Army Form C. 2118.

Place	Date 1918	Hour	Summary of Events and Information	Remarks and references to Appendices
SAULCHOY	June 15th		Condition of horses shew improvement during past week.	
	16th		Sunday Routine. Brigade Church parade at GRAND PREAU at 11 a.m. After the Service, the Corps Commander presented medal ribands to recent recipients of same. Capt G. Dent. (MC) and Sgt L.S. Bull (DCM, MM) 2nd M.G. Sqdn, received the ribands of the M.C. and D.C.M. respectively.	
	17th		Subsection Parades at 8 a.m. Medical Inspection at 10.15 a.m. Afternoon. S.R.R Drill for whole Sqadron.	
	18th		Subsections parades at 8 a.m. Training of Signallers. Range practices (Rifle) for Transport in afternoon.	
	19th		Subsection parades at 8 a.m. Lecture by C.O. to all Officers at 10.30 a.m.	
	20th		Exercise before Breakfast. Baths and Foden disinfector was at SAULCHOY during the morning. Pactical ride for all Officers under the C.O. at 6.30 a.m. "Messages and reports".	
	21st		Exercise at 8 a.m. Certain Officers attended a stuff ride with	

Army Form C. 2118.

WAR DIARY
or
INTELLIGENCE SUMMARY.
(Erase heading not required.)

Place	Date 1915	Hour	Summary of Events and Information	Remarks and references to Appendices
SAULCHOY	June 21st.		Officers of 9th Lancers under the Brigadier. Afternoon, Arms Inspection.	
	22nd.		Range Practices with M.G. carried out at LA NEUVILLE Range. 150 men per gun shot. Party left by lorries about 7.30 a.m. Remainder Exercise and Stables.	
	23rd.		Sunday Routine. Church Parade (C of E.) at SAULCHOY at 12 noon.	
	24th.		Subsection parades at 8 a.m. Medical inspection at 10.15 a.m. Afternoon No.1 Section Shooting for bad rifle shots. Remainder instruction on the M.G. Evening, Squadron Parade for S.B.R drill at 10 p.m.	
	25th.		Subsection parades at 8 a.m. Afternoon as for previous day. "P.U.O." Broken out in Squadron.	
	26th.		Range Practices (M.G.) carried out on LA NEUVILLE Range. 6 men per gun fired. Party left by lorries about 7.20 a.m. Remainder Exercise and Grazing.	[signature]

WAR DIARY or INTELLIGENCE SUMMARY.

Army Form C. 2118.

Place	Date	Hour	Summary of Events and Information	Remarks and references to Appendices
SAULCHOY	1918 June 27th		Early Exercise. Baths at SAULCHOY during morning. Section sports in afternoon.	
	28th		Subsection parades at 8 a.m. Lt. Hibbert and 2Lt. Cheadle attended a staff ride under the Brigadier. Afternoon; Shoppee Saddle inspection. 8 men admitted to Hospital with P.U.O.	
	29th		Exercise and Grazing at 8 a.m. Kit and Equipment inspection at 10.30 a.m. 5 men admitted to Hospital with P.U.O.	
	30th		Sunday Routine. 31 cases of P.U.O. in the Squadron to date. All admitted to hospital. Changes during month: A rank of Major granted to C.O. (Capt. L.N.D. Mather). Establishment increased by 1 officer 27 OR and 26 horses.	

J.N.D. Mather. Major.
Commanding 2nd Machine Gun Squadron.

WX 30

CONFIDENTIAL.

War Diary
of:
2nd Squadron. Machine Gun Corps. (Cavalry).
July. 1918.

Volume No. 30.

WAR DIARY or INTELLIGENCE SUMMARY.

Army Form C. 2118.

(Erase heading not required.)

Place	Date	Hour	Summary of Events and Information	Remarks and references to Appendices
SAULCHOY (Abbeville) (1100,300)	1918 July 1st		Subsection parades at 6am.	
	2nd		Subsection parade at 6am. Section Drill at 11am. Afternoon Garage Drill & all Subsections. 11 OR to Hospital (P.U.O.)	
	3rd		Subsections parades at 8am. Drill. Baths at SAULCHOY during afternoon.	
	4th		Subsection Parade at 6am. Drill. Afternoon Garage Subsection. 5 discharges - P.U.O. 4 OR admitted to Hospital - 5 discharges - P.U.O.	
	5th		Squadron Drill on Aerodrome near KPT CHEPMN. from 7 to 8.30 am. General Drive practised with a view to an inspection by the Commander-in-Chief. 4 new admitted to, and 3 discharges from Hospital. P.U.O.	
	6th		Squadron Drill on the Aerodrome from 6.15 to 9.30am. Parade of all Officers for Sword Drill at 2-3pm. 6 OR admitted to, and 2 discharges from Hospital. P.U.O.	
	7th		Sunday. Parade 5 OR admitted to and 5 OR discharged from Hospital. P.U.O.	

Army Form C. 2118.

WAR DIARY
or
INTELLIGENCE SUMMARY.
(Erase heading not required.)

Instructions regarding War Diaries and Intelligence Summaries are contained in F. S. Regs., Part II. and the Staff Manual respectively. Title pages will be prepared in manuscript.

Place	Date	Hour	Summary of Events and Information	Remarks and references to Appendices
SAUCHOY.	July 8th 1918		Squadron Drill on the Aerodrome from 7.30 to 8.30 a.m. 10/R admitted to and discharges from Hospital – P.O.O.	
	9th		Early Exercise on Blankets at 6.30 a.m. O.C. 2nd/Lt T.J.E. Bone Dep't. taken on the strength. Orders received that the Sqdn are once monthly to send Lancers at 10% Asst. Strength only under Off. of Sqdn. N.C. proceeded by lorries. 10% admitted and 2 discharges from Hospital. P.O.O.	
	10th		Squadron marched to TROHEN-LE-GRAND and was ready to march by the Squadron paraded at SAULCHOY at 8 a.m. and marched via GENNES-IVERGNY and VALENS, then continued via AURI-LE-CHATEAU to billets at BEAUCOURT. (Ref. Maps: ABBEVILLE & LENS, 1/100,000).	
BEAUCOURT.	11th		March continued to SARTON area (Ref. LENS 1/100,000). Squadron paraded at BEAUCOURT at 10.15 a.m. and marched via LUTREBOIS and DOULLENS to billets just E. of SARTON. All horses in Stables in the camp.	
SARTON.	12th		Exercise on Blankets at 7.30 a.m. (cleaning Saddlery and Harness, and work on Camp, etc.	MWR9

WAR DIARY / INTELLIGENCE SUMMARY

Army Form C. 2118.

Place	Date 1918	Hour	Summary of Events and Information	Remarks and references to Appendices
SARTON	July 13th		Exercise at 6 am. Conference at Brigade H.Q. for CO's at 10 am.	
	14th		Exercise at 7 am on Blankets. Reconnaissance between BROWN (D30) and RED (Copse) line carried out daily by Certain Officer, reports on same being forwarded to Brigade HQ.	
	15th		Exercise at 6 am. All Machine Guns and Arms inspected by the Armourer-Sergeant during the day. Independent Belts of same sent to where action immediate.	
	16th		M.G. practice carried out on the Machine Gun Range 4.15.6. (Reg Map Sheet 57D 1/40,000) from 8 am to 12 noon. 6 men per detachment fire all ranks of the squadron to wear SBR's for at least 10 minutes daily during ordinary work. Barrage Drill.	
	17th		Exercise at 6 am. Afternoon. Medical Inspection at 10.30 am.	
	18th		Exercise at 6 am. Subsections in afternoon. Barrage Drill to all Subsections in afternoon. Baths at ORVILLE from 9 am to 12 noon. All SBR's newly issued since last fitting tested at DGO's Hut at 10 am. in the afternoon all sections carried out firing on the field firing range in H.15.d with Machine Guns. Range up to 800 x (about) 3 men per detachment fires	MMS79

Army Form C. 2118.

WAR DIARY
or
INTELLIGENCE SUMMARY.
(Erase heading not required.)

Place	Date	Hour	Summary of Events and Information	Remarks and references to Appendices
SARTON	July 1918 20th		Exercise at 8 a.m. Saddles & Harness cleaned in afternoon.	
	21st		Sunday Routine. Grazing from 8 to 9 a.m.	
	22nd		Subsection Parade at 8 a.m. Equitation Horses. Drill in afternoon.	
	23rd		Squadron moved to Billets at THIÉVRES in morning.	
THIÉVRES			Standings for horses on marshy ground - very bad. Men billetted in village.	
	24th		Exercise at 8 a.m. Heavy rain all day.	
	25th		Paraded in the lines at 7.15 a.m. Machine Gun practice carried out on the Bois Lieux range. Sections came into action and advanced in stages before single baths at ORVILLE in afternoon.	
	26th		103 Section repeated m.g. range practice. Yesterday. Remainder Exercise. Carriage Drill for all Subsections.	
	27th		Squadron arranges to fight Brigade on range in G.116. 103 Section proceeded to range, remainder cavalry going to Sutton quick practice. Weather very bad.	
	28th		Weather — Range going not too very bad. Heavy rain — Inca very Brigade funeral Service at SARTON Sunday Routine. Major L.W.D. Walker proceeds to U.K. 1st S.G. to Mann at Mann.	Wks

Army Form C. 2118.

WAR DIARY
INTELLIGENCE SUMMARY

(Erase heading not required.)

Place	Date	Hour	Summary of Events and Information	Remarks and references to Appendices
THIÉVRES	1918 July 28th		Cavalry Corps Equitation School for 4 days - C.O.'s Course. Capt. A. Mea, M.C. assumes command.	
	29th		Section parade at 6am. Gas Drill at 2pm by O.C. Commander inspects squadron lines during morning stables. V.O. inspects officers chargers, H.Q. and Transport horses. Section parade at 6am. A.D.V.S. Rd. Car. Dn. inspects squadron & C.O. during morning stables. Afternoon inspection of billets.	
	30th			
	31st		Section parade at 6am. Afternoon. Tents and bivouacs dug in lines. Billets etc. cleared up and salvage collected all round. Major E. was washer returned from Country Corps the night. Equitation School. 8 O.R. proceeded on ordinary leave to U.K. During the month. Strength on 1st day of month = 11 officers 241 O.R. Strength last " = 12 " 253 "	

W.S. Mather Major (8th Hussars)
Commanding 2nd Squadron M.G.C. Cavalry

WAR DIARY
of
2nd SQUADRON, MACHINE GUN CORPS, CAVALRY.

AUGUST. 1918

VOLUME No. 31.

CONFIDENTIAL.

WAR DIARY / INTELLIGENCE SUMMARY

Army Form C. 2118.

Place	Date	Hour	Summary of Events and Information	Remarks and references to Appendices
THIÉVRES (Ref Map LENS 1/100,000)	1914 June 1st		No.1 Section took part in a Tactical Scheme with 9th Lancers. Remainder Exercise and Grazing. Stripped Saddle inspection during afternoon.	
	2nd		Rifle Shooting. Squadron spent all day on the range. Was 8 miles away. 19 deadle removed from Hospital, also Major Watson from Cavalry Corps Equitation School.	
	3rd		Evening Ring practice in afternoon cancelled owing to rain.	
	4th		Usual Sunday Routine. Church Parade at 11.45 am. Captain Misa admitted to Hospital.	
	5th		Squadron marched on the night 5/6th from THIÉVRES to KARGNIES via BEAUQUESNE.	
KARGNIES	6th		Remained in billets until 10 pm then marched via VIGNACOURT - ST VAST to the ST SAUVEUR area (Ref AMIENS 1/100,000).	
ST SAUVEUR	7th		Squadron marched to concentration point at LONGEAU.	
CAIX	8th		Squadron marched with the Brigade to CAIX (Ref Sheet 66E 1/40,000) "B" Subsection under Lt. Roberts in action with 4th Dragoon Guards about E.9.D.10.0.1. Later these two	

Place	Date	Hour	Summary of Events and Information	Remarks and references to Appendices
(continued)	8th		Guns moved back to about E.9.6.3.3. They rejoined the Squadron at CAIX at about 6 a.m. on the morning of the 9th inst. "C" Subsection under Lt Hibbet was D Subsection under Lt Page, in action about E.11.c.1. to E.11.d. These guns had various targets including two enemy M.Gs which were silenced. 1 O.R. wounded.	
	9th		Subsection moved at about 1pm via VRÉLY to just behind MÉHARICOURT. D Subsection attached to 9th Lancers who were acting as Advance Guard. Major W.D. NATHEN 1/2th E.G. FRERE wounded, then now both at Brigade H.Q. & Lt White took over command of the Squadron. A, B, & D Subsections in action with 4 D.9K. and 9th guards respectively, S.W. of MÉHARICOURT. E and F Subsections in reserve. 1 O.R. wounded. 10 K. killed and 6 wounded by a shell in Transport lines near CAYEUX. Horse casualties on August 9th = 14 killed.	

Army Form C. 2118.

WAR DIARY
or
INTELLIGENCE SUMMARY.
(Erase heading not required.)

Instructions regarding War Diaries and Intelligence Summaries are contained in F. S. Regs., Part II. and the Staff Manual respectively. Title pages will be prepared in manuscript.

Place	Date	Hour	Summary of Events and Information	Remarks and references to Appendices
CAIX	1918 10th			
	11th		Brigade returned at dawn to point N.W. of CAIX. Received orders to move at 3 p.m. but after going a short distance Brigade returned to previous area. Squadron remained in bivouac in wood near CAIX (ref map sheet 62D 1/40,000) N.26 central until 9.45 p.m. when the Brigade marched via MARCELCAVE and VILLERS-BRETONNEUX to CAMON which we reached and bivouaced there at 3.30 a.m. Capt. Misa rejoined from hospital and Capt. Dent & Lt. Johnson from leave in France.	
	12th		Reveille 10 a.m. Morning Stables. Afternoon bathing, kit & inspection.	
	13th		Exercise and grazing. Saddle inspection.	
	14th		Exercise and grazing. Washing and packing of limbers in the afternoon. The Field Marshal Commanding-in-Chief rode through the Squadron lines about 4.30 p.m.	
BRETEL	15th		Squadron moved to BRETEL (Ref. LENS 1/100,000) Night march. Capt. A. Misa M.C. proceeded to 10th M.G. Squadron. Capt. G. Dent, M.C. assumed command of the Squadron.	
MAIZICOURT	16th		Moved at night to MAIZICOURT. Arrived about 2 a.m. (17th). Where Squadron billeted.	6

Army Form C. 2118.

WAR DIARY
~~INTELLIGENCE SUMMARY.~~
(Erase heading not required.)

Instructions regarding War Diaries and Intelligence Summaries are contained in F. S. Regs., Part II. and the Staff Manual respectively. Title pages will be prepared in manuscript.

Place	Date	Hour	Summary of Events and Information	Remarks and references to Appendices
MATZICOURT	Aug 1918 17th		Usual Routine.	
	18th		Exercise. Afternoon, horses moved under cover.	
	19th		Exercised. Squadron moved at 8.30 p.m. via FROHEN-LE-GRAND – DOULLENS – MONDICOURT to Bivouac at WARLINCOURT-LEZ-PAS.	
WARLINCOURT	20th		Moved at 8.45 p.m. to the Willow Patch. about E.13 (ref. Map Sheet 57D. 1/40,000). Arrived at midnight. Pegged down and off saddles.	
	21st		Saddled up and moved at 4.30 a.m. to JEWEL VALLEY. Brigade moved up and in touch with Infantry to A 20 C. (ref. ERVILLERS Special Sheet 1/40,000) Squadron all from shell fire. Following casualties:- Killed. 4 O.R. – Died of wounds 2 O.R. – Wounded 28 O.R. – Missing and believed killed 3 O.R. – Horses 77 Killed 7 wounded. Mostly in B.C. and F. Subsections. Squadron was withdrawn about 5.30 pm and shortly after moved back to SARTON and bivouacked about 2 am after thick fog all morning.	
SARTON	22nd		Usual Routine.	
	23rd		Exercise. Afternoon Cleaning Saddlery.	
	24th		17 Remounts joined. Usual routine.	

Army Form C. 2118.

WAR DIARY
or
INTELLIGENCE SUMMARY.
(Erase heading not required.)

Place	Date	Hour	Summary of Events and Information	Remarks and references to Appendices
SAIGON	Aug 1918 25th		Usual routine. Lt. M Chenevix M.C. and 2.Lt. Jones from Base	
	26th		Moved at 4.30 pm to MAIZIERES. Arrived at 10.30 pm and billetted	
	27th		Usual routine. Orders received to Stand to at 1½ hours notice to move.	
	28th		Orders to Stand to at 5½ hours notice. Exercise.	
	29th		Usual routine.	
	30th		Usual routine.	
	31st		Usual routine. 8 O.R. arrived from the Base.	
			During the month 1 Officer and 9 O.R. proceeded on leave to U.K.	
			Strength on 1st of month was 12 Offs. 252 O.R.	
			" " 31st " " 10 Offs. 207 "	

G. W. Egerton
Comdg. 2nd Squadron M.G. Cavalry.

Army Form C. 2118.

WAR DIARY
or
INTELLIGENCE SUMMARY.
(Erase heading not required.)

WR 32

WAR DIARY
of
2nd SQUADRON, MACHINE GUN CORPS (CAVALRY).

SEPTEMBER. 1918.

VOLUME No 32.

CONFIDENTIAL.

WAR DIARY
INTELLIGENCE SUMMARY

Army Form C. 2118.

Place	Date	Hour	Summary of Events and Information	Remarks and references to Appendices
MAIZIERES	1/7/18		Exercise. Changed to 1½ hours notice. Later back to 3½ hours notice.	
(Ref: LENS 1/100,000)	2/7/18		Later back to 5½ hours notice. Exercise. 66 Remounts and 12 O.R. joined Squadron. Again ordered to stand to at 1½ hours notice. Later back to 5½ hours notice.	
	3/7/18		Reorganized Transport. Sending back two Limbers to each Subsection. About 10.30 p.m. Back to 1½ hours notice. Later, back to 5½ hours notice. About 12.30 a.m. Warning order to move at 5 a.m. 1 hours notice. About 2 a.m. order cancelled. Back to 5½ hours notice.	
	4/7/18		Exercise. Test carried out with "Expendable" belts.	
	5/7/18		Exercise.	
	6/7/18		Moved to REBREUVE at 2 p.m.	
REBREUVE	7/7/18		Exercise.	
	8/7/18		Sunday routine. 9 O.R. transferred to 1st M.G. Squadron.	
	9/7/18		Usual Routine.	
	10/7/18		Subsection drill.	
	11/7/18		Subsection drill and Mounted Gas Drill.	

Army Form C. 2118.

WAR DIARY
or
INTELLIGENCE SUMMARY.

(Erase heading not required.)

Instructions regarding War Diaries and Intelligence Summaries are contained in F. S. Regs., Part II. and the Staff Manual respectively. Title pages will be prepared in manuscript.

Place	Date	Hour	Summary of Events and Information	Remarks and references to Appendices
REBREUVE	12/6		Subsection drill. Baths in afternoon.	
	13/6	3 pm	Section drill. 10 K remounts to 9th A.V. Sqdn. 10 Remounts joined.	
	14/6	9 am	Exercise on Bleudeck.	
	15/6		Usual Sunday Routine. 10 K taken on strength from 1st M.G. Sqdn.	
WILLEMAN	16/6		Squadron moved to WILLEMAN at 9 am. Staff Ride to G.O.S. in preparation for manoeuvres. 2 OR joined from Base.	
	17/6	4.30 pm	Manoeuvres. Started East from OEUF. Ceased fire about Squadron attacks at CAUMONT.	
CAUMONT				
FROHEN-LE-PETIT	18/6	8½	Moved to FROHEN-LE-PETIT. about 11 am.	
	19/6		Exercise and grazing. Lecture by Officers by G.O.C. in afternoon.	
	20/6	9 am	Exercise. SBR inspection. 2 Remounts taken on the strength.	
	21/6		Usual Routine. 1 OR sent to England for services	
	22/6		Usual Sunday Routine. Hand to Cadet Unit.	

Army Form C. 2118.

WAR DIARY
INTELLIGENCE SUMMARY.
(Erase heading not required.)

Place	Date	Hour	Summary of Events and Information	Remarks and references to Appendices
FROHEN LE PETIT.	23.9.18		G.O.C. 2⁷ᵈ Armd. Bde and O.C. A.S.C. Arms inspected all Transport in morning. Exercises inspection.	
FAMECHON.	24.9.18		Moved to FAMECHON at 7 P.m.	
AVELUY.	25.9.18		Moved to AVELUY at 7 P.m.	
MOISLAINS	26.9.18		Moved to MOISLAINS at 8.45 p.m. (Sheet 62 1/40,000)	
	27.9.18		Usual Routine.	
	28.9.18		Usual Routine.	
HAMELET.	29.9.18		Moved at 4 P.m. to HAMELET. (Sheet 62° 1/40,000)	
	30.9.18		Laid to at 3 hours notice from 8 a.m. until 11 a.m. then at 3 hours notice for remainder of day.	

Aus. Captain
Comdg. 2⁷ᵈ Squadron, Machine Gun Corps.
(Cavalry).

Vol 33

Army Form C. 2118.

WAR DIARY
or
INTELLIGENCE SUMMARY.
(Erase heading not required.)

War Diary.
October 1918.
Volume 33.
2nd Machine Gun Squadron

G. [signature] Major
Commanding 2nd Machine Gun Squadron

2ND MACHINE GUN SQUADRON
31-X-18

Army Form C. 2118.

2ND MACHINE GUN SQUADRON.

WAR DIARY
or
INTELLIGENCE SUMMARY.
(Erase heading not required.)

Instructions regarding War Diaries and Intelligence Summaries are contained in F.S. Regs., Part II. and the Staff Manual respectively. Title pages will be prepared in manuscript.

Place	Date	Hour	Summary of Events and Information	Remarks and references to Appendices
Hamelet. Sheet 62c 140,000 K21.a.Central	1-X-18.		Usual Routine.	
	2-X-18.		Brigade moved up ao far as Villeret, in the morning. Then returned to bivouac at Hamelet.	
	3-X-18.		Usual Routine.	
"	4-X-18.		Usual Routine.	
"	5-X-18.		Brigade moved up to the neighbourhood of NAUROY, and moved back, in the evening to Hamelet.	
"	6-X-18.		Usual Routine.	
(Sheet 62c) L.14.c.8.8.	7-X-18.		Moved in the evening to Hesbecourt, and bivouaced at L.14.C.8.8. (Sheet 62c)	
	8-X-18.		Moved up at 04.15. by Bellecourt, Folemprise Fm, Geneve to Serain. No 1 Section attached to 4th Dragoon Guards. No 2 Section attached to 9th Lancers. No guns in action. Returned to Gouy in the night.	
Gouy.	9-X-18.		Moved up at 06.00 to Le Trou au Soldat. Bivouaced for the night.	
Sheet 67B. V.7.Central	10-X-18.		Moved up to neighbourhood of TROISVILLE and "stood to" until 15.00. Then returned to bivouac at Le Trou au Soldat. (Sheet 67B. V.7. Central)	
Le Trou au Soldat.	11-X-18.		Remained in bivouac.	
	12-X-18.		Remained in bivouac.	
Caulnigny Fm	13-X-18.		Moved back at 08.45 to Caulnigny Farm. (Sheet 62c Q32 a)	
62c Q32.a.	14-X-18.		Usual Routine.	
	15-X-18.		Usual Routine - 4 remounts joined.	
	16-X-18.		Usual Routine - Baths	
	17-X-18.		Usual Routine - 10 remounts joined	
"	18-X-18.		Usual Routine.	
"	19-X-18.		Usual Routine.	
"	20-X-18.		Usual Routine. Section Drill.	
"	21-X-18.		Usual Routine. Section Drill. Gas Drill.	
"	22-X-18.		Usual Routine. No 2 Section on a scheme. 3guns out ao enemy.	
"	23-X-18.		Usual Routine.	

Army Form C. 2118.

2ND MACHINE GUN SQUADRON.

WAR DIARY
or
INTELLIGENCE SUMMARY.
(Erase heading not required.)

Instructions regarding War Diaries and Intelligence Summaries are contained in F. S. Regs., Part II. and the Staff Manual respectively. Title pages will be prepared in manuscript.

Place	Date	Hour	Summary of Events and Information	Remarks and references to Appendices
Cavigny Farm. Sheet 62c Q.32.d	24-X-18		Usual Routine. Drill. Afternoon Gun Drill	
"	25-X-18		Usual Routine. Drill. Afternoon Gun drill	
"	26-X-18		Usual Routine. 6 guns out on enemy for Brigade Officers Scheme	
"	27-X-18		Usual Routine. Drill	
"	28-X-18		Usual Routine. Drill	
"	29-X-18		No 1 Section out on Scheme with 4th Dragoon Guards	
"	30-X-18		12 Guns out on enemy to 9th Cavalry Brigade (Scheme)	
"	31-X-18		Brigade Scheme against hostile M.G.s under G.O.C. 1st Cavalry Division	

WM 34

"CONFIDENTIAL"

WAR DIARY
of
2ND SQUADRON. MACHINE GUN CORPS, CAVALRY.
NOVEMBER, 1918.
VOLUME No. 34.

WAR DIARY
INTELLIGENCE SUMMARY
(Erase heading not required.)

Army Form C. 2118.

Place	Date	Hour	Summary of Events and Information	Remarks and references to Appendices
CAUVIGNY F^m (Ref. Sheet 62^c 1/40.000 – Q.32.d.)	1/7/18		Section Drill. Gas Drill in afternoon	
	2/7/18		Exercise. Arms and Equipment inspection	
	3/7/18		Usual Sunday Routine	
	4/7/18		Section Drill. Horse lasting parade to A.D.V.S. Marston	
	5/7/18		Section Drill. Gun Drill in afternoon. Orders received to be ready to move at 2 hours notice. Saddles and transport packed ready.	
GRAVECOURT	6/7/18		Squadron marched at 08.15 for JEANCOURT – HARGICOURT – LE CATELET – to GRAVECOURT (nr. VALENCIENNES, 1700 am) arrived at about 15.15 which bullited the night.	
GOEULZIN	7/7/18		Squadron marched at 08.30 via MASNIÈRES – CAMBRAI – AUBENCHEUL – CANTIN to GOEULZIN arriving at about 15.30. About billeted the night.	
MONS-EN-PEVELE	8/7/18		Squadron marched at 10.00 via DOUAI – Roche to MONS-EN-PEVELE and billeted the night	
	9/7/18		Remained in bivouac	

Army Form C. 2118.

WAR DIARY
INTELLIGENCE SUMMARY.
(Erase heading not required.)

Place	Date	Hour	Summary of Events and Information	Remarks and references to Appendices
MONS-EN-PEVELE	10/11/18		Squadron received orders to move to an area about NOMAIN (Rly. TOURNAI-MONS). Squadron paraded at 07:30. At NOMAIN, orders were received that the Brigade would continue it's march Eastwards, and Squadron eventually the night at WASMES.	
WASMES	11/11/18		Orders received that the Brigade would march in fighting formation to a wit about BASECLES. The Squadron (less No.2 Section) paraded at 08:00. No.2 Section under L/ 104 Farg. were ordered to report to O.C. Advanced [Squadron] (St. Javans) and come under the orders of O.C. St. Javans at 07:20. Before reaching the line about BASECLES, however, runners were held at about 11:15 and orders were received that an Armistice had been concluded with the Enemy. Orders were then received for the Squadron to billet the night at ELIGNIES-ST-ANNE. No.2 Section rejoined the Squadron at about 13:00.	
ELIGNIES-ST-ANNE	12/11/18		The Brigade marched at 08:45 to an area about MONTAGNE. The Squadron arrived at BELLOY and SIN about 14:20 and billeted with H.Q. in BELLOY	
BELLOY	13/11/18		Remained in billets.	

Army Form C. 2118.

WAR DIARY
or
INTELLIGENCE SUMMARY.
(Erase heading not required.)

Instructions regarding War Diaries and Intelligence Summaries are contained in F. S. Regs., Part II. and the Staff Manual respectively. Title pages will be prepared in manuscript.

Place	Date	Hour	Summary of Events and Information	Remarks and references to Appendices
BELLOY	14/8		Remained in billets. O.C. 2nd Cav Bde inspected all horses of the Squadron at 11.45	
	15/8		Exercise - All rifles washed and cleaned. Orders received that the 1st Cavalry Division would march East to Germany, commencing the march on the 17th inst. in stages of 2 days march and 2 days rest. Captain D. O. G. Duff joined from M.G. Base Depot and assumed the duties of 2 I/C in Squadron.	
	16/8		Stable inspection. All saddles and wagons packed.	
	17/8		The Squadron marched at 07.00, via PERONELZ - STAMBRUGES - S. RAULT to billets at BEUGELETTE.	
BEUGELETTE	18/8		Squadron marched at 07.45 via LOUVIGNIES - NEUFVILLES - SOIGNIES to 6.103.b at NAAST (N. of BRUSSELS 1/100,000) arriving at about 13.30. Major G Dent was proceded to England on 2 months leave. Captain D. O. Duff assumed command of the Squadron.	
NAAST	19/8		Remained in billets. Normal routine and exercise. Men marched during the day.	

Army Form C. 2118.

WAR DIARY
or
INTELLIGENCE SUMMARY.
(Erase heading not required.)

Place	Date	Hour	Summary of Events and Information	Remarks and references to Appendices
BIELLOY	14/11/18		Runners in billets. G.O.C. 2nd Cav Bde inspected all horses of the Squadron at 11.45	
	15/11/18		Exercise. All arms washed and cleaned. Orders received that the 9th Cavalry Division would march East to Germany. Commencing the march on the 17th inst. in stages of 2 days march and 2 days rest. Captain D.S.S. Duff joined from MGC Base Depot and assumed the duties of 2nd in Command.	
	16/11/18		Stable inspection. All saddles and harness packed.	
	17/11/18		The Squadron marched at 07.00, via PÉRONNE - STAMBRUGES - SIRAULT to billets at BLUGELETTE.	
BLUGELETTE	18/11/18		Squadron marched at 07.45 via LOUVIGNIES - NEUFVILLES - SOIGNIES to billets at NAAST. (Pop BRUSSELS 1/100,000) arriving at about 13.00. Major G. Dent M.C. proceeded to England on 2 months leave (Captain D.S. Duff assumed command of the Squadron.	
NAAST	19/11/18		Remained in Billets. Horses routine. Use exercise. More Guard mounted during the day.	

WAR DIARY
INTELLIGENCE SUMMARY.
(Erase heading not required.)

Army Form C. 2118.

Place	Date	Hour	Summary of Events and Information	Remarks and references to Appendices
BELLON	14/11		Remained in billets	
	15/11	9.0.6	2nd in Command inspected all horses of the Squadron at 11.45. Exercised. All inspect washed and cleaned. Orders received that the jrt (Canal Section) would march East to Germany, commencing the march on the 17th inst. in stages of 2 days march and 2 days rest. Captain R & J Duff joined from M.G.C. Base Depot and assumed the duties of 2/ic in Command.	
	16/11		Saddle inspection. All saddles and waggons packed.	
	17/11		The Squadron marched at 07.00 via PERUWELZ - STAMBRUGES - SIRAULT to billets at ROUGELETTE.	
ROUGELETTE	18/11		Squadron marched at 07.45 via LOUVIGNIES - NEUFVILLES - SOIGNIES - HOULLERS at NRAST. (of 1st Bn for BRUSSELS 1/120,000) arriving at about 13.00. Major J. Dent M.C. proceeded to England on 1 months leave. Captain R.J. Duff assumed Command.	
NRAST	19/11		Remained in Billets. Normal Routine. Real Exercise main and rounds name during the day	

Army Form C. 2118.

WAR DIARY
or
INTELLIGENCE SUMMARY.
(Erase heading not required.)

Instructions regarding War Diaries and Intelligence Summaries are contained in F. S. Regs., Part II. and the Staff Manual respectively. Title pages will be prepared in manuscript.

Place	Date	Hour	Summary of Events and Information	Remarks and references to Appendices
NAAST	20/11/18		Light Exercise. Arms Equipment inspection. Normal routine. MC Skil Dehmot's Defaulters	
ROUGELETTE	21/11/18		Continued march at 07.15 to Rouletter ROULETTE	
	22/11/18		March continued at 08.00 to NAMUR. Billets in the Rue de Champs d'Epées (own'd to Rouge being impracticable for motor traffic & instructions) and at BEEZ. (Ref NAMUR 1/100,000)	
NAMUR	23/11/18		No Exercise. Working parties. Divisional tour in Theatre NAMUR at 18.30.	
ENVOZ-COUTHOIN	24/11/18		Continued march to ENVOZ-COUTHOIN at 18.45 (Ref LIÈGE 1/100,000)	
	25/11/18		Remained at ENVOZ. Routine normal. Box Exercise.	
	26/11/18		Routine Normal. 2/Lt Com. Comd O/C D/Coy. 22nd Bn. Lyman to Arty. I/R 5/5x1 5/5. 3 Kings for Carrier Pigeon Inspection of food order and Military Brothels	
SPERMONT	27/11/18		Continued march at 07.45 to SPERMONT.	
	28/11/18		Remained at SPERMONT. 29 Cm promulgates.	

Army Form C. 2118.

WAR DIARY
or
INTELLIGENCE SUMMARY.
(Erase heading not required.)

Instructions regarding War Diaries and Intelligence Summaries are contained in F. S. Regs., Part II. and the Staff Manual respectively. Title pages will be prepared in manuscript.

Place	Date	Hour	Summary of Events and Information	Remarks and references to Appendices
SPRIMONT	27/11		Battalion march to ROY (B) MARCHE 11.00 a.m. Coys. Sundry parties for inspecting the Bougain previous Nough	
			SPA	
ROY	30/11		Remained at ROY	

E.G. Buff
Captain (Steven)
Commanding B Squadron M.G. Camb.

Army Form C. 2118.

WAR DIARY
or
INTELLIGENCE SUMMARY
(Erase heading not required.)

Place	Date	Hour	Summary of Events and Information	Remarks and references to Appendices
SPRIMONT	29/11/18		Continued march to ROY (R) MARCHE - 1/100,000) Offrs. Commanders, Coy's/offrs. inspected the harper pason's troops. SPA	
ROY	30/11/18		Remained at ROY	

D.G. Duff
Commanding B. 22 Squadron

Captain (Stevens)
M.F.C Comdr

Vol 35

WAR DIARY
of
2nd Squadron, Machine Gun Corps, Cavalry.

December 1918.

Volume No. 35.

CONFIDENTIAL.

Army Form C. 2118

WAR DIARY
or
INTELLIGENCE SUMMARY
(Erase heading not required.)

Instructions regarding War Diaries and Intelligence Summaries are contained in F. S. Regs., Part II. and the Staff Manual respectively. Title Pages will be prepared in manuscript.

Place	Date	Hour	Summary of Events and Information	Remarks and references to Appendices
RUY.	1/12/18		March continued into Germany via MALMEDY - WEISMES - BUTGENBACH - ELSENBORN - KALTERHER - BERG - MONTJOIE - to KONZEN. where 5pln billeted. The frontier was crossed at 10-15. (Ref. Map - RHINE VALLEY No.1. 1/250,000.	
KONZEN	2/12/18		Remained at KONZEN.	
KONZEN	3/12/18		Remained at KONZEN.	
BOICH	4/12/18		March continued via SIMMERATH - STRAUCH - SCHMIDT - NIDEGGEN. to BOICH where 5pln billeted for the night.	
GYMNICH	5/12/18		March continued via THUM - FROITZHEIM - VETTWEISS - GLADBACH - ERP - LECHENICH to GYMNICH where 5pln billed for the night.	
COLOGNE	6/12/18		March continued to COLOGNE (Ref. Map. Germany 5L. 1/100,000) via MODRATH - FRECHEN. Location H.2. BONNER STRASSE Barracks. No.1. Section detached to 4th D.G.s for duty on MULHEIM Bridge - No.3. detached to 18th Hussars for duty on Harbour and Hohenzollern Bridge. 1 Sub Section (No 2 Section) detached to 18th Hussars for duty on Railway Bridge BONNER.	Initials
COLOGNE	7/12/18		Remained at COLOGNE.	

1875 Wt. W593/826 1,000,000 4/15 J.B.C. & A. A.D.S.S./Forms/C. 2118.

WAR DIARY or INTELLIGENCE SUMMARY

Army Form C. 2118

(Erase heading not required.)

Place	Date	Hour	Summary of Events and Information	Remarks and references to Appendices
COLOGNE.	8/12/18		Remained at COLOGNE.	
	9/12/18		Remained at COLOGNE. Infantry arrive to take over Bridges.	
	10/12/18		Remained at COLOGNE. Pickets relieved by Infantry. 10 a.m.	
	11/12/18		Remained at COLOGNE.	
REFRATH.	12/12/18		The Squadron marched at 08.30 via the Hohenzollern Bridge - BRUK - to billets at REFRATH. - LUSTHEIDE. - SIEBENMORGEN.	
STUMPF.	13/12/18		Marched onwards via BENSBERG - BECHEN. - DHUNN. - to billets at STUMPF. (Ref map, Germany 2.F. 1/100,000.)	
	14/12/18		Remained at STUMPF.	
	15/12/18		Remained at STUMPF.	
COLOGNE (DEUTZ)	16/12/18		Sqdn. marched at 09.00 to COLOGNE and billeted in the Cavalry Barracks, DEUTZ. Major L.W.D. Rathen rejoined from England, and assumed command of the Sqdn.	
	17/12/18		Cleaning up Barracks etc. Equipment, harness etc.	
	18/12/18		Usual routine.	
	19/12/18		Exercise on blankets at 08.30 a.m.	
	20/12/18		Usual routine. Vy. Exercise 08.30. Mid-day Stables 11.00. Evening Stables 15.30.	LWR

WAR DIARY
INTELLIGENCE SUMMARY
(Erase heading not required.)

Army Form C. 2118

Place	Date	Hour	Summary of Events and Information	Remarks and references to Appendices
COLOGNE	21/12/18		Usual Routine. 4 O.R. to Hospital. Influenza. Arms Inspection 10.a.m.	
	22/12/18		Sunday Routine. 3 O.R. to Hospital. 5 O.R. Leave to U.K.	
	23/12/18		Usual Routine. 4 O.R. to Hospital. Influenza. 3 O.R. Leave to U.K.	
	24/12/18		Usual Routine. Inspection by C.O. of all mares on strength, for retention of Brood Mares. 3 O.R. to Hospital Influenza. 2 O.R. Leave to U.K.	
	25/12/18		Christmas Day. Exercise 07-30 Stables 09-30.	
	26/12/18		Usual Routine, all horses saddled at exercise. 1 O.R. to Hospital. 2 O.R. discharged Hospital. 2 O.R. Leave to U.K.	
	27/12/18		Usual Routine. L.O.C. 2nd Cav. Bgde. inspected the Barracks and visited Stables during Mid-day Stables. A.F.G.C.M. assembled at Sqdn. H.2. to-day, to try No. 47245 Pte STEWART. G. 2nd M.G. Sqn. 2 O.R. to Hospital. Influenza.	MW20
	28/12/18		Usual Routine. Inspection of all O.R's at 10-00 by M.O. 2 O.R. to Hospital. 3 O.R. Discharged. Influenza.	

Army Form C. 2118.

WAR DIARY
or
INTELLIGENCE SUMMARY.
(Erase heading not required.)

Instructions regarding War Diaries and Intelligence Summaries are contained in F. S. Regs. Part II. and the Staff Manual respectively. Title pages will be prepared in manuscript.

Place	Date	Hour	Summary of Events and Information	Remarks and references to Appendices
COLOGNE.	29/12/18		Routine. Kennettes pickling. (1 Ebrenzabern per Section O.R.) 11.00 to discuss "Sports & Recreation. All transport horses placed under command of T.O. (2Lieut CHRISTIE) Lieut E F ROBERTS. M.C. taken on the strength from 74th M.G. Sqn.	
	30/12/18		1 O.R. to Hospital Influenza. H O.R. to Ireland (Demobilisers).	
			2 O.R. Leave to U.K.	
	31/12/18		Usual Routine. All rations (from 29th) drawn by Unit transport from Depôt at L/of COLOGNE (8½ kilos) to O.R. to U.K. (Demobilisers) 10 O.R. arrived as reinforcements and taken on the strength. 10 O.R. to Hospital Influenza. 2 O.R. Leave to U.K.	[signature]

[signature] Major
Commanding 2nd Machine Gun Squadron.

CONFIDENTIAL.

WAR DIARY
— of —
2ND SQUADRON, MACHINE GUN CORPS. CAVALRY.

JANUARY 1919.

VOLUME N° 36.

WAR DIARY
or
INTELLIGENCE SUMMARY.

Army Form C. 2118.

Place	Date	Hour	Summary of Events and Information	Remarks and references to Appendices
DEUTZ COLOGNE	1/1/19		Sunday Routine (Christmas Dinners)	
	2/1/19		Routine and Exercise as usual. Leave to a O.R.'s by Lieut E.E. Roberts on Education. 3 Men Discharged Hospital. 1 Man Leave to U.K.	
	3/1/19		Routine and Exercise as usual. Medical Inspection 13-45. 3 Men Discharged Hospital	
	4/1/19		Routine and Exercise as usual. Inspection of Arms & Equipment.	
	5/1/19		Sunday Routine.	
	6/1/19		Usual Routine. Rations and Forage drawn from this date by Mech Transport. 6 Kilos from Barracks.	
	7/1/19		Usual Routine. Baths. Inspection of Ammunition Belts etc	
	8/1/19		Usual Routine. 4 Men Leave to U.K. 1 Man to Hospital. 2 Men Discharged Hospital.	
	9/1/19		Usual Routine. 6 Stores evacuated, Manfe.	
	10/1/19		Usual Routine. Medical Inspection 13-45 hours. Lecture by O.C. 3rd 6.J.H. on Venereal diseases at 15-45 hours. 3 Men Leave to U.K.	
	11/1/19		Usual Routine. 2 Men Leave to U.K.	
	12/1/19		Sunday Routine.	

Army Form C. 2118.

WAR DIARY
or
INTELLIGENCE SUMMARY.
(Erase heading not required.)

Instructions regarding War Diaries and Intelligence Summaries are contained in F. S. Regs., Part II. and the Staff Manual respectively. Title pages will be prepared in manuscript.

Place	Date	Hour	Summary of Events and Information	Remarks and references to Appendices
DEUTZ COLOGNE	13/1/19		Usual Routine. Squadrons detailed to find one Section always standing to at 3 hours notice for use in the event of disturbances in COLOGNE. No 1 Section duty Section for week. Major L.V.D. WATHEN President of Court Martial at 4th Dragoon Guards. Captain D.F.G. Duff and Lieut E. DAVENALL members of, and under instruction at above Court Martial respectively.	
	14/1/19		Usual Routine. Afternoon, Saddle Inspection and Baths. 27 O.R's as reinforcements from M.G.C. Base Depôt taken on the strength. 4 Men Leave to U.K.	
	15/1/19		Usual Routine. 1 Man Leave to U.K.	
	16/1/19		Usual Routine. Swimming Bath in afternoon. 11 horse casts (sic).	
	17/1/19		Usual Routine. 4 Men Leave to U.K. Inspection by G.O. of duty Section (No1) in marching order.	
	18/1/19		Usual Routine. Medical Inspection at 10.30 hours. Lecture by Viscount Browne R.N. on Kearl's Work, attended by 30 from Squadrons. Major L.V.D. WATHEN and Captain G. DENT President and member respectively of a Court Martial at H.Q. 9th Lancers. 3 Men Leave to U.K.	

Army Form C. 2118.

WAR DIARY
or
INTELLIGENCE SUMMARY.
(Erase heading not required.)

Instructions regarding War Diaries and Intelligence Summaries are contained in F. S. Regs., Part II. and the Staff Manual respectively. Title pages will be prepared in manuscript.

Place	Date	Hour	Summary of Events and Information	Remarks and references to Appendices
DEUTZ COLOGNE	19/1/19		Sunday Routine. Church Parade. C of E at 10.30 hours. Major Fox D.S.O. sub. Guards Lectures at 18.00 hours on "Demobilization and Reconstruction". 1 O.R. Leave to U.K.	
	20/1/19		Usual Routine. A 2 Section relieves No 1 Section as duty Section for the week. Very cold weather begins.	
	21/1/19		Usual Routine. G.O.C. 2nd Cav Bde inspected the horses rugs, nosebags and cavalry horses at 11.00 hours, and all horses were wearing order at 11.45 hours. Both Parades satisfactory and pronounced very smartly by inspecting officer.	
	22/1/19		Usual Routine. Afternoon inspection of all guns and ammo. 2 men to Hospital.	
	23/1/19		Usual Routine. 10 horses dispatched to R.A.E. on loan for officers requirements purposes. Horse evacuated sick. Inspection by A.D of V.S. of Squadron (A 2) in marching order at 15.30 hours.	
	24/1/19		Usual Routine. Medical Inspection 10.30 hours. Baths 4 Men Leave to U.K. 1 Horse destroyed. 1 L.D. taken on the strength.	
	25/1/19		Usual Routine. The Army Commander inspected 4th D.G's and while doing so inspected part of Squadron Barracks. 2 OR's Leave to U.K.	MMcK

(39175) Wt W2358/P561 600,000 11/7 D. D. & L. Sch 53a Forms/C2118/15

Army Form C. 2118.

WAR DIARY
or
INTELLIGENCE SUMMARY.
(Erase heading not required.)

Instructions regarding War Diaries and Intelligence Summaries are contained in F. S. Regs., Part II. and the Staff Manual respectively. Title pages will be prepared in manuscript.

Place	Date	Hour	Summary of Events and Information	Remarks and references to Appendices
DEUTZ COLOGNE	26/9		Sunday Routine. Commenced to snow.	
	27/9		Usual Routine. No. 3 Section relieves No. 2 Section as duty Section. 2 Men leave to U.K.	
	28/9		Usual Routine. Snow and frost interfere with exercise. Layer Riding School now in use.	
	29/9		Medical Inspection at 10.30 hours. Veterinary classification of all horses in groups. GOC 30 Div'n also inspects Canteen accounts. 2 O.R. proceeded to England on leave. 30 OR proceeded to England for Demobilization.	
	30/9		Usual Routine. Swimming Baths in afternoon. Two reinforcements join on the strength from Base.	
	31/9		Exercise at 08.30 hours. GOC Cavalry Corps inspected horses and men of H.Q. Transport and No. 1 Section at Stables at 11.30 hours. 6 OR arrives from Base on leave and 2 taken on the strength. 55 men absent on leave at this date.	WWV[?]

(19275) Wt W2358/P360 600,000 12/7 D.D.&L. Sch. 532. Forms/C2118/15

Army Form C. 2118.

WAR DIARY
or
INTELLIGENCE SUMMARY.
(Erase heading not required.)

Instructions regarding War Diaries and Intelligence Summaries are contained in F. S. Regs., Part II. and the Staff Manual respectively. Title pages will be prepared in manuscript.

Place	Date	Hour	Summary of Events and Information	Remarks and references to Appendices
DEUTZ. COLOGNE	31/1/19		In all 24 O.R. proceeded to England during the month in connection with Demobilization.	
			<u>Honours + Awards</u>.	
			No 41301 Sgt. C.Charles "20th M.G. Squadron. Awarded the Meritorious Service Medal, vide Supplement to London Gazette of 18/1/19.	

M.W.Mathews Major.
Commanding 2nd M.G. Squadron M.G. Cavalry.

CONFIDENTIAL

WAR DIARY

OF

2ND MACHINE GUN SQUADRON

FROM 1.2.19 TO 28.2.19.

VOLUME No. 31.

CONFIDENTIAL.

2ND MACHINE GUN SQUADRON. — FEBRUARY, 1919.

WAR DIARY

INTELLIGENCE SUMMARY.

(Erase heading not required.)

Army Form C. 2118.

GERMANY. 2 L
VOLUME. 3 f.
1/100,000.

Instructions regarding War Diaries and Intelligence Summaries are contained in F. S. Regs., Part II. and the Staff Manual respectively. Title pages will be prepared in manuscript.

Place	Date	Hour	Summary of Events and Information	Remarks and references to Appendices
COLOGNE	1st.		Exercise 8.15 a.m. on Blankets. — Remount & Classification Board classified all horses into groups "X", "Y" and "Z". Began at 12.00 hrs and finished at 15.15 hrs.	S/f
"	2nd.		Sunday Routine. — very cold weather. All leave and Demobilisation temporarily stopped. Squadron ordered to remain at 100% strength now below 75%.	S/f
"	3rd.		Usual Routine. — Saddle inspections ordered for retro hues and hrd. Lecture by C.O. at 14.15 hours on "Formation of New Armies and Bounds".	S/f S/f
"	4th.		Exercise on Blankets at 08.15 hours. All horses treated with Mallein test on return from exercise. — Snow	S/f
"	5th.		All horses inspected by V.O. in the morning in connection with yesterday's test. Exercise in afternoon. 2 men discharged from hospital.	S/f
"	6th.		Exercise. — No 3 Section inspected in Marching Order. 16 Horses marked "D" destroyed. 8 horses struck off strength. No 41304. Pte. Cook. A. transferred to 9th Lancers struck off strength.	S/f S/f
"	7th.		Exercise.	S/f

WAR DIARY
of
INTELLIGENCE SUMMARY.
(Erase heading not required.)

SHEET 2.
FEBRUARY. 1919
VOLUME. 37
Army Form C. 2118.

Place	Date	Hour	Summary of Events and Information	Remarks and references to Appendices
COLOGNE	8th		Exercise — Brood Mares other than TT examined by V.O.	S/b
"	9th		7 men (coalminers) to U.K. for demobilization.	S/b
"	10th		Exercise — All "Y" horses inspected by Remount Classification Board for Pack horses at 14.15 hrs. Lecture on "Small Holdings"	S/b
"	11th		Exercise — Inspection of barracks by G.O.C. Division. Afternoon — foot parade for G.O.C. Division.	S/b
"	12th		Exercise — Lecture on Social Subjects.	S/b
"	13th		Exercise.	S/b
"	14th		Exercise — Lecture on "Prison life in DARTMOOR" — 2 horses evacuated and struck off the strength.	S/b
"	15th		Exercise.	S/b
"	16th		Sunday Routine.	S/b
"	17th		Exercise — Canteen meeting 17.30 hours. — 1 horse destroyed—struck off	S/b
"	18th		Exercise — All "Z" horses inspected by V.O. for reclassification.	S/b
"	19th		Exercise — Riding school for men who joined since 1916.	S/b

SHEET 3. FEBRUARY 1919. VOL. 37. Army Form C. 2118.

WAR DIARY
or
INTELLIGENCE SUMMARY.
(Erase heading not required.)

Place	Date	Hour	Summary of Events and Information	Remarks and references to Appendices
COLOGNE	20		Exercise and Riding School. 1 Officer 3 O.Rs. to HORREM. for demobilization.	S/2
"	21st		1 O.R. granted leave to U.K. 1 horse destroyed and struck off strength.	S/2
"	22nd		Exercise and Riding School. 1 O.R. granted leave to U.K.	S/2
"	23rd		Exercise and Riding School. 1 O.R. granted leave to U.K.	S/2
"	24th		Sunday Routine.	
"	25th		Exercise and Riding School. 1 O.R. granted leave to U.K.	S/2
"	26th		Officers rode for 2nd Army Hypro at 14.30 hrs. Exercise and Riding School. All guns fired during exercise.	S/2
"	27th		Exercise and Riding School. Major L.W.D WATHEN. to U.K. on duty. 3.O.Rs to U.K. for demobilization. 2 horses evacuated and 1 horse died, struck off the strength. - Officers Ride for	S/2
"	28th		2nd Army Hypro at 14.30 hrs. Exercise and Riding School.	S/2

COLOGNE.
1.3.19.

S.T.S. Duff. Captain
Commanding 2nd Machine Gun Squadron.

CONFIDENTIAL. VOLUME NO. 38.

2nd MACHINE GUN SQUADRON.

WAR DIARY
or
INTELLIGENCE SUMMARY.

(Erase heading not required.)

Army Form C. 2118.

March, 1919. GERMANY. 2.L.1/10000

Place	Date	Hour	Summary of Events and Information	Remarks and references to Appendices
	March.			
COLOGNE	1st		Exercise and Riding School. 2 O.Rs. Evacuated sick, struck off the strength.	
"	2nd		Usual Routine. Church parade 11.30 hours. 5 O.Rs. Demobilized. 1 Horse evacuated.	
"	3rd		Exercise and Riding School. Ride for Officers of 2nd Army in the afternoon. Lt. S.G. Hibbert and 1 O.R. granted leave to U.K.	
"	4th		Exercise and Riding School. 1 O.R. Demobilized. 1 O.R. granted leave to U-K. 2 horses evacuated, struck off the strength.	
"	5th		Exercise and Riding school.	
"	6th		Exercise and Riding School. M.Os. inspection at 10.30 hours. 1 O.R. Demobilized.	
"	7th		Exercise and Riding School. 1 O.R. granted leave to U.K. 1 O.R. evacuated sick.	
"	8th		Exercise and Riding School at 08.30 hours. 1 O.R. granted leave to U.K. 1 O.R. transferred to G.H.Q. 3rd Echelon. (Clerk)	
"	9th		Sunday Routine. Church Parade. C of E. at 11.30 hours. 70 "Z" horses despatched by road to BELGIUM. Conducting party of 34 men under 2/Lt. J.G.J. Christie. 1 O.R. from hospital.	
"	10th		Exercise and Riding School at 08.30 hours. Major. L.W.D. WATHEN. from temporary duty in U.K. re-assumes command-	
"	11th		Exercise under Orderly Officer and "next for duty", and Riding School at 08.30 hours.	

Army Form C. 2118.

WAR DIARY
or
INTELLIGENCE SUMMARY.

(Erase heading not required.)

Instructions regarding War Diaries and Intelligence Summaries are contained in F. S. Regs., Part II. and the Staff Manual respectively. Title pages will be prepared in manuscript.

Place	Date	Hour	Summary of Events and Information	Remarks and references to Appendices
COLOGNE	March 12th 1919.		Exercise and Riding School at 08.30 hours. Lecture on "XXXX "AUTHORS" in barracks in the evening.	
"	13th		Exercise and Riding School at 08.30 hours. Medical Inspection at 10.30 hours.	
"	14th		Exercise and Riding School. Usual Routine.	
"	15th		Exercise at 08.30 hours. Cavalry Corps Race meeting at SPA. Special train conveyed Officers and O. Rs.	
"	16th		Usual Routine and Riding School.	
"	17th		Usual Routine and Riding School.	
"	18th		The following horses were transferred to the 4th Dragoon Guards Cadre and struck off the XXXX strength. 10 "A" L.D., 2 S.S. L.D., 1 S.S. Riding, and 4 "Z" Packs.	
"	19th		Usual Routine.	
"	20th		Exercise at 08.30 hours. 1st Ride inspected by C.O. at 08.45 hours and dismissed Riding School. Smoking Concert for the men in the Canteen at 20.00 hours.	
"	21st		Exercise and Riding School at 08.30 hours. Inspection of Arms. (Instead of Saturday as usual)	
"	22nd		Exercise and Riding School at 08.30 hours, Usual Routine.	

Army Form C. 2118.

WAR DIARY
or
INTELLIGENCE SUMMARY.
(Erase heading not required.)

Instructions regarding War Diaries and Intelligence Summaries are contained in F. S. Regs., Part II. and the Staff Manual respectively. Title pages will be prepared in manuscript.

Place	Date	Hour	Summary of Events and Information	Remarks and references to Appendices
COLOGNE.	March. 1919.			
	23rd		Sunday ROUTINE. All further demobilization cancelled by War Cabinet owing to impending strikes in U.K.	
"	24th		Exercise and Riding School at 08.30 hours. 48 "Z" horses from 8th Hussars taken on ration strength. (N.B. not as yet posted to unit)	
"	25th		Exercise and Riding School at 08.30 hours. Order suspending demobilization now cancelled Authority obtained to pay the bonus under Army Order XIV to all officers and O.Rs. on the strength, although releasable.	
"	26th		Exercise under Section arrangements resumed from this date. 2nd ride inspected by C.O. at 08.45 hours for dismissal from Riding School. None passed out. Riding School discontinued for the present owing to the shortage of men for exercise.	
"	27th		Exercise at 08.30 hours. Lecture by Major OSBORNE. 20th HUSSARS. In Artillery barracks on "CAVALRY IN PALESTINE OPERATIONS" at 18.30 hours. 15 O.Rs. and 42 "X" Riding horses from 7thMmachine Gun Squadron taken on the strength.	
"	28th		Reveille 06.00 hours breakfast 06.30 hours for demobilized party 91 N.C.Os. and men paraded at 07.00 hours and proceeded for demobilization. Exercise under Section arrangements (in two lots) at 08.30 hours.	

Army Form C. 2118.

WAR DIARY
or
INTELLIGENCE SUMMARY.

(Erase heading not required.)

Instructions regarding War Diaries and Intelligence Summaries are contained in F. S. Regs., Part II. and the Staff Manual respectively. Title pages will be prepared in manuscript.

Place	Date	Hour	Summary of Events and Information	Remarks and references to Appendices
COLOGNE	March 1919. 29th		Usual Routine. Exercise in two lots. — 5 horses per man at stables..	
	30th		Sunday Routine. 38 O.Rs arrived from the 3rd Machine Gun Squadron on previous night and taken on the strength. All retainable men.—4 horses per man at stables. cold and snowing.	
	31st		Usual Routine. Clothing and equipment inspections in afternoon. Snowed.	
			NOTE. Number of Officers and O.Rs demobilized during the month.	
			OFFICERS. 3	
			Other Ranks. 102.	

W.W. Stellers
Major.
Commanding 2nd Machine Gun Squadron.

120 95/1111/2

1914-1918
1ST CAVALRY DIVISION
2ND CAVALRY BRIGADE.

'H' BTY R.H.A.
SEP 1914 - MAR 1919

'L' BTY R.H.A.
5.8.14 - 19.10.14
extracted to Mr Phillips
(JSL) 11 June '53

Returned

2nd Cavalry Brigade.
1st Cavalry Division.

Joined 2nd Cavalry Brigade 28.9.14.

"H" BATTERY R. H. A.

28th SEPTEMBER to 31st OCTOBER 1914

2/1

a96

121/2489

H. Battery R.H.A.
2/1st Cavalry Division.

Vol III. 20.9. – 31.10.14

nothing for M.T.2

H. Battery. R.H.A.   38

Sept 28.
Detrained at Mont-Notre Dame in the early hours of the morning, after about 48 hours in the train. Marched to Longueval, where the battery joined the II Cav: Bde under the command of Brig: Gen: De Lisle C.B.

Sept 29.
Genrl de Lisle took Maj: Budworth & Capt: Skinner to advanced trenches, about 100 yds distant from those of Germans. Shelled in Vendresse with Shrapnel. Battery came under Fire for first time in Longueval, losing 1 man No. 48059. Driver B. Dowson (wounded) and two horses. 1e 1st Casualties on Aisne.
The IX Lancers alongside lost about 40 men.
Shells were "Heavy Howitzer" H.E.
Fine opportunity afforded of contrasting H.E. & Shrap: fire against villages. Evidence overwhelmingly in favour of H.E.

Sept 30. Moved to and billeted at Bazoches.

Oct 1. Ordered to occupy defensive line at Braine. Marched out, but orders cancelled & returned to Bazoches.

Oct 2. Bde acting in relief of Chassemy position.
Moved to & billeted at Lime.

Oct 3. Moved to & billetted at Courcelles. Reconnoitred & prepared position near Vassemy.

Oct 4. Occupied Vassemy position – called by them "Gibraltar" owing to natural and artificial protection etc afforded.
In evening received sudden orders to march – destination not communicated – marched 10.45. P.m.

Oct 5. During night passed by Serches – Hampstemi. Chausée. Reached Hartennes 1.50. a.m {15 mls}. Marched again at 0.p.m. via Corcy. Forêt de Retz. Fleury. Villers – – Cotterêts and Lavigny to Loyolles where we arrived 1.a.m {17 mls}. Congestion of traffic en route.

Oct 6. Marched 1.P.m. via Vaumoise – Crepy, – Betrancourt and Porte de la Croix to Remy (27 mls) arrived 8.30.P.m.

Oct 7. Marched 9.a.m. Called upon to concentrate rapidly at near Montdidier to support the French. Prepared for, but did not come into action.
Marched via Wacquemoulin. Avencourt. Montdidier and subsequently Gratibus & Malpart, bivouacking close to the fine château of Fulescampe. {30 mls}.

Oct 8. Marched 11.30.a.m passing over River Somme & through Amiens to Vilers – Bocage {25 mls}, where we arrived towards nightfall.

Oct 9. Marched 9.a.m. viâ Rubempré, Puchevillers, Marieux, Halloy, to La Souich {20 mls}.

Oct 10. Marched viâ ~~Mais Bailui~~ Etrée, Maizières, Tingues to Villers-Brulin (15 mls). Arrived 1. P.m.

Oct 11. Marched 8.a.m. viâ Rebreuve, Houdain, Bruay, Marles, Choques, Merville, finally dumping down in the Forest of Nieppe {30 mls} about 11. P.m.
The Bde picketting the line Merville - Hazebrouck.

We have now attained our Concentration area. The above marches were made with new men - new Horses - new Harness and new Vehicles and constituted a useful if painful process of "Hardening up" morally and physically! Having come through successfully, the battery can now afford to undergo severer trials.

Oct 12. Striking during night.
The II Cav: Bde ordered to advance by bounds - Strazeele was easily taken, but German guns between Merris & Bailleul then checked progress.
Took 2 guns into action, Lt Imbert-Terry & Grant Suttie being also present.
Position close to Strazeele.

41

In order to draw the fire off the 18th Lancers, the guns were taken rapidly into action.

We soon found ourselves engaged in a duel with 2 to 4 German guns.

Out of 12 men serving guns:

- No. 13242. Saddler Peters was killed
- " 53150 Sergeant Freeman .. severely wounded
- " 39780 Corporal Boatman .. " "
- " 50465. Bombardier Loveday .. " "
- " 53205. Gunner Langstone .. slightly ..

The guns maintained their fire in spite of a loss of ½ of their strength.

Nearly all the casualties were caused by one shell passing between No 2 gun & wagon.

One horse was also lost.

Saddler Peters was buried on the Gun Position.

In spite of their wounds, all the wounded appeared concerned solely with how they were to get back to their own battery when recovered.

Guns withdrawn at dusk.
Rounds fired 104.

Oct 13. In action in two Half Batteries on a little Hill near St Dyzeele supporting attack against Merris - Bailleul - Meteren - Berthen -- Fired 124 Rds. Subsequently occupied position of assembly near Flêtre.

climatic conditions (rain) 42
and topographical conditions (mud)
bad. Billetted at a neighbouring
Farm.

Oct 14. Dampness of rain and fog of
tactical situation vied with each
other. Came into action — notably
at Mont Noir — several times, but
did not fire.
Finally billetted on the borders
of France and Belgium at a
Chateau near Boere. —
"Chateau de la Douve".

Oct 15. Remained in billets.

Oct 16. II Bde under orders to cross
the river Lys. Heavy fog clogged
proceedings. Passed this. Dranoutre
& Neuve Eglise.
Right Section came into action
near Ploegsteert and fired
38 Rds into the fog.
Marched back to the "Chateau
de la Douve" in inky darkness.

Oct 17. No. 35143. Driver Goodarn was
wounded during the night,
while on sentry duty.
Marched before daylight to support
attack of II. Bde: against enemy
holding River Lys.
Came into action in two half
batteries near Ploegsteert.
Fire reported v. accurate.
In afternoon Germans obtained
accurate range of Rt Half
battery, but not of Left.

One "Coal box" fell within 5 yds of a Gun & several others very adjacent, but without causing damage.
Fired 279 Rds.
Late at night retired to billet at Petit Pont.

Oct 18. Moved out to continue attack before daylight.
Came into action in usual formation of two half batteries both entrenched near village of St Yves.
The Germans obtain range of one half battery, this permits fire to be maintained with other. A free use is made of sacks in entrenching & the position prepared as far as possible before the guns come into action.
H. battery was this day enabled to put in some v. effective fire — the reports received from IX. Lancers & IV. DGˢ with whom it was in close touch being highly satisfactory.
Fired 433 Rds.
Billeted near Ploegsteert.

Oct 19. Ordered to occupy gun pits of D. Bty R.H.A. near Messines. Where we fired 180 Rds locating and silencing the fire of some German howitzers.
Billeted at Neuve Eglise.

Oct 20. Reoccupied position at Messines under orders of 1st Cav. Bde.
Desultory fire in morning, but in afternoon Germans commenced to push on.
Observed from Messines Ch. Tower which was rendered somewhat "unhealthy" spot by enemy's shells
The population rapidly cleared out.
Apparently our 1st Bde was heavily shelled in its trenches and had to retire.
Late in the afternoon judging from messages received and other evidence things became somewhat critical.
A line of Horse Artillery guns was formed in rear of Messines to which H joined itself, nothing apparently remaining between it & the Germans.
Rain & night came down together to the accompaniment of a constant roar of guns & rattle of rifles.
The advance was however checked & we "shook out" and awaited orders on the road.
After some vicissitudes we succeeded in finding an occupied farm near Ploegsteert
Fired 532 Rds.

Oct 21. Sounds of war commenced early. Occupied a position on Hill 63, [now closely packed with Fd & Heavy batteries.] Fired 116 Rds. Coal boxes and lesser shells well in evidence. [Turcos] sent forward a single gun to closely support Inf, but in neither case was it required. Our fire reported effective — a pleasant surprise — as Fog much in evidence. Billetted close to Wulverghem.

Oct 22. Marched before dawn to Wytschaete and made arrangements for its close Artillery defence. Fired 81 Rds. Retired at P.M to a farm between Wytschaete & Wulverghem.

Oct 23. Occupied Messines position before dawn, observing from a house on outskirts of village. Desultory fire all day, terminating with a grand display of fireworks after dark. The whole line blazing with Rifles. Did some night firing — which one was enabled to observe reasonably well. Fired 657 Rds.

Oct 24. Firing broke out in the early morning, but soon ceased.
During the day German guns were busy, our Observing Station coming in for slight attention. Fired 44 Rds.

Oct 25. Relieved at 6.30. a.m & retired into neighbouring Farm.

Oct 26. Ordered to move S to support of II Corps. Marched at 11. a.m via Neuve Eglise – Steenwerck and Estaires, reaching the Chateau of Werppe near Lannoy and Gonnehem about 6.40. P.m. {21 mls}. Billetted.

Oct 27. Ordered to move out to support of III Div: near Neuve Chapelle. State of affairs apparently somewhat critical. Battery halted at Neuve Chapelle.
Bde: conference at Richebourg St Vaast. No demand apparently for guns, but Rifles badly wanted, and made preparations to send up Riflemen in case of emergency. They were not however required. Battery remained in Readiness all night.

Oct 28. Stood fast all day, anticipating orders.

Oct 29. A fierce attack directed on the left of the r. div., but just as the 60th Rifleman were preparing to go up, attack died away, thanks to action of the II Bde., who covered themselves with glory. Marched N again and returned to billets near Neuve Eglise.

Oct 30. About 11. a.m. were suddenly ordered off to Wytschaete — again made preparations for its defence, but soon after dark we were ordered back to Kummel.

Oct 31. Sent for Earby to II Bde HQ. Severe German attack impending.
Moved to Wytschaete & placed Left Half Battery in action N of that place — At the request of the O.C III Cav. Bde these guns were withdrawn, when the Germans attained within 600 yds of that place. They then occupied a position Pt 75.
The Rt Half Bty occupied a position E of Wytschaete, where they were somewhat heavily shelled, they were subsequently

transferred to Pt. 75.
The fire was directed against Germans massing N & N.E of Messines and the efficacy of their fire was subsequently mentioned in general orders.
Except to change position the battery remained in action without ceasing fire throughout the day and night, supporting later in the day the attack of the London Scottish on Messines.
At midnight 31 Oct/1st Nov it was still in action and firing, while a stream of wounded & unwounded men came up from the direction of Messines. The latter were collected & placed in position about the windmill Pt 75.
Capt. the Honble H.R. Scarlett was attached to the battery from Oct 24th.

L. E. Beadon
Lt. Col. RHA
O.C. II RHA

2nd Cavalry Brigade.

1st Cavalry Division.

"H" BATTERY R.H.A.

NOVEMBER 1914.

H. Battery, R.H.A.
                Diary for November.
Nov 1st. Found the battery still in
action at P.76 and firing slowly.
In the early hours of the morning
news arrived that the Germans
had broken through between
Messines and Wytschaete.
Verification that something of
the sort had occurred was not
wanting.
All unwounded men who fell
back were collected and placed
under the command of an
officer in the neighbourhood of
the windmill.
The rate of fire was increased.
At dawn orders were received
    from the O.C II Cav: Bde to
retire towards Lindenhoek
and come into action in the
    vicinity of the other H.A Batteries.
NW I.7.D.3. The retirement covered
    by one Gun, was carried
    out under desultory rifle
fire.
From the position now occupied
    the advancing Germans presented
    a favourable target.
    About 10.30, the German
advance had evidently come
to a standstill and permission
    was asked and obtained
from the O.C II Cav: Bde to
    re-occupy P.76 from which

more effective fire could be brought to bear on Messines. The advance was carried out without casualties and the Battery continued in action on Pt 75 until ordered by the O.C. II Cav: Bde to fall back on Wulverghem about 3 p.m. March to Neuve Position. The Battery had not ceased firing for further over 33 hours — although the rate of fire was at times very slow).

Total Rds. Fired 1482.

The destructive effect of the fire of the R.H.A. I Cav: Div.d was subsequently mentioned in Corps. orders.

Nov 2. Ready to move 5.a.m. Occupied Position on mont Kemmel to deal with a possible German advance. Did not fire. It being anticipated that a night attack would be made against the II Cav: Bde (holding the roughly Nulverghem - Pt 75) from direction of Messines, took forward, under cover of darkness 3 guns of H. Battery to Pt 75, with the object of repelling any such attack by direct fire. Pt 75 was held by III Faust and the advanced outpost line. The night passed quietly

and the Guns were withdrawn
at dawn to Mont Kemmel.
Nov 3. Fired from Mont Kemmel
in support of the French
against a somewhat feeble
German attack.
Subsequently moved forward
to Lindenhoek in support
French counterattack against
Messines.
Relieved by D. Battery at 7.30 p.m
and went back to billets at
Dranoutre. billets difficult
to procure.

Nov 4. Remained in billets
Nov 5. News came to hand today
that in gazette dated Oct 30th
every officer in "H" was promoted.
Moved to Lindenhoek at 4 p.m
and took over from D. Battery
about 5 p.m; a noisy
bombardment by the Germans
Opened fire in support of
the French about 5.15 p.m.
only fired 25 Rds.

Nov 6. Passed day + night in
action firing at intervals
in support of French attack,
which was not pressed
home. Fired 222 Rds.
Varied + ineffective bombardment
by German artillery.

Nov 7. Passed day in action in support of French attack which was not apparently pressed. In evening relieved by J. Battery & went into billets close to Bailleul.

Nov 8 - Remained in Billets
Nov 9 - Reconnoitred as C.R.H.A. Triangle
I. Div. Ploegsteert - Messines. Wolverghem.

Nov 10. Moved forward to Neuve Eglise - billetted in neighbourhood

Nov 11. In readiness - Returned to Bailleul in evening, and received orders to march for Ypres about 9.30 p.m.

Nov 12. Marching all night - cold & rain. deep mud and roads congested with traffic.
Passed round Ypres and after a long halt, dumped ourselves down in a field in the wind & rain.
Set to work to rig up shelters with rather scanty material, most things being already in possession of French troops. Towards night fortunate enough to find reasonable shelter in small farm buildings near Brielen.

Nov 13. Marched 5.20 a.m. and returned to our old dumping

ground N of Ypres. Shells fell somewhat promiscuously during day, but with our usual luck we only had a couple of horses wounded, while the R.G.A. in next field had several men hit.

~~[struck through lines]~~

As our Cav: Regts were ordered this night into the trenches & the guns were not required, volunteered to assist and furnished 1 officer, and some 12 men to each Regt:
Remainder of Battery retired to Billets.

Nov 14. Guns not required - did our best to assist cavalry Regts in other ways.

Nov 15. Abominable weather. Snow - sleet. Guns still not required - as in most other places it is rifles rather than guns which are wanted.

Nov 16. Stood fast all day. Intermittent shelling.

Nov 17. In afternoon about 3.45 started to fight our way back to Bailleul through

mud and traffic.
Marched via Watnertinghe.
Renninghelst. Westoutre.
Billetted just short of Bailleul

Nov. 18 } In billets near Bailleul
" 19 }
Nov 20 }
" 21. Marched to Neuve Eglise
to assist 27 Bde R.F.A.
Country frozen and progression
difficult.
Came into action S of Neuve
Eglise & remained in action
throughout night.

Nov 22. Remained in action
all day & night.
Weather v. cold.

Nov 23. Relieved at 8.30. a.m.
& billetted at farm close
to Romarin road.

Nov 24. Marched back via
Bailleul to farm between
Meteren & Berthen and
S of Pt 68.

Nov 25. Billet defective in size

Nov 26. Moved into new billet
nearer to Meteren
Officers granted 72 hrs leave
to England, Sent off Captain.

Nov 27 }
" 28 } Battery settling down
" 29 } into Winter Quarters.
" 30 } Building Stables. Cookhouses.
Improving communications etc.

2nd Cavalry Brigade.

1st Cavalry Division.
========

"H" BATTERY R. H. A.

DECEMBER 1 9 1 4.

H. Battery, R.H.A.
Diary for December.

During this month H. Battery remained in billets near Nd. Meteren.
Cookhouses - Shelters - Ovens etc were built for the men, who slept in barns.
Stables were built for the horses.
On Dec 2nd the Battery was inspected and addressed by
F.M. The Commander-in-Chief Sir John French.
On Dec 3rd the Battery took part in the review on the occasion of H.M. King George V Visit to his Army in the field.
Place between Meteren and Flêtre.
On Dec 19. the Battery was inspected by the G.O.C Cavalry Corps. General E.H Allenby.

E.B. Edmunds
Lt Col R.H.A
O.C. H.Bty.

1st Cavalry Division

121/4194

"H" Battery RHA.

Vol V. January 1915

"H" Battery R.H.A.

Diary Jan. 1915

The battery remained in billets during the month, the time being employed in the usual routine of training and in perfecting the arrangements for the comfort of men and horses in billets.

The following changes took place among the officers of the battery.

Jan 5th Lieut Colonel C.E.D. Budworth M.V.O. transferred to England on promotion

Jan 9th Captain H.B. Imbert Terry transferred to 4th Divisional Artillery on promotion.

Jan 30th Captain H.F. Grant Suttie transferred to 2nd Divisional Artillery on promotion.

Jan 4th Lieut J.D. Mackenzie joined from 22nd Brigade R.F.A.

Jan 8th Lieut K.D. Wells Cole joined from 127th Battery R.F.A.

E.J. Skinner
Major R.H.A.
Commanding "H" Battery R.H.A.

1st Cavalry Division

12/4559

"H" Battery R.H.A.

Vol VI 1 – 28.2.15

Diary February 1915
"H" Battery R.H.A.

During the month of February the battery remained in billets. Usual routine work was carried out.

Feb. 7th Lieut. A. R. Schreiber joined the battery.

Feb. 23rd Two officers, Capt Hermon Hodge and Lieut Wells Cole with sixteen men proceeded to the trenches with the 2nd Cavalry Brigade to fire trench mortars.

E. J. Skinner
Major R.H.A.
Commanding "H" Battery R.H.A.

121/5099

Ac
196

1st Cavalry Division
2nd " Bde
"H" Batty: R.H.A.
13 — 28.4.15
Vol VII 1 — 30 Ap 65

Diary
"H" Battery R.H.A.

March 1915

March 1st – 6th A party consisting of two officers, Capt. HERMON HODGE, Lieut WELLS COLE and 19 N.C.Os & men were in the trenches S.E of YPRES with the regiments of the 2nd Cavalry Brigade. This party was employed with trench mortars. There were no casualties.

During the month, the battery remained in billets. Usual routine work was carried on.

April 1915

April 1st – 22nd The battery was in its winter billets, doing the usual routine of training.

April 23rd Marched with the 2nd Cavalry Brigade to vicinity of ELVERDINGHE about 4 miles N.W. of YPRES in order to be ready to support the French who had been attacked and forced to retire on the line STEENSTRAATE —

— BOESINGHE. Bivouaced there for the night.

April 24th Went into action one mile S.W of WOESTEN in cooperation with the French artillery. Fired 26 rounds.

April 25th In action in same place. Fired 12 rounds.

April 26th In action in same place. In cooperation with French artillery shelled villages of LIZERNE and HET SAS preparatory to assault by French infantry. Fired 573 rounds.

April 27th Still in action. Fired 410 rounds. On this day had the following casualties. —
No 29508 Gr H. DIVERS, No 12194 Gr J. WEBB (slightly) and No 65315 Dr. A. WILFORD (severely) wounded. Three horses, two of them chargers of Captain HERMON HODGE and Lieut SHREIBER were killed, four horses wounded.

April 28th Came out of action at 4-30 A.M. Marched to rest billet at RIETVELD near WORMHOUDT.

April 29th-30th Remained in billets.

E.J. Skinner
Major R.H.A.
Commanding "H" Battery R.H.A.

92/a56

121/5508

1st Cavalry Division.

"H" Batty: R.H.A.
W VIII 1 — 31.5.15.

Army Form C. 2118.

WAR DIARY
or
INTELLIGENCE SUMMARY.
(Erase heading not required.)

"H" Battery R.H.A.
2nd Cavalry Brigade.

Instructions regarding War Diaries and Intelligence Summaries are contained in F.S. Regs., Part II. and the Staff Manual respectively. Title pages will be prepared in manuscript.

Hour, Date, Place	Summary of Events and Information	Remarks and references to Appendices
May 1st - 2nd	Battery was in billets at RIETVELD N of CASSEL	
May 3rd	Marched to new billets between STAPLE and WALLON CAPPEL	
May 3rd - 6th	Remained in billets.	
May 7th	Marched to old wooden billets near METEREN.	
May 8th	In billets.	
May 9th	Received orders 1-30 A.M. at 3-30 A.M. Bivouacked in a field S.W of village.	
May 10th-11th	Stood ready to move at shortest notice in same bivouac.	
May 12th	Left section moved into action to relieve 69th Battery R.F.A. east of canal N.E. of YPRES.	
May 13th	Left section fired 144 rounds. Driver MADDAMS of Ammunition Section wounded. One horse killed, three horses wounded. Right and centre sections came into action 8.30 p.m on the right of the left section.	
May 14th	Fired 254 rounds in support of the Cavalry who were in the trenches near POTIJZE E of YPRES. Enemy used asphyxiating gas.	

WAR DIARY
or
INTELLIGENCE SUMMARY.
(Erase heading not required.)

H. Battery R.H.A.

May 1915

Army Form C. 2118.

Hour, Date, Place	Summary of Events and Information	Remarks and references to Appendices
May 15th	Still in action. Received congratulatory telegram from G.O.C. 1st Cavalry Division on effective support rendered to Cavalry.	
May 16th	Quiet day. Did not fire.	
May 17th	Left section was heavily shelled about 4 a.m. by 6 in. guns of the enemy. Quiet day. Fired a few rounds registering.	
May 18th	Quiet day. No firing.	
May 19th	Under G.O.C. 5th Cavalry Brigade. Fired a few rounds registering.	
May 20th – 23rd	Quiet day. No 34322 Bdr. W.L. SAMS wounded by shrapnel bullet when mending telephone wires. Still in action. Fairly quiet days. Fired some rounds daily in registering targets. Supporting infantry, Cavalry having been relieved.	
May 24th	Enemy began an attack about 3 a.m. under cover of gas. Our infantry forced to retire a little. Fired 1145 rounds. Hot day's work. Telephone communication with trenches repeatedly cut by shell fire. Maintained all day, though wires were repeatedly cut by shell fire.	
May 25th	Fired 103 in continuation of action of previous day. Battery was shelled by a heavy howitzer about 7 a.m. No 19173 Gunner C.V. BIRD (Captain's servant) wounded. Two horses killed.	

3

May 1915

H. Battery R.H.A.
3rd Cavalry Brigade

Army Form C. 2118.

WAR DIARY
or
INTELLIGENCE SUMMARY.
(Erase heading not required.)

Instructions regarding War Diaries and Intelligence Summaries are contained in F.S. Regs., Part II. and the Staff Manual respectively. Title pages will be prepared in manuscript.

Hour, Date, Place	Summary of Events and Information	Remarks and references to Appendices
May 26th 27th	Quiet days except for the usual shelling by the enemy. Did not fire.	
May 28th	Quiet day. Left and centre sections went out of action being relieved by two Batteries 1st Northumbrian Bde R.F.A.	
May 29th	Quiet morning. Right section to be relieved at 9 p.m. At 7 p.m. heavy gun fire on the left by the French. Enemy replied vigorously. Relief postponed. 10 p.m. quiet again. Teams came up, shelling resumed. Section got out of action without any casualties. Trekked at 11-30 p.m. for new billets N of CASSEL.	
May 30th	Arrived in new billets at 4-30 a.m.	
May 31st	In billets.	

E.J. Munro Major R.H.A.
Commanding H. Battery R.H.A.

June 1st 1915.

13/6111

a2
096

1st Cavalry Division

"H" Batty RHA
Vol IX
1-30-6-15

WAR DIARY
or
INTELLIGENCE SUMMARY.

"H" Battery R.H.A. Army Form C. 2118.
2nd Cavalry Brigade

Hour, Date, Place	Summary of Events and Information	Remarks and references to Appendices
June 1915	During the whole of this month the battery was in billets at RIETVELD about 5 miles N of CASSEL. Usual routine work was carried out, having recruits &c. The battery was inspected with the 3rd Cavalry Brigade by Field Marshal Sir JOHN FRENCH and was complimented by him.	

E J Skinner
Major R.H.A.
Commanding "H" Battery R.H.A.

1st Cavalry Division

12/6272

"H" Battery R.H.A.

Vol X

July no name
1-31 — Aug 1-15?
nn

Army Form C. 2118.

"H" Battery R.H.A

WAR DIARY
or
INTELLIGENCE SUMMARY.   July 1915

(Erase heading not required.)

Instructions regarding War Diaries and Intelligence Summaries are contained in F. S. Regs., Part II. and the Staff Manual respectively. Title pages will be prepared in manuscript.

Hour, Date, Place	Summary of Events and Information	Remarks and References to Appendices
July 1915.	The battery was in billets at ZEGGERS CAPPEL N of CASSEL during the whole of this month. Usual routine work was carried on. On July 30th one officer (Lieut O.R. SCHREIBER) and 40 men were employed with detachments from the regiments of the 3rd Cavalry Brigade in digging trenches near YPRES	

E.J. Thomson Major R.H.A.
Commanding "H" Battery R.H.A.

2/1st Cavalry Division

1st/6993

"H" Battery: R.H.A.

Vol IX

August & Sept. 15

WAR DIARY
or
INTELLIGENCE SUMMARY.
(Erase heading not required.)

H. Battery R.H.A.
2nd Cavalry Brigade.

Army Form C. 2118.

Instructions regarding War Diaries and Intelligence Summaries are contained in F. S. Regs., Part II. and the Staff Manual respectively. Title pages will be prepared in manuscript.

Hour, Date, Place	Summary of Events and Information	Remarks and References to Appendices
August 1915	The Battery was in billets at ZEGGERS CAPPEL. During the month a party mounted at a strength of 50 was employed digging trenches near VLAMERTINGHE.	
Aug 11th	No. 38264 Gr. B. HUTCHINS & No. 847,35 Gr. H. BUCKLEY & No. 64197 Gr. S. JARROLD rewarded by adopted while entrenching twenty.	
Aug 8th	No. 19668 Sgt. H. WEEKES received a commission in R.F.A. and left the Battery 19th Regt.	
Aug 21st	No. 29815 Bdr. A. SHAFE awarded medal of St George (4th class) by H.I.M. the Emperor of Russia for gallantry and distinguished conduct in the field.	
Aug 30th	Battery under orders to march.	
Aug 31st	Marched to WARDRECQUES and bivouaced for the night.	

E. J. Munro
Major R.H.A.
Commanding H. Battery R.H.A.

Sept I

September

WAR DIARY
or
INTELLIGENCE SUMMARY.

"H" Battery R.H.A. 2nd Cavalry Brigade.

Army Form C. 2118.

(Erase heading not required.)

Instructions regarding War Diaries and Intelligence Summaries are contained in F. S. Regs., Part II. and the Staff Manual respectively. Title pages will be prepared in manuscript.

Hour, Date, Place	Summary of Events and Information	Remarks and References to Appendices
Sept 1st	Marched to MARLES LES MINES and bivouaced. Very wet	
Sept 2nd		
Sept 3rd At MARLES LES MINES	Battery marched to NOEUX LES MINES. Advanced party to GRENAY where the battery was to come into action to prepare position	
Sept 4th	Advance party working on position. Guns came into action in evening	
Sept 5th	Working at position. Observation station in a house at MAROC near trenches facing LOOS	
Sept 6th	Fired 54 rounds registering points in the village of LOOS. Work on gun pits continued	
Sept 7th	Fired 24 rounds, objective LOOS.	
Sept 8th	Fired 13 rounds registering.	
Sept 9th	Did not fire	
Sept 10th	Fired 13 rounds ↄn LOOS	
Sept 11th	Fired 12 rounds at a battery near windmill in LOOS. At 6.p.m were shelled from direction of windmill in LOOS. presumably by battery engaged in the morning.	
Sept 12th	Some shrapnel fired on battery	
Sept 13th	Vicinity of battery heavily shelled by 6 in gun. Enemy's shell found to have still now, presumably common fuzing.	
Sept 14th	Fired 44 rounds at Enemy's battery. Tried high explosive for first time	

Army Form C. 2118.

September

WAR DIARY
or
INTELLIGENCE SUMMARY.

(Erase heading not required.)

H Battery R.H.A.
2nd Cavalry Brigade

Instructions regarding War Diaries and Intelligence Summaries are contained in F. S. Regs., Part II. and the Staff Manual respectively. Title pages will be prepared in manuscript.

Hour, Date, Place	Summary of Events and Information	Remarks and References to Appendices
Continued		
Sept. 16th	Fired 29 rounds at various points in LOOS. Received orders to be prepared to go out of action.	
Sept. 16th	On action but did not fire. Turned out of action 10.30 p.m. to NOEUX LES MINES. Arrived 12.30 A.M. Sept 17. During the time the battery was in action work on gunpits etc never stopped and on the 16th the battery was dressing in, great quantities of material were used for props, over garden etc.	
Sept 17th	Marched from NOEUX LES MINES to MORBECQUE	
Sept 18th	Marched to ZEGGERS CAPPEL	
Sept 19 - 22	In billets at ZEGGERS CAPPEL	
Sept 23rd	Marched at 10.30 p.m. around WISERNES 4 a.m. Sept 24th	
Sept 24th	Marched 9.30 p.m. around CUHEM 3.30 a.m. Sept. 25th	
Sept 25th	Marched at 2 p.m. around VAUDRICOURT 12.30 AM Sept. 26th very wet and tedious march	
Sept. 26th	Changed our bivouac to FOUQUIERES LES BETHUNE.	
Sept 27-29th	At FOUQUIERES standing ready to move at 2 hours notice.	
Sept 29th		
Sept 30th	Marched to LAPUGNOY to find billets for Regiment.	
	At LAPUGNOY	
	Sept 7th No 12975 Bt. T GIBBS died in hospital at CALAIS of dysentery, was battery storeman and his death a great loss to the battery.	

E. J. Sherwin Major R.H.A
O.C H Bty R.H.A

121/7599

2/1 1. Cavalry Division

"N" Batty R.H.A.
Oct 1915

Vol XII

H. Battery R.H.A.

WAR DIARY
or
INTELLIGENCE SUMMARY.

October 1915

Army Form C. 2118.

(Erase heading not required.)

Hour, Date, Place	Summary of Events and Information	Remarks and References to Appendices
Oct. 1-2	In billets at LAPUGNOY	
Oct. 3rd	Marched to LIGNY LEZ AIRE	
Oct. 4th – 19th	In billets at LIGNY LEZ AIRE	
Oct. 20th	Marched to REMILLY WIRQUIN	
Oct. 20 – 31st	In billets at REMILLY WIRQUIN	

E.J. Skinner
Major R.H.A.
Commanding H. Battery R.H.A.

"H" Battery R.H.A.
Nov — Dec 1915.
Vol. XIII 11+12

CR. 778/8216

WAR DIARY
or
INTELLIGENCE SUMMARY

H Battery R.H.A.

for November 1915

Army Form C. 2118.

(Erase heading not required.)

Hour, Date, Place	Summary of Events and Information	Remarks and References to Appendices
1st to 15th	In billets at REMILLY WIRQUIN. Usual routine work being carried out.	
16th	Marched to BEUSSENT to new billets. Very cold march, snow on ground.	
28th	Received notes to march next morning to go into action under G.O.C. Artillery IVth Corps.	
29th	Marched to DILETTE. Long, trying march, roads very slippery - heavy rain following most.	
30th	Marched to LABUISSIERE, and billetted there.	
	The officers of the battery :- Major E.J. SKINNER R.H.A. Lieut. C.N. WELLS COLE R.H.A. (temporary Captain) Lieut. O.R. SCHREIBER R.H.A. Lieut. P. WRIGHT R.F.A. Lieut. Hon. L.E. BINGHAM. R.F.A. attached 2/Lieut. J.N.H. WILSON R.F.A. 2/Lieut. K.F.G. STRONACH. R.F.A.	

E.J. Skinner
Major R.H.A.
Commanding H Battery

Army Form C. 2118.

WAR DIARY
or
INTELLIGENCE SUMMARY.

H. Battery R.H.A.

For December 1915

(Erase heading not required.)

Hour, Date, Place	Summary of Events and Information	Remarks and References to Appendices
Dec 1st	At LABUISSIERE. Preparations being made to go into action the following morning.	
2nd	Went into action 5.30 p.m N of LENS-BETHUNE ROAD near QUALITY STREET. Wagon line in the streets of NOEUX-LES-MINES. Dressing station in old German gun line trench called POSEN STREET.	
3rd	In action. QUALITY STREET very heavily shelled.	
4.5	In action at the same place until 4.30 p.m. when the battery moved to a fresh position at VERMELLES. Dressing station and wagon lines same as before.	Dec 15th No 61464 a/sjt. C. J. WHITE severely wounded, died of his wounds same evening. Buried at NOEUX-LES-MINES.
5th – 31st	In action at VERMELLES	
31st	Number of rounds fired during December 3308	
	The officers of the battery:—	
	Major E. J. SKINNER R.H.A.	
	Capt N. W. NELLS-COLE R.H.A. (temporary Captain)	
	Lieut O. R. SCHREIBER R.H.A	
	Lieut P. WRIGHT R.F.A	
	2nd Lt Hn L.E. RINGHAM R.F.A attached	
	Vet Lieut J.M.J WILSON R.F.A	
		E.J. Skinner Major R.H.A
		Commanding H. Battery R.H.A

"H" Bty R.H.A.
Jan 1916 -
Vol. 13

WAR DIARY
or
INTELLIGENCE SUMMARY.

(Erase heading not required.)

H. Battery R.H.A. Army Form C. 2118.

January 1916

Hour, Date, Place	Summary of Events and Information	Remarks and references to Appendices
January 1-5	In action at the same position in VERMELLES as during December 1915.	
January 6th	Dismounted Cavalry Division came into the trenches. Battery joined the 4th Dismounted Division. 2nd Brigade in action in a new position in VERMELLES.	
January 7th	The other 2 batteries went into new position. Observation post in a support trench called DEVON LANE. Wagon line moved to VERQUIGNEUL	
Jan 7th - 31st	Battery in action in this position. 3228 Rounds fired during the month.	
	Major E.J. SKINNER Lieut. O.R. SCHREIBER } Mentioned in Despatches London Gazette 1.1.16	Officers with the Battery
	No 39687 B.Q.M.S W.R. BELL No 34322 B.S.M W.L. SAMS	Major E.J. SKINNER R.H.A Captain N.W. WELLS COLE R.H.A Lieut. O.R. SCHREIBER R.H.A Lieut. P. WRIGHT " Hon. L.E. BINGHAM } R.F.A. Lieut. K.F.G. STRONACH } attached " J.N.H. WILSON
	Lieut O.R. SCHREIBER awarded Military Cross 14.1.16.	

E.J. Skinner Major R.H.A.
Commanding H Battery R.H.A.

WAR DIARY • H Battery R.H.A Army Form C. 2118.
or
INTELLIGENCE SUMMARY.

(Erase heading not required.)

Instructions regarding War Diaries and Intelligence Summaries are contained in F. S. Regs., Part II. and the Staff Manual respectively. Title pages will be prepared in manuscript.

Hour, Date, Place	Summary of Events and Information	Remarks and References to Appendices
Feb. 1st to 21st	The battery in action at VERMELLES in the same position as in the previous month.	
Feb. 21st	At 6 p.m. The Right Section went out of action being relieved by a section of 9th Battery R.H.A.	
Feb. 22nd	Remaining two sections relieved by 9th Battery R.H.A. Marched to ANNEZIN near BETHUNE and billeted there for the night. Snow fell all day.	
Feb. 23rd	Battery marched to THEROUANNE. Very cold and hard march in driving snow.	
Feb. 24th	Marched to billets at BEUSSENT. Roads very slippery after snow and of frost.	
Feb. 25th – 29th	In billets at BEUSSENT.	Total rounds fired during February = 1418 Shrapnel. Battery thanked by G.O.C. for "very prompt and efficient support".

E J Skinner
Major R.H.A
Commanding H Battery R.H.A

March 1916

H Battery R.H.A.

WAR DIARY or INTELLIGENCE SUMMARY

Army Form C. 2118.

(Erase heading not required.)

Hour, Date, Place	Summary of Events and Information	Remarks and References to Appendices
March		
BEUSSENT	During the month the battery was in billets at BEUSSENT. The battery carried out training.	
March 5th	Major SKINNER and Lieut WRIGHT with 36 N.C.O's and men were attached to 11th Corps. The party left at 3.15 pm for DESVRES.	
March 6th	Proceeded by train to BETHUNE and billeted there for the night.	
March 7th	Joined C Battery 157 Brigade 35th Division in action about ½ mile S.E. of RICHEBOURG St VAAST. Drawing rations at the "SAVOY" in the RUE DU BOIS.	During its time the detachment was in action though only 2400 yards from the German trenches, there was practically no shelling on the part of the enemy
March 7-15	The party was employed on instructing and assisting the battery to which it was attached. On evening of March 18th the detachment took two 18 pr guns to a forward position and on the following morning March 14th proceeded to cut the German wire. Range 1600 yards. 200 rounds fired, result armed good.	
March 16th	Detachment returned to billets via BETHUNE and DESVRES.	
March 18th	A party consisting of two N.C.O's proceeded to the 39th Division to assist the batteries of that Division	

E J Skinner Major RHA
Major Battery RHA
Commanding H Battery RHA

WAR DIARY or INTELLIGENCE SUMMARY.

H Battery RHA. Army Form C. 2118.

April 1916

(Erase heading not required.)

Hour, Date, Place	Summary of Events and Information	Remarks and references to Appendices
BEUSSENT	The battery was in billets during the whole of the month. Usual routine work was carried out. On Monday April 17th the battery with the 1st Can. Division were inspected by the G.O.C. 1st Army	

E J Skinner Major RHA
Commanding H Battery RHA

WAR DIARY
or
INTELLIGENCE-SUMMARY.
(Erase heading not required.)

"H" Battery R.H.A.   Army Form C. 2118.
May 1916.

Hour, Date, Place	Summary of Events and Information	Remarks and References to Appendices
May 1916	The battery was during the whole of the month in its rest billets at BEUSSENT. Usual training was carried out.	Lieut. P. WRIGHT left the Battery to command a Battery in the 39th Division. He was succeeded by Lieut. C.C. RYAN. Lieut. Hon. L.G. BINGHAM, Adjutant R.H.A. 1st Cav Divn 17.5.16. Succeeded by Lieut. J.C. COLTRIM.

E.J. Skinner
Major R.H.A.
Commanding H. Battery R.H.A.

WAR DIARY "H" Battery R.H.A. June 1916.

Vol 18

Date	Entry
June 1st	Marched to EQUIHEN a seaside camp.
June 2 – 18th	Drill and training on sands at EQUIHEN.
June 19th	Returned to Billets at BEUSSENT.
June 24th	Marched 8-45 p.m.
June 25th	Arrived RAYE EN AUTHIE at 4-50 A.M. Marched at 9-15 p.m.
June 26th	Arrived MEZEROLLES 4 a.m. Marched at 8-30 p.m.
June 27th	Arrived BERTEAUCOURT LES DAMES at 2-15 A.M. Marched at 8-30 p.m.
June 28th	Arrived at QUERRIEU 3-30 A.M.
June 29–30	In bivouac at QUERRIEU.

Nothing unusual to report during early part of month. During the night marches weather conditions bad.

E.J. Thinner
Major R.H.A.
Commanding "H" Battery R.H.A.

Vol 19

WAR DIARY

of

"H" BATTERY. R.H.A.

for the Month of

JULY. 1916.

VOLUME. XXIV.

CONFIDENTIAL:

Army Form C. 2118.

WAR DIARY
or
INTELLIGENCE SUMMARY

H. Battery R.H.A.

(Erase heading not required.)

Hour, Date, Place	Summary of Events and Information	Remarks and References to Appendices
July 1st 5.15 A.M.	Marched from QUERRIEU to BRESLE returning to QUERRIEU in same evening.	At QUERRIEU and BUIRE the battery was in bivouac for the greater part of the time ready to move at short notice.
July 2nd ". " "	In bivouac at QUERRIEU	
July 5th 7.45 AM	Marched to billets at L'ARBRE-A-MOUCHES	
July 11th 7.45 pm	Marched to QUERRIEU	
July 13th 6.0 pm	Marched to BUIRE.	
July 24th 9.0 AM	Marched to QUERRIEU.	

E.J. Skinner Major R.H.A.
Commanding H. Battery R.H.A.

Vol 20

WAR DIARY
of
"H" BATTERY. R.H.A.
for the Month of
AUGUST. 1916.
=================

VOLUME XXV.
==========

CONFIDENTIAL.
=============

WAR DIARY Volume XXV   Army Form C. 2118.
or
INTELLIGENCE SUMMARY.
(Erase heading not required.)

Hour, Date, Place	Summary of Events and Information	Remarks and References to Appendices
QUERRIEU.		
Aug 1st to Aug 8th	With 1st Cav. Div. awaiting orders -	
4.30 am Aug 9th	Marched to PONT REMY. (30 miles) arriving 1.30 pm	Very 1st day very hot march.
5.15 am Aug 10th	Marched to GOUSSEAUVILLE (20 miles) arriving 11.15 am	Very hot day.
Aug 11th to Aug 31st	Resting in billets -	Fine dry weather - Heavy rain Aug. 29th & 30th.
GOUSSEAUVILLE		
Aug 12th	Major E. J. SKINNER. D.S.O. left the Battery to take up appointment Bde Major R.A. 49th Div.	
Aug 18th	Major T. H. CARLISLE arrived to take over command on posting from 14th Div -	
Aug 19th	LIEUT J. H. COLHOUN RFA. (attached RHA) posted to R.J.H.A.	

J M Maclean Major RHA

Confidential

War Diary
of
"H" Battery R.H.A 1st Cavalry Division
September 1916.

Volume No. XXVI

Army Form C. 2118.

WAR DIARY
or
INTELLIGENCE SUMMARY.
(Erase heading not required.)

Hour, Date, Place	Summary of Events and Information	Remarks and References to Appendices
GOUSSEAUVILLE. Sept 1st to 5th	Resting in bivouac.	
Sept 6th 10.30 am	Marched to ALLERY arriving 3.15 pm. bivouac for night.	
ALLERY. 10 am Sept 7th	— LANEUVILLE arriving 1 pm.	
LANEUVILLE. Sept 8th to 14th	Remained in bivouac at LANEUVILLE.	
7 am Sept 14th		
CARNOY. Sept 15th & Sept 15th	Marched to bivouac in CARNOY VALLEY, arriving 4 pm. Remained in bivouac, harnessed up standing ready to move.	
3 pm Sept 17th	Marched back to LA NEUVILLE arriving 7.30 pm.	
LANEUVILLE Sept 18th to 22nd	Remained in bivouac.	
7.30 am Sept 23rd	Marched to L'ETOILE arriving 3 pm.	
8.30 am Sept 24th	Marched to DUBRUMETZ arriving 4.30 pm.	
8 am Sept 25th	Marched to FRESNOY arriving 10.30 am.	
FRESNOY. Sept 26th to Sept 30th	Resting in billets & bivouac —	
Sept 3rd	Lieut. C.C. Ryan RHA (attached RHA) left Battery on [?] to 116 Horse Battery.	
Sept 5th	Lieut. K.E.G. STRONACH RHA joined Battery on [?] from 1st Bde RHA-Am in col.	

J. Manley Major RHA
[signature] H. Beth. RHA

(0 29 6) W 3332—1107 100,000 10/13 H W V Forms/C. 2118/10.

Vol 22

CONFIDENTIAL.

WAR DIARY.

of

"H" BATTERY. R.H.A.

for the month of

OCTOBER. 1918.

VOLUME. XXVII.

WAR DIARY or INTELLIGENCE SUMMARY

Army Form C. 2118.

Place	Date	Hour	Summary of Events and Information	Remarks and references to Appendices
FRESNOY	Oct 1st - 18th	&c	Resting & training in billets at FRESNOY.	
BOFFLES	19th - 20th	8.15am 9.30am	Marched to BOFFLES arriving 2 pm. Marched to ST. LEGER les DOMART arriving 2.45 pm.	
ST. LEGER les DOMART	22nd	7.30am	Marched to SOMME area going into action at 4pm near MESNIL with wagon line near MARTINSART. Teams left behind in DOMART area to come up later.	
MESNIL	24th	-	Attached to 18th Divn. Artillery - registered one on zone N of THIEPVAL.	
"	"		In action. Registration carried out.	
"	31st		Occupying an old position with fair gun pits. Very quiet. One gas shell & occasional heavy shell fell near Battery, but no casualties. One section 91 Battery in some pits making up an 8 gun battery. Remainder of Bde in action close by.	

J Hornie Major RFA
O.C. 91st Batt

Confidential

War Diary
of
"H" Battery Royal Horse Artillery
for
November. 1916.

Volume XXVIII

Vol 23

WAR DIARY
or
INTELLIGENCE SUMMARY
(Erase heading not required.)

Army Form C. 2118.

Place	Date	Hour	Summary of Events and Information	Remarks and references to Appendices
MESNIL	Nov. 1st to 12th		In action against German posts in outskirts the ANCRE. attached to 18th Div Artillery. Repairing damages & preparing for the attack by Y Army on 13th Nov.	
	13/14th		Took part in damages for the attack on PIERRE DIVON & BEAUCOURT.	
	18th/19th		Again took part in a further attack commenced 6am 18th against GRANDCOURT.	
	21st	6am	In action working with 95th Bde Art. & I Battery to RUBEMPRÉ arriving 1pm. During our stay in action at MESNIL the Battery fired 8897 rounds and received the thanks of the G.O.C. 32nd & 19th Div's for their help & good work.	A
RUBEMPRÉ	22nd	9am	Marched to BERTAUCOURT arriving 12.30pm	
BERTAUCOURT	23rd	8am	Marched to St RICQUIER arriving 12.30pm. Very cold weather	
St RIQUIER	24th	6am	Marched to QUILEN 38 miles arriving 4pm.	
QUILEN	25th	11am	Marched to ERGNY 5 miles arriving 12.30pm. Heavy rain.	
ERGNY	26th to 30th		Resting & refitting in permanent billets at ERGNY. Guns all sent to 10M for overhauling. Exchange of Recruits for time served soldiers from Battery & Column commenced. No casualties except three horses killed by shell fire. No guns out of action during the month.	

JM Tankel Major RHA
Cmdg H.B.A.T.

Confidential

War Diary
of
"H" Battery Royal Horse Art:
December. 1916.

Volume No. XXIX.

Vol 24

Diary A

19th Division No. G.223.

Headquarters,
1st Cavalry Division.

Will you please convey my thanks to the 7th R.H.A. Brigade and Warwickshire R.H.A. Battery which worked with my Division during the recent operations.

The efficacy of their enfilade fire was of the greatest service to the Division in the attack on the 18th November.

D.H.Q.   (Sgd) T. BRIDGES, Major-General,
22/11/16.   Commanding 19th Division.

2.

1st Cavalry Brigade.
2nd Cavalry Brigade.
9th Cavalry Brigade.
Warwickshire Battery R.H.A.
C.R.H.A.

G.S. 817.   24/11/1916.

For your information.

B.D. Fisher
Lieut-Colonel,
General Staff,
1st Cavalry Division.

1ST CAVALRY DIVISION
2ND CAVALRY BRIGADE

'H' BATTERY R.H.A.
JAN - DEC 1917.

Confidential

War Diary
of
"H" Battery. Royal Horse Art.
January. 1917.
Volume N⁰ XXX

Army Form C. 2118.

WAR DIARY
~~INTELLIGENCE SUMMARY.~~
(Erase heading not required.)

Place	Date	Hour	Summary of Events and Information	Remarks and references to Appendices
2nd Army Artillery School. TILQUES.	Jan 1st to 31st		Attached to II Army Artillery School as Depot Battery — Weather exceptionally cold, with snow and frost — Horses all slipped in shoes — Out when ordered to go to the gun 195 Kt. 2/Lt LUMSDEN R.F.A. (attached) reported for hospital 13/1/17 and went to I Battery for instruction in the line — J.W.Fraser Major RHA Commanding "H" Battery R.H.A.	

Confidential

War Diary
of
"H" BATTERY
Royal Horse Artillery
February 1917

Volume No XXXI

WAR DIARY
INTELLIGENCE SUMMARY

Army Form C. 2118.

Place	Date	Hour	Summary of Events and Information	Remarks and references to Appendices
II Army ARTILLERY School TILQUES.	February		Acting as Depôt Battery at II Army Artillery School.	
	Feb. 26th		Weather very severe. Frost thaws up to 12th inst. Oct. rations cut down to 9 lbs per horse. Hay to 10 lbs. Horses lost condition during the cold. Owing to short food: Capt. Wills-Cole admitted to Hosps; on 31/1/17. Came back 26/2/17. 2Lt. Stamack passed course at R.H.A. School — Cavalry Corps. 2Lt. Wilson left for R.H.A. School Cav. Corps. to press course. 24/2/17. The Battery was inspected & discounted by Maj. Gen. Franks, C.R.A. II Army, who complimented them on their smartness & thanked them for their help at the School.	

JMBarker
Major R.H.A.
Commanding "H" Battery R.H.A.

Confidential

War Diary

of

"H" Battery

Royal Horse Artillery

March 1917

Volume XXXII

Army Form C. 2118.

WAR DIARY
or
INTELLIGENCE SUMMARY.
(Erase heading not required.)

Instructions regarding War Diaries and Intelligence Summaries are contained in F. S. Regs., Part II. and the Staff Manual respectively. Title pages will be prepared in manuscript.

Place	Date	Hour	Summary of Events and Information	Remarks and references to Appendices
TILQUES	March 1st		Depot Battery at II Army Artillery School –	
	March 8th	9 am	Marched to ERGNY – arriving 3pm. Snowing hard & very cold. 21 mile march –	
ERGNY	March 9th to 17th		Resting at ERGNY –	
	March 17th	9–2 pm	Marched to WIERRE au BOIS on changing billets – arriving 2pm –	
WIERRE au BOIS	March 18th to March 31st		Resting in billets – weather very cold with snow & frost –	
	March 2nd		2Lt. G.S. BULLEN. R.H.A. posted to joined the Battery – 2Lt. J.N.H. WILSON R.H.A. left the Battery in posting to H.Q. 7 Bde C.O. Orderly officer to C.R.H.A. 1st Cav Div	

J.W. Stanleye
Major R.H.A.
Commanding "H" Battery R.H.A.

Confidential

Vol 28

War Diary
of
"H" Battery
Royal Horse Artillery
April - 1917
Vol. XXXIII

Army Form C. 2118.

WAR DIARY
or
INTELLIGENCE SUMMARY.
(Erase heading not required.)

Instructions regarding War Diaries and Intelligence Summaries are contained in F.S. Regs., Part II. and the Staff Manual respectively. Title pages will be prepared in manuscript.

"H" BATTERY
No 304/4
Date 1/17
ROYAL HORSE ARTILLERY

Place	Date	Hour	Summary of Events and Information	Remarks and references to Appendices
WIERRE AU BOIS	1st April		Resting in both Willets.	
	5th "		Left by march for ERGNY. arriving 12-noon. Very cold day, horses frost chipt on road.	
ERGNY	7th "		Left 6.30 a.m. arrived MONCHY - CAYEUX 11.30 a.m.	
MONCHY	8th "		Left 12-noon arriving FREVENT - CAPELLE 6.30 p.m. Billet's Horses bivouacked in fields. Weather very cold, front hard hard frosts showers.	
FREVENT CAPELLE	10th "		Marched at 3.30 p.m. to polder Bde in fighting formation in support of 14th Cav Bde into ARRAS & woods ATHIES - Passed R.w. St LAURENT BLANGY at 12 midnight. bivouacked just N. of Railway Embankment. A snow blizzard then came on the whole of the afternoon & night. Battery left when horses very exposed, no shelter of any kind made affair especially trying. 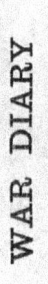 R.A. Brigade front line systems.	
ST LAURENT BLANGY	11th "		Shood closely at hour to work up in support of 1st Bde at ATHIES & FAMPOUX. were not required to spent night on sunken Road terrace. Again snow & bitter cold wind.	
FREVENT CAPELLE	12th "		2nd Bde moved back to FREVENT-CAPELLE at 9am arriving 3pm. Same bivouac.	
			Put in cold wind rain storm for 5 days. Pump pay appeal, horses most affected.	
LINZEUX	17th "		Left at 7am for LINZEUX arriving 12.30 p.m. Crew very cold stores	
	19th "		Lt & 8ths am for LOISON sur CRÉQUOISE arriving 1.30 p.m. Commanding the Battery R.H.A.	

Major R.H.A.

Army Form C. 2118.

WAR DIARY
or
INTELLIGENCE SUMMARY
(Erase heading not required.)

Instructions regarding War Diaries and Intelligence Summaries are contained in F. S. Regs., Part II and the Staff Manual respectively. Title Pages will be prepared in manuscript.

Place	Date	Hour	Summary of Events and Information	Remarks and references to Appendices
LOISON	19th April		and going into billets in Petit BEAURAIN & LOISON. All wires down under snow — Houses very much pulled down — mainly roof & beam roads — No wires left from Telephone —	
	29th		Petit BEAURAIN firm up & tell battery Wattel in LOISON. O/C 2nd Can Bde inspected lines on 24th inst. B.G RA Cav Corps inspected lines 28th inst. 2/Lt. K.E.J. STRONACH appointed to RHA 5/4/17. 2/Lt. G.V. HOLT. R.F.A. attached battery joined 7/4/17. From 20th April to 30th April weather beautiful, hot & sunny, things improving rapidly	

J.W. Carlisle Major RFA
Cmdg A.H. Batt.

Confidential

Vol 29

War Diary
of
"H" Battery
Royal Horse Artillery
May 1917.

Volume No. XXXIV

WAR DIARY
INTELLIGENCE SUMMARY

Army Form C. 2118.

Place	Date	Hour	Summary of Events and Information	Remarks and references to Appendices
LOISON	1/5/17	6.12.5/17	In permanent billets resting -	
PETIGNY	13/5/17	6-0 am	Marched to PETIGNY - Battery arriving 1.10 pm. Very hot day.	
ST. HILAIRE	14/5/17	7.45 am	Marched to ST. HILAIRE - COTTES arriving 11 a.m. - & billetted for night.	
QUENTIN	15/5/17	7.45 am	Marched to QUENTIN arriving 1 pm.	
	16/5/17		Resting in bivouac.	
	17/5/17	2.15 pm	Marched to wagon line at LOCON - being 2nd Div. Bde. (who go into the line for work dismounted) toming under orders O.C. 7th Bde. R.H.A.	
LOCON	18/5/17	8-0 pm	Right Section went up into action in Rue de L'EPINETTE, relieving a section of 38th Bde.	
LE TOURET	19/5/17	8-0 pm	Left & Staff Sections went up into action & completed the taking over of Battery & zone. Battery in action & shooting on friendly portion of the line. Six Boche aeroplanes flying very low. Some tract wandering round the trenches otherwise no activity. Weather fine & very hot - Battery fired about 100 rounds per day -	
Rue de L'EPINETTE	31/5/17		Party were knocks helping build the line near here. Gen. L. Messer R.A. 1st Army visited Battery. Foreign his said lines looked well & shewed good.	

J Macleod RMM
Cmdg A Batt

Confidential

Vol 30

War Diary
of
"H" Battery
Royal Horse Artillery
June 1917
VOLUME No. XXXV

Army Form C. 2118.

WAR DIARY
or
INTELLIGENCE SUMMARY
(Erase heading not required.)

Instructions regarding War Diaries and Intelligence Summaries are contained in F.S. Regs., Part II. and the Staff Manual respectively. Title Pages will be prepared in manuscript.

Place	Date	Hour	Summary of Events and Information	Remarks and references to Appendices
FESTUBERT	June 1st		In action in Rue de L'Épinette, covering the 66th Division.	
	June 2nd	9/pm	Right Centre Section withdrawn from action to wagon lines.	
	June 3rd	9/pm	Left Section withdrawn to wagon line. Battery relieved by C/246 R.F.A.	
LOCON	June 4th	10.am	Marched to Quentin on rejoining 2nd Can. Bde.	
	5th		Resting in wagon line at Quentin.	
QUENTIN	June 11th	2/pm	Marched to wagon line at LE HAMEL.	
LE HAMEL	June 15th	9/pm	Battery went into action in Rue de L'Épinette. Same position as before.	
	16th to 18th		In action. Supporting 66th Div. again.	
FESTUBERT	19th	10/pm	Battery withdrawn from action to wagon line at LE HAMEL.	
LE HAMEL	21st	9:30 am	Marched to Petit Sains arriving 12.30/pm, & billetted.	
PETIT SAINS	24th	6/pm	Battery went into action in ANGRES in support of 46th Div.	
	to 30th		In action. Shooting in to Hill 65 & Lorettes Ridge. Took part in attack & capture of Hill 65 in 28.E Weather fine throut with without thunder showers, rain on 25th & y29E.	

J. M. [illegible] R.M.T.
Cmdt 11th Batt.

Confidential

Vol 31

War Diary
of
"H" Battery
Royal Horse Artillery

July 1917.

Vol. XXXVI

Army Form C. 2118

WAR DIARY
or
INTELLIGENCE SUMMARY

(Erase heading not required.)

"H" BATTERY ROYAL HORSE ARTILLERY
No. 24
Date 7/7/17

Instructions regarding War Diaries and Intelligence Summaries are contained in F. S. Regs., Part II. and the Staff Manual respectively. Title Pages will be prepared in manuscript.

Place	Date	Hour	Summary of Events and Information	Remarks and references to Appendices
ANGRES	1/7/17		Battery in action. Supporting A6B Div in attack on Hill 65 & outskirts of LENS.	
PETIT SAINS	3/7/17	12 noon	Guns withdrawn to wagon line at Petit SAINS.	
	4/7/17	9 am	Battery marched to ESTAIRES arriving in wagon line 2.30 pm.	
ESTAIRES	5/7/17	7.30 pm	Centre section went into action at CROIX BARBEÉ	
	6/7/17	8 pm	Right & left sections went into action at CROIX BARBEÉ. The Battery relieved C/245 Bde RFA and were supporting the Portuguese in the Neuve Chapelle Sector.	
	7/7/17		Wagon line moved to new billets at LA GORGUE.	
	15/7/17	10 pm	Guns withdrawn from action & whole battery moved to new billets at QUENTIN. Rejoined 2nd Cav. Bde. in rest area.	
QUENTIN	19/7/17	9 am	Battery moved to new wagon lines at Mt. BERNENCHON.	
MOUNT BERNENCHON	22/7/17		Battery inspected by G.O.C. R.H.A. Cavalry Corps. to whom attached.	
	31/7/17		In rest billets at Mt. BERNENCHON. Guns repaired in 10th workshops. 13 Reinforcements joined during the month. Weather very hot. Thunderstorms.	
	27/7/17		2/Lt. G.V. Holt, RFA (attached) left Battery on posting to 20th Div. R.F.A.	

J. Marlatt Major RHA
Cmdg. H Batt.

Copy of letter received from
G.O.C. Cavalry Corps.

With reference to my recent inspection of the horses of the 7th R.H.A. Bde.

Will you please inform your Battery Commanders and Ammunition Column Commander how pleased I was with the very great improvement in the condition of the horses that has taken place since my last inspection.

This result could only have been obtained by really hard work and good horsemastership, and I congratulate all concerned.

H.Q. R.H.A.
Cav. Corps
28 July 1917.

Sd. H.S. Seligman
Brig. General.
G.O.C. R.H.A.
Cavalry Corps

Confidential

WA 32

War Diary
of
"H" Battery
Royal Horse Artillery
Volume XXXVII — August. 1917

Army Form C. 2118.

WAR DIARY
or
INTELLIGENCE SUMMARY.
(Erase heading not required.)

Instructions regarding War Diaries and Intelligence Summaries are contained in F. S. Regs., Part II. and the Staff Manual respectively. Title pages will be prepared in manuscript.

Place	Date	Hour	Summary of Events and Information	Remarks and references to Appendices
MONT BERNENCHON	16/7		In rest billets with 2nd Cav. Bde. in reserve to C.E.F. in NEUVE-CHATELLE sect.	
VINCLY	27/8/17	7.15am	Marched to VINCLY with 2nd C.B.	
	28/8/17	6.45am	Marched to MENTY (SOMMER area) arriving 2.30 pm. Very wet detaining day. A bad march for horses.	
MENTY	29/8/17		In billets at MENTY	
	30/8/17			
	31/8/17			
	1/9/17		2nd Lieut A.H. Hamilton-Gordon posted to Battery from I Batt. RHA	

J.K.Dunlop
Major R.H.A.
Commanding "H" Battery R.H.A.

Confidential

Vol 33

War Diary
of
"H" Battery
Royal Horse Artillery
September 1917.

VOLUME XXXVIII

Army Form C.2118.

WAR DIARY
or
INTELLIGENCE SUMMARY
(Erase heading not required.)

Place	Date	Hour	Summary of Events and Information	Remarks and references to Appendices
MONTY	Sept 1st to 30th		Resting, training in billets. — Good manoeuvre ground. Weather fine. —	
	2/9/17		Lieut. G.B. VAUGHAN-HUGHES. M.C. R.H.A. joined the Battery from I. R.H.A. & took over Mobile Sect.	
	3/9/17		Capt. N.W. WELLS-COLE R.H.A. left to join 28th Bde R.F.A. & assumed command 65th How Battery R.F.A. Lieut. J.A. COLQUHOUN R.H.A. left to join A8th Div & he 2nd in command of B/231 R.F.A.	
	5/9/17		Capt. C.F. FORESTIER-WALKER. M.C. R.H.A. joined from 65th Battery R.H.A. as Captain R.H.A. 2nd Lieut. K.F.G. STRONACH promoted Lieut. 1/7/17.	
	Sept 1st		Corps Horse Show. — Best Gun Team won by "B" Protection Gun team.	

J. Mackie
Major R.H.A.
Commanding "H" Battery R.H.A.

Confidential

Vol 34

War Diary
of
"H" Battery
Royal Horse Artillery
October 1917.
Volume XXXIX

Army Form C. 2118.

WAR DIARY
or
INTELLIGENCE SUMMARY

(Erase heading not required.)

Instructions regarding War Diaries and Intelligence Summaries are contained in F. S. Regs., Part II. and the Staff Manual respectively. Title Pages will be prepared in manuscript.

Place	Date	Hour	Summary of Events and Information	Remarks and references to Appendices
MENTY	4th Oct		Battery inspected by G.O.C. 1st Cav. Div. at Drill & Manoeuvre.	
	6/10/17	5:45am	Battery left MENTY & marched with 2nd Cav. Bde. to WATTEN arriving 4:45pm. Very wet day.	Very wet day
WATTEN	7/10/17		Continued march to HOUTKERKE area arriving 3:30pm. Very wet horrid day.	
	8/10/17	8:30am	Bivouacked in small farm - water very bad. Horses standing in mud & wet. Felt jeremy & change & weather very much.	
HOUTKERKE	12/10/17			
	12/10/17	8.0am	Marched into 2nd Cav. Bde. trek to WATTEN area & billeted for night at RUMINGHEM.	
RUMINGHEM	13/10/17	8.0am	Continued march trek to old billets at MENTY. Exceptionally wet horrid day, rain all day. Into last charms - arrived 11.0pm.	
MENTY	15/10/17	8.30am	Left for new billets at HUCQUELIERS arriving 1pm. Horses all put under cover in sheds & stables, men comfortable.	
HUCQUELIERS	25/10/17		Inspection of horses by A.D.V.S. + Brigadier 2nd Cav. Bde.	
	28/10/17		Presentation of Medals by Brig. Gen. Reade Baron D.S.O. Cmdg. 2nd Cav. Bde.	
	29/10/17		Lieut K.F.G. STRONACH R.H.A. left battery on posting to Amm Col I Battery R.H.A.	

W. Marshall
Major R.H.A.
Commanding "H" Battery R.H.A.

Confidential

WK 35

War Diary
of
"H" Battery
Royal Horse Artillery

November – 1917

Volume XL

Army Form C. 2118.

WAR DIARY
or
INTELLIGENCE SUMMARY.
(Erase heading not required.)

Instructions regarding War Diaries and Intelligence Summaries are contained in F.S. Regs., Part II. and the Staff Manual respectively. Title pages will be prepared in manuscript.

"H" BATTERY — No. 30/XI/17 — ROYAL HORSE ARTILLERY

Place	Date	Hour	Summary of Events and Information	Remarks and references to Appendices
MUCQUELIERS.	10/11/17		Marched with 2nd Cav Bde to LEBIEZ arriving 1-30pm.	
LEBIEZ	11/11/17		Marched at 9am to BARLY arriving 5-15pm. Very long march, cold day, roads very heavy.	
BARLY	12/11/17		Marched at 12.45pm to RAVINCOURT arriving 6.45pm. Hot day.	
BAVINCOURT.	13/11/17		Marched at 3.15pm to ETINEHEM arriving 9pm. Roads heavy, rest day, fed at night.	
ETINEHEM.	14/11/17		Marched at 3.15pm to COURCELLES near PERONNE arriving 9.15pm. Horses in standings, men in huts.	
COURCELLES	15/16/17/18/19		Resting in COURCELLES preparing for Gap Scale.	
	19/20/11/17		Marched at 12 mn to FINS arriving in bivouac 5 am.	
FINS			Marched at 9 am with 2nd Cav Bde. as leading Bde 1st Cav Div. 1st Section (Centre) went with the leading Regt. (4th D.Gds.) 1st hit HAVRINCOURT WOOD. (Lewton Brittle took 6.20 am. Hindenburg front line & support reported captured 8 am. Remainder retired forward.) 2nd Bound to RIBECOURT where leading Regt went on to NINE WOOD. Remainder Bde bivouacked for night between MARCOING & RIBECOURT. Pouring wet night. Germans still holding FLESQUIERES. 4th D.Gds in action at NOYELLES. Germans did not leave its action. Quite section rejoined at night fall.	
MARCOING.	21/11/17		Battery went into action N of MARCOING at daylight. Supporting attacks on CANTAING & NOYELLES.	
	22/11/17		Battery withdrawn on relief by 61st Div Artillery & marched to METZ EN COUTURE. arriving 6.30pm.	
METZ	23/11/17		Resting in bivouac at METZ.	

Major RHA.
Commanding H Battery, RHA.

Army Form C. 2118.

WAR DIARY
or
INTELLIGENCE SUMMARY

(Erase heading not required.)

Instructions regarding War Diaries and Intelligence Summaries are contained in F. S. Regs., Part II. and the Staff Manual respectively. Title Pages will be prepared in manuscript.

Place	Date	Hour	Summary of Events and Information	Remarks and references to Appendices
METZ EN COUTURE	24/11/17		Marched at 3 pm with 7th Bde RHA to BEUGNY arriving 8 pm. (2nd Lar Bde Sect) BTC who was wounded in support of 9 to Car Bde.) Guns went straight into action in support of 56th Div in the killing was BOURSIES on BAPAUME–CAMBRAI Road in support of 56th Div in the hilling Sectn INCHY EN ARTOIS – 'MOEUVRES – hope hues in BEUGNY.	
BOURSIES	25/11/17 to 30/11/17		In action. responded in attack in TADPOLE COPSE on 25th firing 1100 rounds in barrage. Casualties on 24.11.17. Majors & Trumpeter hues both killed, one other wounded. One Syrielle wounded (slightly at duty) The man slightly wounded at BOURSIES 26/11/17.	

[stamp: BATTERY 30/11/17]

J M ...... RMA
Major

.... M Batt.

Confidential

WM 36

War Diary

of

"H" Battery

Royal Horse Artillery

December 1917.

VOLUME XLI

Army Form C. 2118

WAR DIARY or INTELLIGENCE SUMMARY

Place	Date	Hour	Summary of Events and Information	Remarks and references to Appendices
BOURSIES.	1/12/17	2.30am	Still under 56th D.A. Battery Shelled with Gas Shells and H.E. and following men were wounded No 64951 Gr WILLETT (died of wounds). No 31794 Sgt GIBBINS. No 295715 Sgt WENSLEY, No 102713 Gr DAGNELL No 152715 Gr BURROUGHES. No 136638 Gr BYRNE, and No 66396 Br WISE.	
DOIGNIES	3/12/17	6.0am	Moved guns into new position here owing to withdrawal of our line which rendered the old position untenable. New position ably heavily reconnoitred and found the following day to be in view. Moved again to position semi-circled behind LOUVERVAL. Position in open field.	
LOUVERVAL	4/12/17		Enemy "Plane dropped bombs on and near Bryn line (BEDGNY). Wounded Bram. No 70615 Br HILL. (Since died of wounds) No 72519 Br BURRELL No 96330 Br CHAPMAN. That night (5th - 6th) enemy shells at A.R.P. near village with H.V. gun. Gas shells fell which began his killing 2 horses astrophit and 4 have had to be destroyed. One of the Prize team had been wounded by the bomb.	
	5/12/17	3.0pm		
BEUGNY.	7/12/17		Major CARLISLE left for a Course in ENGLAND. Battery relieved by a Field Battery and withdrawn to wagon lines. Marched out next morning at 8.30am. Leaving the command of 56th D.A.	
BEUGNY.	8/12/17		Marched by ROCQUIGNY and PERONNE to BOUCLY a suburb of TINCOURT-BOUCLY.	
BOUCLY	8/12/17	4.08pm	Coming under the orders of 24th D.A. and the Cavalry Corps.	
	9/12/17	2.0pm	The Centre Section went into action at TEMPLEUX-LE-GUERARD relieving a section of "C" Battery R.H.A.	

WAR DIARY
or
INTELLIGENCE SUMMARY.

Place	Date	Hour	Summary of Events and Information	Remarks and references to Appendices
TEMPLEUX	10/14/17	10 a.m.	Remainder of Battery went into action relieving the remainder of "C" R.H.A. We have one section (the Right) detached about 300 yds from remainder of Battery. Both parts of the battery are amongst the ruins of the village. The front is very quiet and all registration and a little sniping is done by the Battery during the remainder of the march. The position is unknown until being seen in front of any work carried to the danger of its turning the shear screw the position.	
	3/14/17		Major CARLISLE returned from the course in England and assumed temporary command of the Brigade.	

A. Maule Salmon
Captain
for Mods "H" Battery R.H.A.

Confidential

Vol 37

War Diary
of
"H" Battery
Royal Horse Artillery
January – 1918

VOLUME XLII

WAR DIARY or INTELLIGENCE SUMMARY

Army Form C. 2118.

Place	Date	Hour	Summary of Events and Information	Remarks and references to Appendices
TEMPLEUX le GUERARD	1/1/18 to 22/1/18		In action with 7th Bde R.H.A. in support of 24th Division - Heavy enemy Hpoot - very little firing.	
JEANCOURT	23/1/18 to 31/1/18		Moved position to JEANCOURT on joining Cavalry Dismounted Division - who were holding the line South of RUBY WOOD. The gun pit took a direct mt 30/1/18 - No casualties to personnel.	
	25/1/18		2/Lt. A.H. HAMILTON-GORDON R.F.A. left the Battery on posting to B/107 Bde R.F.A.	
	27/1/18		2/Lt. E.F. MAUDE R.F.A. joined the Battery on attachment.	
	31/1/18		2/Lt. S.V.C. BOWERS R.F.A. joined Battery on attachment.	

Manville Major
Cmdg H Bty

Confidential

War Diary
of
"H" Battery,
Royal Horse Artillery.
February 1918.

Volume XLIII

WAR DIARY
or
INTELLIGENCE SUMMARY

Army Form C. 2118.

Place	Date	Hour	Summary of Events and Information	Remarks and references to Appendices
JEAN COURT	1/2/18		In action with Cavalry Dismounted Division.	
	4/2/18		About 11 pm we were called on to fire an S.O.S. Barrage.	
	10/2/18		Enemy pill raid on Bremen trenches near Buisson - Guilain Farm in which we took part by firing a barrage.	
	18/2/18		Battery position shelled with 5.9 in Hows. Little damage done.	
	27/2/18	2.56 am	Called on to fire S.O.S. barrage for enemy raid which was repulsed.	
	31/1/18		2nd Lieut St.C. Bower RFA joined the Battery on attachment from England. Weather during the month on the whole very dry & cold. A good deal of frost.	

Marchie Major RHA
Andy A Bett.

"H" BATTERY
No. 28/2/18
ROYAL HORSE ARTILLERY

Confidential

2 Cav Bde
1 Cav Div

War Diary

of

"H" Battery

Royal Horse Artillery

March - 1918

VOLUME XLIV

WAR DIARY or INTELLIGENCE SUMMARY

Army Form C. 2118.

Place	Date	Hour	Summary of Events and Information	Remarks and references to Appendices
JEANCOURT	9th Aug 1st to 5th		In action at same position - Moved fwd position to VRAIGNES.	
VRAIGNES	13/14th to 14/15th	wk	Battery pulled out of action on relief by "A" Battery RHA. Moved to support lines at VRAIGNES.	
MONS	15th	9.0am	Battery moved to MONS-EN-CHAUSSÉE, rejoined the 2nd Cav. Bde.	
	21st	4.0 pm	Battery moved in Gap Organisation to the support of 66 Div who were being heavily attacked, and led their line broken - came into action just S of ROISEL.	
ROISEL	22nd	9.0am	Fired during the night heavy harassing. [Thick fog] the Germans again pushed their attack & drove 66 Div & the remnant position at G.B and it were NOBESCOURT FARM to defend ROISEL during the afternoon of Germans advancing in troops. Some fine Targets heavy losses in open sights & in the open to HERVILLY on ridges W of HERBÉCOURT. Shooting with open sights & did good execution, stopping several waves of attack — About 3pm, word took to position near BRULE to defend from two attacks to get on ridges about NOBESCOURT FARM which Germans occupied that evening. Ordered to march to BRIENCOURT but on arrival there disarmed it was a wrong map. was told to take action at LE CATELET at dawn. Another position fully knowing if the Germans again advanced — did not exist far from position — marched to BRIE to see that all bridges were blown up about 2pm. Third Bn who were not likely	
BRIE CRAIG	22nd	12 mn		
LE CATELET	23rd	8.0am	Troops crossed & bridges were blown up about 2pm. Third Bn who were not likely lost his 2 lorries in the river when he stumbled across with his 3d rallied — the Germans came all the best on opposite bank about 2500 yds range & he again had good targets for open fire shooting — On the whole we moved hourly fired on by F.A. with machine guns.	

Army Form C. 2118.

WAR DIARY
or
INTELLIGENCE SUMMARY
(Erase heading not required.)

Instructions regarding War Diaries and Intelligence Summaries are contained in F.S. Regs., Part II. and the Staff Manual respectively. Title Pages will be prepared in manuscript.

Place	Date	Hour	Summary of Events and Information	Remarks and references to Appendices
PARIS			We left this position about 5pm when last battery to leave the forward slope of the hill.	
BARLEUX	24th	3am	Came into action again at BARLEUX.	
		3pm	Moved position again on canal crossing. Forced [illegible] again to BERNY & came into action by 1st Bde RHA – fired at ridges during the night.	
BERNY-EN-SANTERRE			German attack morning succeeded in crossing the river. Battery fired barrages all day until the enemy succeeded in getting into the ridge nr VILLERS-CARBONNEL. Battery was then heavily shelled but succeeded in withdrawing by hand guns by gun after firing all ammunition. Retired to position at SOYECOURT where we stayed for the night.	
SOYECOURT	25th		Attack developed again in the early morning & after firing for 2½ hours in morning we moved back to FOUCAUCOURT & came into action astride the main road.	
	26th		Fritz stopped his F. about 4 a.m. then further attack to VAUVILLERS where we dropped into action but did not fire 2 rounds – moved back again. He afterwards via HARBONNIERES to CAIX & came into action just E of CAIX	
			entering ROSIERES & the railway station. Stayed the night & the enemy put a few shell into the wagon lines & hit 2 horses but cleared the other.	
CAIX	27th		Successfully moved up to a new forward position behind ROSIERES where we put down a 3 hour barrage stopping 3 german attacks then at escarpment of the enemy withdrew to our position near CAIX WOOD – still there the night. 5pm we moved Battery up to Railway near	

Place	Date	Hour	Summary of Events and Information	Remarks and references to Appendices
CAIX	28th		HARBONNIERES in support of a counter attack by Whitehounds of 66. 84. 50. Divs. R/R firing for about ½ an hour. We were recalled in a hurry & rattled away to help another heavy attack in the sector in POZIERES. Pulled out at dawn & rushed back to a position W of CAIX to cover the ridge CAIX – VRELY. Shortly later kind f 2 hours did good execution, were shelled slightly but were lucky in having no casualties. Moved back again to a position about 1000 yards back E of BEAUCOURT. Here we held up the enemy again for a time. Th infantry were very cooked & came back down the main road but formed a thin again in front from our position. We again started to LAWS at DOMART till dark. Recommg. on ways our infantry skirmishing there were two infantry fronts in byhyd in front of us. The Bde reserves & arms the drive to EASTELL where we arrived 3 am.	
CASTELL	29th		At dawn moved up to a position in the line about HAILLES & came thro over. Cover up at THEZY & HAILLES. Did not fire. Moved up again at 9pm to a position at HANGARD in support of 66 & 2n he Bde horses haking under 8– Div Artillery. Came into position & remained in Bois de HANGARD	

WAR DIARY or INTELLIGENCE SUMMARY

Army Form C. 2118.

Place	Date	Hour	Summary of Events and Information	Remarks and references to Appendices
HANGARD	29th		At 5:45 am enemy attacked down the main road with N of BOIS de HANGARD, shortly on AUBERCOURT. He came opposite the ridge about AUBERCOURT – VILLERS-BRETONNEUX wood & we had some excellent shooting on their right. Again machine took about 1000 and kept a barrage on the ridge. About 4 pm burst up once more in support of a bomb attack by the regts dismounted, which cleared the enemy off the ridge.	b-c
CACHY	30th		Battalion was CACHY in the afternoon. Retired to DOMART took up a position near the Church - Blank Have the Enemy attacked down infantry. He took down the main road in DOMART he again caught the enemy coming on the ridge, but open fire at 2700 and kept them behind the ridge. Virtually he retired about 2000 and kept up our barrage on the east till nightfall. Remained in action during the night. The 2nd Cav. Div. made a combined attack at 9am & cleared the enemy.	
GENTELLES	31st		2 Battalions staying at 6 of the DOMART woods established on this again on the west of the ridge. The battery fired barrages for this attack & had some good sniping shots at enemy massing in the woods.	

WAR DIARY or INTELLIGENCE SUMMARY

Army Form C. 2118.

Place	Date	Hour	Summary of Events and Information	Remarks and references to Appendices
GENTELLES	March 31st		Remained in action in same position for the night.	
	April 1st		Found to be too forward position just N.G. DOMART from the line which our infantry was held in the night.	
	2nd	3pm	Pulled out to again 2nd line Role at DAOURS supper.	
			During the whole 13 days between us fighting was in progress. Its battery occupied 28 different positions and fired execution on the enemy at times. The weather was very bad for the 1st week but latterly hoty I wet days. On 30th position was shelled at BERNY, CAIX, 4 DOMART, but luckily escaped serious damage. began here was shelled at CAIX & BEAUCOURT. Casualties were. 1 Off wounded (Capt.) 9 men wounded, 1 missing. Trick 27 horses wounded short. The Battery were thanked for their services by B.G. R.A. 66th Div. & B.G. R.A. 8th Div.	

M. Marshall Major RFA
Cmdg A/Bty.

Army Form C. 2118.

WAR DIARY
or
INTELLIGENCE SUMMARY.

APPENDIX "A"

(Erase heading not required.)

Instructions regarding War Diaries and Intelligence Summaries are contained in F. S. Regs., Part II. and the Staff Manual respectively. Title pages will be prepared in manuscript.

Place	Date	Hour	Summary of Events and Information	Remarks and references to Appendices
	March 21st.		OPERATIONS OF "H" BATTERY R.H.A. FROM 21st. MARCH 1918 ONWARDS	
			The Battery was in billets at MONS EN CHAUSSEE. At about 2 p.m. orders were received to move to reinforce the 66th. Divisional Artillery. The situation on the 66th. Divisional front at the time was that the enemy had penetrated the line and was holding TEMPLEUX LE GEURARD and the high ground at FERVAQUE FARM. At about 5 p.m. the Battery came into action just South of ROISEL, where it remained during the night firing an occasional barrage across the COLOGNE River.	
	22nd.		The enemy attacked about 9 a.m. As no information was forthcoming the Battery fired a map barrage. The wagon line about 600 yards behind the Battery received a certain amount of the heavy bombardment which fell about ROISEL, but no damage was done. At 10 a.m. the Battery moved back through HAMELET into a position on the high ground North of NOBESCOURT FARM. At 11 a.m. the morning fog lifted, and the enemy was engaged over open sights as he advanced down the slopes from HESBECOURT to HERVILLY in waves. Good execution was done. 1,600 rounds (21 wagon loads) were fired from this position. At about 4 p.m. the Battery moved and came into action just South of BRUSLE to cover the 50th. Division in the defence of the GREEN LINE. Up to dark the enemy was engaged about NOBESCOURT FARM, which they occupied, and afterwards as they came swarming through the wire along the main road. During the evening	

March
22nd. while watering at BRUSLE, a heavy shell fell on the bridge among the teams causing them to stampede. The drivers during this displayed great gallantry and steadied their horses well. Owing to an incorrectly worded order which was received at midnight, the Battery marched North across the river at COURCELLES and went by BUSSU to DRIENCOURT. Here a message was received to the effect that the former order was wrong, and the Battery was ordered to be back at GATELET by dawn.

23rd. The Battery arrived in action just West of BIAS cross roads about 8 a.m. A retirement across the SOMME was now ordered, and at 9 a.m. the Battery moved by LE MESNIL and BRIE to a position about 500 yards West of the river to cover the infantry crossing the BRIE bridge. At about 3 p.m. the enemy appeared on the high ground South of LE MESNIL and on the main AMIENS road. They were engaged with open sights and prevented from advancing over the crest. Considerable difficulty was experienced this day in finding 13-pdr. ammunition with which to replenish the wagons. While in action the Battery was continually engaged with Machine Gun fire from low flying aeroplanes in flights of six or eight at a time. The Battery Lewis gunners claimed one aeroplane, which fell about 600 yards behind the Battery, with both its pilot and observer wounded. Lieut BOWER with a signaller and horseholder were left on the East side of the river on patrol duty when the bridges were blown up. They succeeded in getting across the damaged bridges and almost got one horse across, but it fell into the river at the last moment. The Battery left its position at about 5 p.m. being the last to leave the Eastern slopes of the ridge and came into action just South of BARLEUX, covering the crossing at ETERPIGNY.

24th. At 3 a.m. the Battery was ordered to retire to a position North of BELLOY WOODS on the BARLEUX - ASSEVILLERS Road. During the morning the enemy was fired on as he was reported to be crossing the river at ETERPIGNY and LA CHAPPELLETTE. 2/Lieut.LUMSDEN was forward observing at LA MAISONETTE but owing to enemy shell fire communication was difficult to keep up.
BARLEUX was heavily shelled and a Field Artillery wagon line stampeded past the Battery.

25th. At 3 p.m. the Battery was ordered to leave the 66th.Divisional Artillery, and join the 16th.Brigade R.H.A. under Lieut.Colonel ALLARDYCE, who was working under the 8th.Divisional Artillery. A position was taken up at dusk just North of BERNY EN SANTERRE. Here the Battery stayed for the night, but moved a short distance in the early morning to get defiladed from the high ground near MARCHELEPOT. As the enemy attacked during the morning the Battery fired barrages across the BRIE bridge until the enemy was reported to be almost on the VILLERS CARBONNEL ridge. As the Battery was now being fairly heavily shelled, two guns in trouble with buffer springs were run back by hand to cover in a sunken road and the advanced wagon line was moved to the same place. The Battery remained in action covering with its fire the withdrawal of the other Batteries of the Group. After firing all their ammunition the guns were finally withdrawn by hand and limbered up in the sunken road. The Battery then moved back through ESTREES and got into action at dusk West of SOYECOURT. The night was spent covering the line which ran through the spinneys round DENIECOURT.

26th. A further retirement was ordered. After covering the withdrawal of "A", "Q" and "U" Batteries, the Battery came into action near the cemetery at FAUCAUCOURT, where a stay of about half an hour was only made, the objective still being DENIECOURT. The retirement continued through RAINCOURT AND FRAMERVILLE to a position

March 26th.	South East of VAUVILLERS firing in the direction of LIHU. At about 2 p.m. the Battery retired again through HARBONNIERES to a position just East of the wood North of CAIX covering ROSIERES and the railway. The wagon line got shelled at dusk, but little damage was done before it moved.
27th.	In the early morning two sections were moved forward about 1,000 yards towards ROSIERES. The position was in the open and was immediately ranged upon, but only about a dozen rounds were fired at the Battery. These guns stayed in position during the day and fired S.O.S. barrages for three hours repelling a series of very strong attacks on ROSIERES. These attacks, according to the infantry, were completly broken up by artillery fire, and very heavy casualties were inflicted on the enemy. At about 5 p.m. the whole Battery moved to a position close to the railway crossing on the CAIX - HARBONNIERES Road to support a counter attack on VAUVILLERS made by detachments of the 8th., 50th. and 66th.Divisions. After firing for about half an hour the Battery was recalled to the CAIX position to help repel another heavy attack on ROSIERES. The Battery stayed all night in this position where it was subjected to a good deal of casual shelling. No damage, however, was done.
28th.	The Battery moved at dawn to a position about 1,000 yards South West of CAIX to cover the VRELY - CAIX line. The Battery fired hard for two hours on the enemy, who crossed the railway and were coming through ROSIERES in great strength. The observation station at CAIX was cut off by shell fire. The right and left flanks gave, the infantry retiring from the direction of BEAUFORT - VRELY and WIENCOURT - MARCELCAVE. 2/Lieut. LUMSDEN with six men was sent off to get touch with the enemy in the direction of WIENCOURT. They returned three hours later with very useful information. The Battery was lucky in escaping casualties in this position, its neighbours suffering heavily. About 2.p.m. the Battery moved to the high ground East of BEAUCOURT WOOD. Here the Infantry fell back to a line about 500 yards in front of the guns. The enemy attacked strongly on the right forcing back the French troops, who were on that flank, through LE QUESNEL. The Battery moved down the road to BEAUFORT under shell fire, losing 4 men and 4 horses hit. The Infantry retired at the same time. Orders were now non-existent, and a general retirement was taking place towards AMIENS. The cross roads at MAISON BLANCHE were heavily shelled from the North and South. The Battery waited at HOURGES for orders. After dark the Battery moved up the road to take up a position on the high ground South West of DEMUIN. However, as it was reported that the French had also retired across the river at MOREUIL and that there was no Infantry line between the Battery and BEAUFORT, a move was made through THENNES to CASTEL.
29th.	Battery moved at dawn to a position near Point 105 East of DOMMARTIN to cover the river crossings at HAILLES and THEZY. The enemy did not appear during the day, and at 9 p.m. the Battery moved through BERTEAUCOURT to a position of readiness in the BOIS DE HANGARD.
30th.	At 6 a.m the enemy attacked down the LUCE. The Battery moved into action West of BOIS DE HANGARD, and fired a barrage across the river East of AUBERCOURT. Our troops fell back and the enemy appeared on the crest along the AUBERCOURT - MARCELCAVE Road. Here they were held by shell fire, the Battery firing at they with open sights at a range of 2,500 yards. At midday as the Infantry still fell back, the Battery moved about 1,000 yards further WEST, being slightly shelled as it left the position. Later on two sections were advanced again to support a counter attack by the "GREYS", which restored the situation and established our line along the AUBERCOURT Ridge. The Battery retired to a position near CACHY. The night was very wet and cold and no rations were forthcoming. The men and horses were much exhausted.

March
31st.   At dawn the Battery moved forward to a position in the valley close to DOMART Church to cover the line Point 104 at the cross roads on the MAISON BLANC - DOMART Road to DEMUI. The enemy developed his attack during the morning and our Infantry retired about noon towards DOMART. This village and the Battery position were heavily shelled. One of the gun wheels was broken and a casualty or two were incurred. The enemy Infantry appeared on the crest and were again engaged over open sights. After covering the withdrawal of another Battery, a move was made to a position South of GENTELLES where the Battery fired till dark and stayed for the night.

April
1st.   A counter attack by the 2nd.Cavalry Division at 9 a.m. was supported. This was most successful. The enemy Battalions were driven out of the large wood North of MOREUIL and a line was established round the Eastern and Southern edges of the wood. Large enemy concentrations behind the woods in this district were fired on by the Battery throughout the day. Some horses of the Battery were wounded by shell fire while refilling with ammunition west of GENTELLES Wood. The Battery remained in action all night firing at intervals on enemy communications.

2nd.   A position was taken up in the valley just North of DOMART to cover the line between the main ROYE - AMIENS Road and HANGARD village. At 2 p.m. the Battery was ordered to rejoin the 1st.Cavalry Division at DAOURS. While withdrawing through GENTELLES some casualties were incurred from shell fire.

During the 13 days of continuous fighting described above, the Battery fired from 28 different positions It got through upwards of 10,000 rounds. Buffer trouble accounted for guns being out of action accasionally but at no period were less than three guns in action.

Food and Ammunition supply was extremely difficult owing to frequent change of position. Cold during the first week's fighting was severe at night, and little sleep was possible even when the opportunity occurred.
Total casualties:-
1 Officer and 10 O.R.wounded
24 horses killed and wounded

Army Form C. 2118.

WAR DIARY
or
INTELLIGENCE SUMMARY

(Erase heading not required.)

Instructions regarding War Diaries and Intelligence Summaries are contained in F.S. Regs., Part II. and the Staff Manual respectively. Title Pages will be prepared in manuscript.

Place	Date	Hour	Summary of Events and Information	Remarks and references to Appendices
AMIENS	4/7/16		March from VECQUEMONT to WILLE on Southern edge of AMIENS. Bde returned at 2 hours notice to move.	
	9/7/16		Owing to hostile shelling with long range guns, which caused us several casualties, moved to RENANCOURT about 2 miles further west.	
RENANCOURT	10/7/16	3 pm	Battery ordered to move North, marched at 3 pm. Arriving at ROUGEFAY at 2 am 11/7/16 after a very long tiring march of 35 miles.	
ROUGEFAY	11/7/16	2 pm	Marched to AUBROMETZ where we billeted.	
AUBROMETZ	12/7/16	2.30 pm	Marched to LISBOURG arriving 7.30 pm.	
LISBOURG	14/7/16	5.45 pm	Moved billets to FIEFS.	
FIEFS	16/7/16	1 pm	Moved billets to GREUPPE (SOMY)	
GREUPPE	27/7/16	9. am	Moved billets to CUHEM.	
	12/7/16		Lieut A.G. RUNDLE RFA joined the Battery on attachment.	
	16/7/16		2/Lieut E.F. MAIDE RFA posted & proceeded to "C" Battery RHA	
	22/7/16		Inspection of horses by Maj. Gen. Mullins Cmdg 1st Car. Div.	
			The following awards were given to officers & men of the Battery for operations from 22nd Mch onwards.	
			D.S.O. Major T.H. Carlisle MC. Military Cross: Lieut G.B. Vaughan-Hughes. 2/Lieut H. Kumeden.	
			D.C.M. B.Q.M.S. A.F. Purser.	
			M.M. Sgt A. Beck. Bomb: A.F. Stockwell. Pr. H. Buckby. S.S. F. Ramsey. Dr. J. Galloway.	

Mullins-Orr
Major Cmdg
Commdg "H" Batty RHA

WAR DIARY
or
INTELLIGENCE SUMMARY

Army Form C. 2118.

Place	Date	Hour	Summary of Events and Information	Remarks and references to Appendices
ERGNY	Dec 12th		Refitting in permanent billets.	
ERGNY	Dec 16th	9.30 am	Marched to LUMBRES, arriving 1 pm.	
	17th	9.30 am	Marched to TILQUES, arriving 12.30 pm for duty as Depot Battery at II Army Artillery School.	
TILQUES	22nd		2/Lt. H. LUMSDEN R.F.A. joined for duty.	

J.M. Mardile Major RFA
Cmdg HQ Rct.

Confidential

War Diary
of
"H" Battery
Royal Horse Artillery
April — 1918

VOLUME XLV

Confidential

APPENDIX I

Army Form C. 2118.

WAR DIARY
or
INTELLIGENCE SUMMARY.
(Erase heading not required.)

Instructions regarding War Diaries and Intelligence Summaries are contained in F. S. Regs., Part II. and the Staff Manual respectively. Title pages will be prepared in manuscript.

Place	Date	Hour	Summary of Events and Information	Remarks and references to Appendices
ST. REMY AUX BOIS	June 1918.		Resting & training in Billets. Weather wonderfully fine - An epidemic of P.U.O. attacked Battery on 18/5/18 lasting till end of month. Up to 80 men per day out of action from this alone - A small Battery Horse Show held on the 19th. 2nd Lieut. A.S. BARSDORF R.H.A. joined & attached 21/5/18. Lieut. J.F.S. BULLEN R.H.A. proceeded to Cav. Corps. Equitation School, Cayeux. 28/5/18. Lieut. H.LUMSDEN M.C. R.H.A. proceeded to Cav. Corps Tactical School nr. Dieppe. 29/5/18. Presentation of medals received for recent fighting by the Cav. Corps Commander at 2nd Cav. Bde. parade service on Sunday June 16th.	

WAR DIARY
or
INTELLIGENCE SUMMARY.
(Erase heading not required.)

Army Form C. 2118.

Place	Date	Hour	Summary of Events and Information	Remarks as references to Appendices
SUSSANES	6.7.16	5 am	Left at dark & Blow and marched to the Saulx village. Orders at that time for our arrangement for the taking of the	
VITRY LE FRANCOIS	15.7.16	3am & 8am	leave to be cancelled. Arrived at [illegible] and here given billets. We marched the next morning from at 9 am	
FAVRE-LE-GRAND	17.6		by AUXI-LE-CHATEAU to FROHEN-LE-GRAND where we arrived at 12.0 noon.	
CANAPLES	27.16		We left again next morning at 8 am and marched SOUTH on BERNAVILLE and arrived at CANAPLES at 11.0am. Billets were not good but only the [illegible] were slept by the horses. The following day the Captain went forward to LEAUVILLERS to reconnoitre and on	
LEAUVILLERS	27.16	4pm	he horses were marched from CANAPLES eastwards to LEAUVILLERS where [illegible] afield to E. of the village taking over the lines of a Bde. of the 17th D.A. who were about to be relieved. We were here acting in connection	
			with the 3rd R.H.A. Bde as Dv. Arty. to the 17th Division. Were in V Corps front. Officers reconnaissances were carried out daily from the ground in the Battle zone	
	6.7.16. 10.7.16		We left LEAUVILLERS on relief by the Bde of the 7th D.A. and marched NORTH WEST to RAINNEUVAL where we bivouaced in a field North West	

Army Form C. 2118.

WAR DIARY
or
INTELLIGENCE SUMMARY.
(Erase heading not required.)

Place	Date	Hour	Summary of Events and Information	Remarks and references to Appendices
RAINEUVAL	6.7.18	2 am	We were shelled under 21st Division who was left 3rd Rifle Bde on their arty. There was artillery fire meanwhile owing to P.U.O. Our 2 batteries C (P.U.O. was given almost first aid though we had 5th without the Mobile Section of the R.A.C. owing to trailers) (from Meuma Rennes) were again carried out. The weather broke and we were somewhat uncomfortable under these circumstances.	
RAINEUVAL			General Franke (R.A. 3rd ARMY) visited the Battery and conferences the Major & the Interallied.	
	22.7.18		Left 21st Div. and rejoined our Division at THIEVRES.	
THIEVRES	23.7.18. 24.7.18.	11:00am	The Batteries now came under New Bde. Ratio. The Division is in 1000h Mobile reserve into 3rd ARMY and reconnaissances have been carried out over the ARMY Battle Zone.	
	25.7.18		Casualties:— Lieut. E.P.N. JONES M.C. joined from 5th Div. Bty. 7.7.18. R.H.A. 2nd Lieut. S.C. BOWER RFA left for attachment to I R.H.A. 8.7.18. MAJOR. T.H. CARLISLE D.S.O. M.C. R.H.A. 24.7.18. { forwarded A. Lieut. G. Mc. SWINEY. R.H.A. 25.7.18. } Gooch.	

APPENDIX 'A'

Army Form C. 2118

"H" RHA

WAR DIARY
or
INTELLIGENCE SUMMARY

(Erase heading not required.)

Place	Date	Hour	Summary of Events and Information	Remarks and references to Appendices
THIEVRES	4.8.18		Lieut. T.F.S. BULLEN RHA rejoined the Battery from the Cavalry Corps School of Equitation.	
	5.8.18	9 P.M.	The Battery accompanied the Bde on its march Southwards, the mission of the Bde being unknown. Arrived in early morning at HAVERNAS where it remained during the day.	
HAVERNAS	6.8.18	1.45 A.M.		
S'. SAUVEUR.	7.8.18	2.45 A.M.	The march was continued the following night to S'. SAUVEUR. Here a divisional conference divulged for the 1st time the operations planned for the next day.	
GUISY-LONGEAU	8.8.18	4.0 A.M.	Marching through AMIENS during the night the Battery (with the Cav. Bde.) arrived at the forward concentration area which it left again about 6.0 A.M. passing to a point just North of CACHY. The 2 Cav. Bde. was in reserve and followed the Divisional Headquarters between while the other two Bdes were spreading at first behind the infantry N. & S. of the AMIENS — CHAULNES railway.	
		6 A.M.	The Battery, marching last of the fighting troops in the Bde. Column, proceeded via MARCELCAVE, WIENCOURT L'EQUIPEE and GUILLAUCOURT towards CAIX.	
		1.0 P.M.	Here the Battery hung back in order to cover the Cavalry who CAIX if necessary but did not come into action as CAIX was entered without resistance. The Battery then moved to the western outskirts of CAIX.	
		2.30 P.M.		At 2.30 P.M. the Centre Section under Lieut E.P.M. JONES MC RHA was brought into action in

WAR DIARY or INTELLIGENCE SUMMARY.

Army Form C. 2118.

Place	Date	Hour	Summary of Events and Information	Remarks and references to Appendices
CAIX	8.8.18	2.30PM	the top of the hill just N. of CAIX and fired on enemy horse and motor transport on the VRELY-WARVILLERS road. The Cavalry having now reached their objective, which was the line of the old OUTER AMIENS DEFENCE, the remainder of the Battery came into action just West of the village of CAIX and lines were laid out by observation, covering the Bde. front.	
		5.0PM	Detached section fired on an enemy one gun (77mm) in action against HARBONNIERES from a point just south of ROSIERES. The gun was silenced and the enemy gunners seen to disperse. This gun was captured the next day. Shortly after this the detached section was withdrawn to the main position W. of CAIX.	
		5.15PM		
		8.35PM	In the evening at 8.30PM. a light barrage was put down by the Battery in response to SOS signals. All quiet at 8.35PM. During the night and early morning enemy snipers were active on the trolley of the LUCE River and men had to be moved 3 times.	
CAIX	9.8.18	7.50AM	At 7.30 AM the Battery fired on some movement of men just W. of VRELY. At 9.30 AM the Battery came into action and remained in the same place waiting with the Cavalry for a further move forward.	
		9.36AM		

WAR DIARY or INTELLIGENCE SUMMARY

Army Form C. 2118.

Place	Date	Hour	Summary of Events and Information	Remarks and references to Appendices
CAIX VRELY	9.8.18	5.0 PM	The Cav. Bde. moved forward and the Battery followed through CAIX and towards VRELY. Battery trotted into action just W. of VRELY and fired against an enemy counter attack on the line MEHARICOURT - ROUVROY. Observed from the Bascule just S. of VRELY.	
	9.8.18	5.45 PM	One Section (the LEFT) under Lt. A.G. RUNDLE R.F.A. was put into action S. of VRELY in order to reach FOUQUESCOURT more easily. There were no further targets so line were laid out approximately covering the Bde front as darkness fell. An enemy aeroplane dropped a row of 12 bombs close to but just missing the Battery & also a row close to the Bde. was withdrawn and the Battery, coming out of action, marched	
	10.8.18	6.0 AM	to a point on the LUCE RIVER from about ½ a mile W. of CAIX. Here the Battery was rejoined by Major T.H. CARLISLE D.S.O. M.C. R.H.A. and Lieuts G.R.N. SWINEY and H. LUMSDEN M.C. R.H.A. from leave and the Cav. Corps Tactical School respectively.	
		4 PM	The Bde. was ordered to saddle up & move to WARVILLERS with remainder of 1st Cav. Div. Movement was subsequently cancelled - Battery remained in bivouac for the night.	
	11.8.18	12 noon	Wasted hirness a few hundred yards North in search of grazing. My range fine. 2 lines syphilis ill.	

WAR DIARY
or
INTELLIGENCE SUMMARY.
(Erase heading not required.)

Army Form C. 2118.

Instructions regarding War Diaries and Intelligence Summaries are contained in F. S. Regs., Part II. and the Staff Manual respectively. Title pages will be prepared in manuscript.

Place	Date	Hour	Summary of Events and Information	Remarks and references to Appendices
MIX.	11/8/18	9 pm	Bde. ordered to withdraw to area E. of AMIENS. Marched via cross tracks to VILLERS BRETONNEUX. Thence via BOIS L'ABBEE & main road to CAMON arriving about 5 am. Enemy aeroplanes very active thro' night & driven off by several casualties from bombs.	
CAMON	12/8/18		Resting in bivouacs in ground railway emb. LT. Isaacs joined batty. to train.	
	13/8/18		LIEUT. EPN JONES M.C. went on leave to England.	
	14/8/18		C in C. visited Brigade - Congratulated Un-B Heavy Bde. on appearance & performance. Says Men looked very well.	
			B.Q. Capt. Ger Ops. Saw Battery Horses.	
GEZAINCOURT	15/8/18	9 pm	Bde. marched North to GEZAINCOURT via AMIENS. THENNES & BEAUVAL arriving 3 am. water much up on the road near BEAUVAL. No damage done Enemy airmen.	
BEAUVOIR RIVIERE	16/8/18	8.45 pm	Bde. marched to BEAUVOIR-RIVIERE via HEM & FROHEN LE GRAND arriving 12 noon. Horses were joined by our P. Schelsea (Heavy Baggage)	
	17/8/18		Rested in Billets. Guns exchanged for Hotchkiss guns.	
	18/8/18			
WARLINCOURT	19/8/18	9 pm	Bde. marched to WARLINCOURT arriving 3.15 am. a Filling function.	
	20/8/18	9 pm	Marched to concentration area W. of FONQUEVILLERS arriving 12 mn. The Bde. was to take part in operations with 3rd Army to commence on 21st.	
	21/8/18	5 am	Marched by tracks to rally gun of AYETTE, from more or less the word S.E. Courcelles. World British & German front lines to objective just N. of BOIS DE LOGEAST. The morning was very foggy & did not clear till 11.30 am. The infantry went on well & captured COURCELLES but did not cross the railway line - Tanks & infantry had great difficulty but did not cross the railway line - Tanks & infantry had great difficulty through thick construction, the cavalry had to keep close behind.	

WAR DIARY
or
INTELLIGENCE SUMMARY.

Army Form C. 2118.

Place	Date	Hour	Summary of Events and Information	Remarks and references to Appendices
SARTON.	22/8/18		The Infantry advanced via LOGEAST WOOD as soon as the Infantry (2nd Bn) had cleared close range fire. Guns from GOMMECOURT was enfiladed the valley between ABRAINZEVILLE & DOURCELLES to good purpose. Officer Staff. Cavalry suffered a good many casualties from M.G. fire. The enemy put up a strong resistance on the line of the railway all became clear that there was no point in Cavalry operations. Bde withdrew at 4 pm to rally. N.2 ADAINZEVILLE telegraphed to SARTON. Under B./F DOULLENS. arriving at 8 pm. The horses of the Bde has all been with but rather since.	
	23/8/18		Rest at WARLINCOURT left at 30 mins were badly in want of it - Moving off at 2.02 a/r 4h. TP Bgd Hosc. per bnfall left at earlier	
	24/8/18		Resting in bivouac.	
	25/8/18		Major's Ball FIELD Bn. moved round the Bde bivouac. Rhnaah arrived.	
	26/8/18 5pm		Resting in bivouac.	
			Marched Northwards to GOUY EN TERNOIS arriving 11.45pm - Very hilly road.	
GOUY EN TERNOIS	30/8/18		No bills in area except draft. Horse trecks. Horse not doing well.	
	31/8/18 2pm		Changed billets to ETREE-WAMIN. good walk in with CANCHE. Trumpeter BARRETT & Gunner DAVIES awarded M.M. for operations. Aug 8", 9"-10"- Casualties 2 m/r wounded & 2 horses kild.	

Appendix A

Army Form C. 2118.

WAR DIARY
or
INTELLIGENCE SUMMARY.
(Erase heading not required.)

Instructions regarding War Diaries and Intelligence Summaries are contained in F. S. Regs., Part II. and the Staff Manual respectively. Title pages will be prepared in manuscript.

Place	Date	Hour	Summary of Events and Information	Remarks and references to Appendices
ÉTRÉE – WAMIN	Sept 1918		Resting in billets at start of this month.	
	21/9/18	8.30 am	Marched with the 91st Bde to LINZEUX - bivouacked for the night.	
LINZEUX	17/9/18	9.0 am	Took part in a Div Arty Scheme shooting up near Abbev. le Chateau. Bivouacked for night at VILLEROY sur AUTHIE	
VILLEROY sur AUTHIE				
MEZEROLLES	18/9/18	11. am	Marched to MEZEROLLES.	
	24/9/18	8 pm	Marched by night to BARTON - with 2nd Can Bde - billetted there	
BARTON	25/9/18	6.45pm	Marched by night to AMELUY + bivouacked.	
AMELUY	28/9/18	9.15pm	Marched by night to BOIS de VAULX near MOISLAINS - bivouacked there - arriving 4.0 am	
FAUX WOOD				
			LIEUT. W. MURE. R.H.A. joined the Battery on posting from 2nd Bde R.H.A.	
	29/9/18	4pm	Marched with 2nd Can Bde to HAMELET via Rvest and bivouacked. Very wet muddy fields.	
HAMELET	30/9/18		Resting in Bivouac	

H. Billington Lt.
O.C. "A" Bty.

Army Form C. 2118.

WAR DIARY
or
INTELLIGENCE SUMMARY.
(Erase heading not required.)

Place	Date	Hour	Summary of Events and Information	Remarks and references to Appendices
ROISEL.	1st Oct.		Moved East via HERMLEY & FERMAIQUE FARM with the 9th Cav Bde. in support of infantry attack.	
	2/10/18	9:30 am	Returned to bivouac about 2 pm.	
	3/10/18	11:30 am	Moved East again by same route to South of canal near BELLICOURT. Returned to PC [Bivouac] at 2 PC [unclear]	
HESBECOURT	5/10/18	2:05 pm	Joined Sub-section & Personnel to east of HESBECOURT.	
	8/10/18	6:00 am	Moved up to BELLICOURT & ESTREES with 2nd Car Bde. [unclear] to support of infantry attack. 1st Car Bde working up to the main LE CATEAU road in close support of infantry attack by IX & XIII Corps. The Bde reached southern edge of SERAIN while their passed thro the infantry but were held up by hostile machine guns. Infantry did in advance the two ELINCOURT - DEHERIES for section of the Battery was sent to left flank front to the right. The section moved forward to G [unclear] to left of SERAIN against the Battery left. A team moved forward to Asinois [?] was surprised just SW of SERAIN. Horses of the Brigade & Battery teams were shot. Attacked by hostile Machine guns & Infantry & for casualties caused but the cavalry could not advance - the Brigade Went down to Serain & thence was Gouy - St Martin to the way back below present town & BEAUREVOIR the Battery was heavily bombed by EA 3 basic times but 15 [unclear] with some of the teams drawing went through out confusion & was dispatched by the fact that Aeroplanes was on the same road was hit in fact by the bombs of the machine. Guns up against line casualties. 2 Guns 1 G [unclear] 1 Machine 4 men killed & 23 WIA 3 MIA ORs and 4 men killed. 18 men wounded [unclear] [unclear] die Hun Village.	

WAR DIARY or INTELLIGENCE SUMMARY

Army Form C. 2118.

Place	Date	Hour	Summary of Events and Information	Remarks and references to Appendices
GOUY- ST- MARTIN	9/10/18		The Bttn. Left GUY ST MARTIN, marched off with the Brigade which was formed into a mobile force under Brigadier Gen. Bethell. Were held up about 4700 of the Rue left in the day in the enemy. The enemy were attacked by Bde Armed. Cars. Lewis gun teams with limbers were in Empty 4 used up in Empty 4 and teamed up to Bn H.Qs. B.H.Q. and 2nd Lon Bn & 3rd Lon Bn to 142 Troop our soldiers south of MARETZ and VENDELLES NORD for the night.	
MARETZ	10/10/18		Moved up with the Bde. Mx. Bns. & CATTIGNY to a position where TROISVILLES and REUMONT to take the position advanced in the day in support of Cav Div. Returned to bivouac at MARETZ at dusk, having the Regiment in touch with infantry.	
	13/10/18		Moved back to BELLENGLISE and VENDHUILE & formed an Civilian escort a week of about 30 miles. Remained some time	
COULAIN- COURT	14/10/18 to 21/10/18		Resting & training in COULAINCOURT area.	
	30/10/18		Presentation of medals by Our Corps Commander at TEMPLEUX. Awarded Medals of the M.M. given to Cpl Britten, Gunner Davis, PTE Dunn, H. Davis, & Dmrr T. Ball for gallantry on 10th & Oct. 8th attack. Le Roi de Guerre awarded to BSM L. Cook R.A.V. for gallantry in action.	

Wm D.V.H. Jenkin Capt
Adjt R. B. Bn

Appendix 'A'
Army Form C. 2118.

WAR DIARY
or
INTELLIGENCE SUMMARY
(Erase heading not required.)

Instructions regarding War Diaries and Intelligence Summaries are contained in F. S. Regs., Part II. and the Staff Manual respectively. Title Pages will be prepared in manuscript.

Place	Date	Hour	Summary of Events and Information	Remarks and references to Appendices
COULAIN-COURT	1st Nov to 6th Nov		Resting in billets.	
CREVE COUER	6/11/18	9.0	Marched with 2nd Car. Bde. to CREVE COUER. Long march every wet day.	
GOEULZIN	7/11/18	9.0	Marched via CAMBRAI to GOEULZIN.	
MONS EN PEVELE	8/11/18	10.30	Marched via DOUAI to MONS EN PEVELE. Got horses under cover.	
VEZON	10/11/18	8.45	Marched to VEZON. Roads bridges blown up. Bitterly cold day. Lieut. W. Milne posted to & joined Battery RHA	
BELOEIL	11/11/18	8.45	Marched to BELOEIL where 2nd Car. Bde. was in support of 9th Bde. who were in action with enemy on ATH - SOIGNIES line. Head official news of Armistice when near BASECLES at 10-15 a.m. Bivouacked for night near BELOEIL Château.	
BELOEIL	12/11/18	8.45	Marched Sno. via PERUWELZ to MORTAGNE near ANTOIGNE where Battery bivouacked in the ruins of the village.	
MORTAGNE	17/11/18	8.45	Commenced our March to Germany. 1st Cav Div acting as Advance Guard to II Army. Marched via PERUWELZ to LENS billeted for the night. M.Th. Bethune horse column, with Lieut. A.S. BARLOW in charge left the Battery & rejoined the 4th Bde RHA horse column. A bitterly cold day.	
LENS	18/11/18	9.0	Marched via SOIGNIES to billets near MIGNAULT where we stayed 3 days.	

WAR DIARY
or
INTELLIGENCE SUMMARY
(Erase heading not required.)

Army Form C. 2118.

Place	Date	Hour	Summary of Events and Information	Remarks and references to Appendices
MIGNAULT	24/11/18	8.15	Marched via Ensile - Braes to WAGNELEE & stayed the night.	
WAGNELEE	25/11/18	9.0	Marched to DHUY and stayed one day.	
DHUY	26/11/18	8.0	Marched to WANZE via HUY on the Meuse and stayed 2 days.	
WANZE	27/11/18	8.45	Marched to FRAITURE near COMBLAIN-au-PONT - last day very heavy roads and hilly country.	
FRAITURE	29/11/18	8.30	Marched via AYWAILLE & SPA to MOULIN DU ROY. near FRANCORCAMPS. about 3 miles W of the frontier - wooded mountainous road & very heavy.	
MOULIN DU ROY	30/11/18		Resting in billets. During the whole of this march the British troops have been most enthusiastically received by the Belgian populace. Villages were all decorated & the village bands played the National Anthems of the Allies. Owing the cheering people - Dances and processions were organized in many towns for the soldiers. At SPA the international Armistice Committee were sitting. Several Officers of all nationalities watched the Brigade pass through. German guards were still in the town. Going east from SPA we had to climb the biggest hill I have seen taken a Battery u/p.	

J.N. Scoville Capt. RHA
Cmdg. H Batt.

APPENDIX A.

Army Form C. 2118.

WAR DIARY
or
INTELLIGENCE SUMMARY

(Erase heading not required.)

Instructions regarding War Diaries and Intelligence Summaries are contained in F. S. Regs., Part II. and the Staff Manual respectively. Title Pages will be prepared in manuscript.

Place	Date	Hour	Summary of Events and Information	Remarks and references to Appendices
MOULIN-DU-RUY	3/12/18	8.30 am	Marched via MALMEDY and MOUNT JOIE to HÖFEN arriving 5 p.m. Crossed the German frontier about 4 miles west of MALMEDY. HÖFEN was our first billett in Germany where we stayed 3 days.	
HÖFEN	4/12/18	8.0 am	Marched via GEMUND to HEIMBACH. A very pretty village. Roads good but very hilly. Country very wooded, mountainous but extremely pretty.	
HEIMBACH	5/12/18	9.0 am	Marched to WISSERSHEIM arriving 3 p.m. On easy march as we were rapidly getting out of the hills into the Rhine Valley.	
WISSERSHEIM	6/12/18	8.0 am	Marched to COLOGNE and billetted in MUNGERSDORF - just outside the city. Stayed here in good billetts till 12th. Had a chance to clean up & harness improved rapidly with less regular routine.	
MUNGERSDORF COLOGNE	12/12/18	9.0 am	Marched thro' Cologne & crossed the Rhine by the Hohenzollern Bridge while the 1st Div (1st 1st Divison) was inspected by G.O.C. 11th Army as it crossed the Rhine. Billetted for the night in BERG-GLADBACH.	
BERG GLADBACH	13/12/18	8.45 am	Marched to KURTEN on the perimeter of the Cologne Bridgehead with cavalry outposts in front. Gave stayed 2 days in very bad billetts - Rain every day.	
KURTEN	16/12/18	9.45 am	The relief by Infantry marched back to Cologne reached Artillery Barracks at 2.0 p.m. where we are stationed. Stabling & gun parks very good also barrack rooms.	

WARDIARY

Army from Cologne

COLOGNE.

And so ends our march into Germany. which has been full of interest. Country is pretty especially the part where we crossed the mountains of the Northern spur of the ARDENNES. Horses have stood the 6 weeks marching well and are now hard & fit. only 2 were evacuated since the start-

The impression of the German population are that they all look for & well fed. there is no appearance of scarcity or starvation. Our returned prisoners have come through work very different there have been obviously deliberately starved

Xmas fare was provided for the men in Barracks & they are now completely housed for the winter.

J.M Brett RHA
Major

Curly M Brett RHA

Confidential

War Diary
of
"H" Battery
Royal Horse Artillery
May - 1918
Volume — XLVI.

WAR DIARY or INTELLIGENCE SUMMARY

Army Form C. 2118.

Place	Date	Hour	Summary of Events and Information	Remarks and references to Appendices
CUHEN	1/5/18 to 6/5/18		In rest Billets.	
			Moved with to PETIGNY (BONY)	
PETIGNY	21/5/18		Marched South with 2nd Line Bde to ST MICHEL, Vn 1st days vr duty march.	
ST MICHEL	22/5/18		Marched to ST REMY AUX BOIS.	
	21/5/18		Lieut G.A.N. SWINEY. R.H.A. posted to us from I Battery. Lieut G.B. VAUGHAN-HUGHES proceeded to 33rd Div: for duty as Captain.	

J. White RHA
Major
Commanding "M" Bty RHA

Army Form C. 2118.

"H" Bty, R.H.A.
Jan – Mar 1919

WAR DIARY
or
INTELLIGENCE SUMMARY.
(Erase heading not required.)

January 1919

Instructions regarding War Diaries and Intelligence Summaries are contained in F. S. Regs., Part II. and the Staff Manual respectively. Title pages will be prepared in manuscript.

Place	Date	Hour	Summary of Events and Information	Remarks and references to Appendices
COLOGNE on the RHINE. GERMANY.	1.1.19.		The Battery remained throughout the month of January in the ARTILLERY BARRACKS at COLOGNE. The Barracks were very fine and furnished. On our arrival but they are much better and the men are being comfortable and the horses in good stabling. Demobilization went on steadily throughout the month. 8 men left Battery in all.	
	20.1.19		The Major General Commanding the 1st Cavalry Division inspected the Battery, Speeches, the horses in the Stables, Gun-Park, and Billets, and enquiring into interior economy, and in the afternoon he saw a dismounted parade.	
	21.1.19			

Afforesto Buckham
Capt R.H.A.
for O.C. "H" Bty, R.H.A.

Army Form C. 2118.

WAR DIARY
or
INTELLIGENCE SUMMARY.
(Erase heading not required.)

February 1919

Instructions regarding War Diaries and Intelligence Summaries are contained in F.S. Regs., Part II. and the Staff Manual respectively. Title pages will be prepared in manuscript.

Place	Date	Hour	Summary of Events and Information	Remarks and references to Appendices
COLOGNE	1.2.19 to 28.2.19		The Battery remained stationed in the Artillery Barracks Cologne, throughout the month. November	
	10.2.19		The Ammunition carried in the echelons was evacuated to the 2nd Army dump, pending the march of the Battery to the Coblenz area. This march was eventually cancelled. The ammunition was again drawn from the Army dump.	
	28.2.19		Demobilisation went very slowly though at the month, only one man, a Student being released. Influenza again attacked the personnel of the Battery and on the 26th inst G.r HANSFORD No 155862 died in hospital. He was buried with military honours at SUDFREDHOF Cemetery	

[signatures]

WAR DIARY
or
INTELLIGENCE SUMMARY.

Army Form C. 2118.

March 1919.

Place	Date	Hour	Summary of Events and Information	Remarks and references to Appendices
COLOGNE.	16/3/19		Major T.H. Carlile D.S.O., M.C., R.H.A. ⎫ posted to "E" Battery R.H.A. Capt. C.F. FORESTER-WALKER M.C. R.H.A. ⎬ after reconstitution of that unit. Capt. E.R.N. JONES M.C. R.H.A. ⎭ Lt. Capt. FORESTER-WALKER Lieut H. RAMSDEN M.C. R.H.A. leave the Battery for "E" R.H.A.	
	27/3/19		"G" Battery R.H.A. arrived to take over equipment and certain categorys of men these from GHQ Batterys preparatory to this Battery's early departure to the Padre area.	
	31/5/19		Transfer of equipment etc nearly completed.	

Reginald Culler
Lieut. R.H.A.
Cmdg. "H" Battery R.H.A.

100 95/1111/3

1 Cav Bde

1st Cavalry Division.

"L" Battery R.H.A. disembarked BOULOGNE 17.8.14:
Returned to U.K. 19th October 1914.

"L" BATTERY R. H. A.

5th AUGUST to 19th OCTOBER 1914

WAR DIARY
or
INTELLIGENCE SUMMARY

Army Form C. 2118.

2nd Cavalry
1st Bde

Page 1

Hour, Date, Place	Summary of Events and Information	Remarks and References to Appendices
Aldershot. Aug 5th 1914	Received orders to mobilize.	
" 15th 12.30pm	Entrained S. Officers, 200 NCOs & men, 228 horses, 6 guns, 12 Ammn Wagons, 1 G.S. Wagon, 1 water cart, 73 revolvers, 78 rifles.	
16th 3 am	Entrained Southampton, embarked SS ROWANMORE	
10 am	Sailed	
8.30 pm	Arrived at BOULOGNE.	
FRANCE 17th 8 am	Disembarked and marched to Rest Camp	
19th 5 pm	Entrained at BOULOGNE.	
20th 9 am	Arrived MAUBEUGE – marched to billets near RIBES, arriving 2 pm	
21st	Marched with Cav¹ Div¹ I,D,&E batteries RHA en route for QUVRY. Arrived at that place. It was sent forward to join 1st Cav Bde (Information given by Gen¹ ALLENBY that about 7000 Germans were reported marching S.W. Towards MONS) were pushed up with 1st Cav Bde N.W. of	H.W.B.

WAR DIARY or INTELLIGENCE SUMMARY

Page 2

Hour, Date, Place	Summary of Events and Information	Remarks and References to Appendices
21st Aug (cont?)	HARMIGNIES and moved with them via ST SYMPHIRIEN to BOIS-DE-HAVRE. Reconnoitred position. Cavalry holding the canal to the N. No encounter with enemy. Battery returned to HARMIGNIES about 5.30 p.m. 1st Division with the rest of the RHA.	
Aug 22nd	Ready start 4 am. Moved west at midday, after going 2 miles battery orders to join Mt Cav Bde. Found it at VILLERS-ST-CHISLAIN. Took up a position to cover possible retirement. (No German shell arrived 12.55 pm on our right) Returned to HARMIGNIES 6 pm. Marches 8 pm and arrived QUIEVRAIN 3.30 am	
Aug 23rd	Billeted in full battery. Alarms all day. "I" battery left in the afternoon to join 4th Cav. Bde. Marched at 8 pm with D. & E batteries arriving in a field nr BAISIEUX about midnight.	W.T.B.

WAR DIARY
or
INTELLIGENCE SUMMARY

Army Form C. 2118.

Page 2.

Hour, Date, Place	Summary of Events and Information	Remarks and References to Appendices
Aug 24th contd	Moved at daybreak to WIHERIES (about 3 miles) E. and to join DE LISLE'S 2nd Cav. Bde near ELOUGES. Came into action south of Railway & east & just E. of ELOUGES & shells enemy's dismounted troops detraining on railway line south of THULIN (range 1800 yards). Enemy (in small numbers) retired when shells burst near them. Hostile aeroplane came over battery & soon afterwards shells. Battery retired [illeg], 4 guns followed by 2 and then moved went with 2nd Cav. Bde (less 18th H'rs) through AUDREGNIES towards ANGRE. About 2 hours later (information having been received that strong infantry div'n. have left near'd about ELOUGES, beyond assistance to enable them to retire) DE LISLE sent battery on to the high ground between AUDREGNIES and ELOUGE WM. of 18th Hrs. The battery arrived there & halted. DE LISLE soon after came there himself. Subsequently heavy rifle and shell fire was opened on it from QUIEVRAIN and east of that towards DE LISLE ordered CO. to take up fire position & support his brigade. W.J.B.	

WAR DIARY
or INTELLIGENCE SUMMARY

Army Form C. 2118.

Page 4.

Hour, Date, Place	Summary of Events and Information	Remarks and References to Appendices
Aug 24th (cont.)	Battery galloped into action in a field S.E. of AUDREGNIES on the open, losing 2 wagons on the way one from shell fire and the other whilst crossing a sunken road. Fired on infantry advancing in closely formed lines from QUIEVRAIN + east of that town, a very clear target range 2000–2300 yds. Enemy broke and retired losing heavily, came on again and again broke. Meanwhile 9th L. and 4th D.Gs charged across the front of the battery & apparently got behind some mounds seen on the way, they did come in small detached teams. The battery continued firing on hostile infantry (enemy guns which kept up a continuous fire, could not be located) till ammunition was nearly exhausted. When an order was given by Capt HAMILTON GRACE of Brigade Major to retire. The guns were then forward about 20 or 30 yards to a help & extricated by single fired in succession. (This Dummy forward from the salvation of the battery if could not have hindered of where it was.) The horses were returned to the shelled long after the battery had left. Horse infantry which was worked up the the valley from QUIEVRAIN has stated in the attack of AUDREGNIES Battery.

4743

Army Form C. 2118.

WAR DIARY
or
INTELLIGENCE SUMMARY
(Erase heading not required.)

Page 5.

Instructions regarding War Diaries and Intelligence Summaries are contained in F. S. Regs, Part II. and the Staff Manual respectively. Title pages will be prepared in manuscript.

Hour, Date, Place	Summary of Events and Information	Remarks and References to Appendices
	Fired 450-600 rounds. Jones up with DE LISLE and about 2 squadrons + howlers to RUESNES arriving ? See map of at Dark.	action on next page.
	Casualties.	
	Wounded.	
	2/Lt J. E. MARSTON	
	7 NCOs & men	
	Missing	
	2 men	
	No high explosive shell fell in the battery. The gun shield afforded protection to the detachments from shrapnel bullets	hub

Army Form C. 2118.

WAR DIARY
or
INTELLIGENCE SUMMARY

(Erase heading not required.)

Instructions regarding War Diaries and Intelligence Summaries are contained in F. S. Regs., Part II. and the Staff Manual respectively. Title pages will be prepared in manuscript.

Page 6

Hour, Date, Place	Summary of Events and Information	Remarks and References to Appendices
	ROUGH SKETCH TO ILLUSTRATE ACTION ON AUG 24.	A. First position of battery. B. Enemy's advance from Thulin in morning. C. Position of battery behind it, then fire opened in afternoon. D. Position of battery in action supporting Cav? in afternoon. E. Infantry attack in the afternoon. F. Direction of charge and retirement of Cavalry. G. Mounds at Sugar factory. H. Retirement of battery in afternoon.

Ground sloped gently down from South to North.

Army Form C. 2118.

WAR DIARY
or
INTELLIGENCE SUMMARY
(Erase heading not required.)

Page 7

Hour, Date, Place	Summary of Events and Information	Remarks and References to Appendices
Aug 25th	Marched at 1 a.m. to WARGNIES-LE-PETIT & from there to a position north of ORSINVAL and took up a position with that of 2nd Cav'y Bde to cover retirement. Fell back during the day and, after coming into action several times, joined up with Cav'y Div'n west of VERTAIN? About 5 p.m. 1st Cav'y Bde with D.E. & L. batteries moved through the village when a violent attack from the north developed. There was great confusion in the French contingents. British Infantry, transport & RFA. We eventually moved out south over the next ridge & waited there till the infantry transport etc had cleared. Heavy shell fire was poured in the rest of the Cav'y Div'n west of VERTAIN? Eventually we marched "L" in rear, at dusk & a sunken road & the darkness apparently saved the column as German Infantry were out about 400 yds behind it. Marched through LE CATEAU (full of British Infantry) and, after much	A718

Army Form C. 2118.

Page 7.

WAR DIARY
or
INTELLIGENCE SUMMARY.
(Erase heading not required.)

Hour, Date, Place	Summary of Events and Information	Remarks and references to Appendices
Aug 25th (cont)	countermarching eventually halted in a field South? of the town with 10th Cav Bde in the early morning.	
Aug 26.	Moved off at 4 am to ―― halted till 7 am. We went now on the right flank of Genl SMITH-DORRIEN'S CORPS and 6 miles off the right flank was the left flank of the 1st Army. We (the 19th Bde L & E batteries) had orders to fill this gap. We moved out came into action north of a village & remained there for some hours, sending out 2 sections to other positions. Took on various objectives at long ranges & were shelled after having been located by aeroplanes; no casualties. We held on till dusk & the 2nd Corps had retired. Marched in heavy rain to ―― ? arriving about 2 am.	HMS.

Army Form C. 2118.

WAR DIARY
or
INTELLIGENCE SUMMARY.
(Erase heading not required.)

Page 8

Hour, Date, Place	Summary of Events and Information	Remarks and references to Appendices
Aug 27th	Started 4 am with 1 Cav. Bde & marched slowly to ST QUENTIN passing through the scattered remains of an exhausted ammunition column. At ST QUENTIN got supplies and horses ar shod, men milling & halted in the high ground S.E. of the town till dusk when we went into billets at ESSANCOURT.	[VDAG. 11/7]
Aug 28th	Moved out about 4:30 am towards ST QUENTIN & remained in a hollow with patrols out most of the day. In spite of the evening a great many stragglers passed through us. We moved south in the evening to BERLANCOURT & Bivouac.	
Aug 29th	Ready to move at dawn. The 2 Cav. Bde was close by to the W. & N.W. About 11 am we were suddenly attacked from the north	H2B

79
3298

Army Form C. 2118.
Page 9

WAR DIARY or INTELLIGENCE SUMMARY

Hour, Date, Place	Summary of Events and Information	Remarks and references to Appendices
Aug 29th (cont)	Our one section not + engaged enemy's cavalry 1200-1500 yards & then retired with that section + joined up with the other 3 guns on a ridge about 1 mile to the south. Soon again retired with while battery along the NOYON road & came into action on either side of the road under cover. McLeod's Bty & the 1st + 2nd Cav. Bde. to the most of the road. Fired a lot of ammunition on enemy's cavalry & landed "fire into" ridge we had just left (range 1800-2500 yards). Enemy's shell-fire however. Opened & retire + did so to top of a high ridge + remained in position. Face to a long time. Sent one section back to previous position but it did not fire.	hy13

WAR DIARY
or
INTELLIGENCE SUMMARY.

(Erase heading not required.)

Army Form C. 2118.

Page 10

Hour, Date, Place	Summary of Events and Information	Remarks and references to Appendices
	rejoined. Received information that the 2 Brigade were returning & that 2nd Brigade had passed we remained & halted as column to clear the road, having been told that the enemy were not coming on. However the (1st?) R.B. were shelled on their way over the ridge, a pity we were not in action. Marched through NOYON to BAILLIE where we bivouaced with 1st Cav Bde.	
Aug 30th	Started at 4.30 am & marched unmolested through forest country to CHOISEY-AU-BAC bivouaced on the south side of the AISNE & lot of outpost & sniping at night.	
Aug 31st	Marched at 5 am, crossed the OISE at COMPIEGNE & joined up with rest of Cav Div at a Rendez-vous south of the D. in ROUTE D'AMIENS. Remained there several hours — came into	AHB.

WAR DIARY or INTELLIGENCE SUMMARY

Army Form C. 2118.
Page 11

Hour, Date, Place	Summary of Events and Information	Remarks and references to Appendices
Aug 31st (cont?)	Action but did not fire. Eventually marched with Cav. Bde. - crossed the OISE at VERBERIE and went into bivouac at dusk at NERY. Protection for the night "L" had a piquet on ??? ??? ??? also picqueted the road to the ???. Cavalry responsible for the rest of the bivouac.	
Sept 1st	Ready to start at 4.30 a.m. Orders received from G.O.C. to "stand fast" and the men to turn out ½ hours notice. Bdr had not been horses saddled and the battery started watering at a ??? ??? by sub-sections. About 5.5 a.m. a heavy shrapnel, machine gun and rifle fire was suddenly opened onto the horses from a ridge 700-800 yards on the right flank and right rear of the ???	See map on page 15

WAR DIARY or INTELLIGENCE SUMMARY

Army Form C. 2118.
Page 12.

Hour, Date, Place	Summary of Events and Information	Remarks and references to Appendices
Sept 1st (cont)	entire line of guns. It had been a misty morning and the fog who only just beginning to rise. Some of the men took cover behind vehicle, haystacks and in the road, those who were intrying horses were unable to get back. Major Slater-Booth was at the guns and was knocked out by a shell when running back to the battery. The rest of the battery Officers, all of whom were in or near the bivouac and several NCOs and men who were handy made a push under a heavy fire and got off 3 guns which were galloped to the enemy's side & the left of a small wood. In fact they were just about to be led away by Captain Bradbury. One of the guns was however not at once. Another was soon fitted & fired very heavy into their front & fled so after firing a few rounds,	See map on page 15

Army Form C. 2118.

WAR DIARY
or
INTELLIGENCE SUMMARY.
(Erase heading not required.)

page 13

Hour, Date, Place	Summary of Events and Information	Remarks and references to Appendices
Sept 1 (cont'd)	The Hund. which had been very quickly got into action by Sgt Nelson a L.A. Sergt. shoe, kept up a good fire & the enemy advanced. Capt Bradbury & Lieut Campbell him-self & others being supplied by Sergt Osborne. Capt Bradbury and Lieut Campbell were killed, Lieut Munby and Sergt Nelson very severely wounded. Meanwhile the L/49 B.C.s went about the enemy's right flank. The XIth Hussars and Bays insured the village, sunken road and upper battery. A machine gun did great execution amongst the enemy's gunners - under this captured defence the enemy did not advance after first opening fire & their guns eventually ceased firing. Subsequently MGB probably	See note on page 15

79
3298

(9 26 6) W 257-976 100,000 4/12 H W V

WAR DIARY of INTELLIGENCE SUMMARY

Army Form C. 2118.
Page 74

Hour, Date, Place	Summary of Events and Information	Remarks and references to Appendices
Sept 1st (cont'd)	Reinforcements arrived. I battery RHA, Mhows Cavalry, 1 Squadron 19th Hussars and Middlesex Regt, who captured 10 German field guns and a number of prisoners. Both teams from I battery, the 6 guns and personnel under Sergt Major Dorrell joined the 2nd Bn RFA. Amongst the Officers wounded Capt Brown and bivouaced forth near for the night. The wounded were taken away by the medical authorities. Casualties. Killed — Wounded Capt Bradbury — Major Sclater-Booth Lieut Campbell — Lieut Giffard [died 2 days later] " Munday [died 2 days later] 20 NCOs & men — 29 NCOs & men Horses killed & lost about 150.	See note on page 15. NB. The account of today is compiled from accounts given by various survivors of the engagement. WM—

Army Form C. 2118.

WAR DIARY
or
INTELLIGENCE SUMMARY.
(Erase heading not required.)

Page 15

Instructions regarding War Diaries and Intelligence Summaries are contained in F.S. Regs., Part II. and the Staff Manual respectively. Title pages will be prepared in manuscript.

Hour, Date, Place	Summary of Events and Information	Remarks and references to Appendices

Rough sketch of Reargd Action at NERY on Sept 1st

(8 German guns) ⚬ ⚬ ⚬ ⚬ ⚬ ⚬ ⚬ ⚬ (2 German guns)
" " " "

Rough lines of German attacks → ← 2 machine guns

"L" R.H.A.
⚬ ⚬ ⚬ ⚬ haystacks
(8th R.H.Q) (XI Hr Bde Q)
Queens Bays bivvies
old farm
Nery

↑ (A)
→ 1 batt'n R.H.A.

(C) ↑
(B) ↓

Country quite open, high ground to the N. and a ridge commanding the village running along the line of enemy's attack. Standing corn & turnips.

(A) Line of advance Howitzd Bat'y
(B) Direction of attack by 5cdi
(C) " " " Midlsex
(M) Queen's Bays machine guns

N (approx) ↑

High ground

Army Form C. 2118.

Page 16

WAR DIARY
or
INTELLIGENCE SUMMARY.
(Erase heading not required.)

Hour, Date, Place	Summary of Events and Information	Remarks and references to Appendices
Sept 2nd	Marched 1am with 14th Bde Amm Col and bivouaced 10 pm	
" 3rd	Marched at 9 pm & joined up with 32nd Bde RFA under J/Col Biddulph. 1/c 6 guns sent to A.O.D. ST NAZAIRE	
" 4th	Order from G.H.Q. to move to CHAMPS via JOSSIGNY BUSSY and TORCY — marched at noon, arrived 5 pm. Here 106 NCOs & men had rejoined, arrives 5pm handed horses over to 7th Bde Amm Col. One G.S. wagon & water cart joined up after 10 days absence. Water cart handed over to D of I. Formed.	
" 5th	Marched at 3 am & arrived MORMONT about 9 p.m. 1/4/14	
" 6th	Left 1 am in LORRIES, arrived MELUN. 3.30 am entrained 10.30 am arrived LE MANS 4 pm & came under the base Commandant Colonel EASTWOOD	

WAR DIARY
or
INTELLIGENCE SUMMARY.
(Erase heading not required.)

Army Form C. 2118.

Page 17

Hour, Date, Place	Summary of Events and Information	Remarks and references to Appendices
Sept 8th to Oct 12th	Two parties of approximately 60 each employed at A.O.D. MAROC fitting up guns haunters &c	
Oct 12th	Telephone message received from D.A.G. Base as follows :- Detail on party of "L" battery RHA on to to relieve from duties at base transport depot and A.O.D. MAROC. Battery billeted at a future system.	
Oct 17th	Entrained at Le MANS. B.S.M. BORRELL & men.	
Oct 18.	Arrived HAVRE	
Oct 19.	Arrived SOUTHAMPTON 10 am arrived WOOLWICH by train 8.45 p.m.	

130 q5/1111/4

1917
1ST CAVALRY DIVISION

2ND CAVALRY PIONEER BATTN

JAN - MAR 1917

1917
1ST CAVALRY DIVISION

Army Form C. 2118

WAR DIARY
~~INTELLIGENCE SUMMARY~~
(Erase heading not required.)

Instructions regarding War Diaries and Intelligence Summaries are contained in F. S. Regs., Part II. and the Staff Manual respectively. Title Pages will be prepared in manuscript.

Place	Date	Hour	Summary of Events and Information	Remarks and references to Appendices
			War Diary of 2nd Cavalry Pioneer Battalion for the month of January. 1917.	

C.J. Thackwell Major
Commanding 2nd Cavalry Pioneer Battalion.

Army Form C. 2118

WAR DIARY
~~INTELLIGENCE SUMMARY~~
(Erase heading not required.)

Instructions regarding War Diaries and Intelligence Summaries are contained in F. S. Regs., Part II. and the Staff Manual respectively. Title Pages will be prepared in manuscript.

Place	Date	Hour	Summary of Events and Information	Remarks and references to Appendices
TINCQUES	11th January. 1917.		Huts and Billets. Parades:-Work on railway continued. Two muck trains are now running on the section of line,prepared by the Battalion,so we should not be delayed so much in future by traffic on the permanent line. Three Other Ranks joined the Battalion; two Other Ranks to Hospital.	
TINCQUES	12th January. 1917.		Huts and Billets. Parades:- Work on the railway continued;three trains now available on our own line;work proceeded without interruption. The Corps Commander visited the Battalion and inspected the work in progress. Orders received for the 9th Lancers detachment to evacuate TINCQUETTE tomorrow and billet in TINCQUES; 14 Other Ranks rejoined their Units today and struck off strength	
TINCQUES	13th January. 1917.		Billets. Parades:- Work on Railway continued.The detachment 9th Lancers moved into billets at TINCQUES today. One Officer(Captain D.G.F.Darley,4th Dragoon Gds) and One Other Rank rejoined their Regiments today and struck off strength of the Battalion.	
TINCQUES	14th January. 1917.		Billets. Parades:-Work on Railway continued.Divine Service after completion of work. More satisfactory results are now being obtained,now that we work on our own railway lines. Two Other Ranks taken on strength of Battalion. One Officer 2/Lieutenant Pink,18th Hussars), and four Other Ranks to Hospital,and are struck off strength.	
TINCQUES	15th January. 1917.		Billets. No work on Railway: Battalion had baths and employed on cleaning billets,etc. A case of Measles in Battalion. All precautions to prevent spread of disease taken by M.O. Four Other Ranks to Hospital and Two Other Ranks to Units,are struck off strength of Battalion. One Other Rank (servant to 2/Lieutenant Pink),struck off strength.	
TINCQUES	16th January. 1917.		Billets. Work on Railway continued. One Other Rank to Hospital and struck off strength.	
TINCQUES	17th January. 1917.		Billets and Huts. Work on Railway continued. A heavy snowstorm last night,and some of the billets in very bad state in consequence; 100 Other Ranks,9th Lancers,had to vacate their barn and go to huts at TINCQUETTE temporarily.	
TINCQUES	18th January. 1917.		Billets and Huts. Work on Railway continued. G.O.C.,2nd Cavalry Brigade inspected billets and work on railway.	

Army Form C. 2

WAR DIARY
INTELLIGENCE SUMMARY
(Erase heading not required.)

Instructions regarding War Diaries and Intelligence Summaries are contained in F. S. Regs., Part II. and the Staff Manual respectively. Title Pages will be prepared in manuscript.

Place	Date	Hour	Summary of Events and Information	Remarks and references to Appendices
TINCQUES	19th January. 1917.		Billets and Huts. Work on Railway continued. One Officer,(Captain H.deGrey Warter,4th Dragoon Gds) one horse and one Other Rank,struck off strength;one Other Rank to Hospital and struck off strength.	
TINCQUES	20th January. 1917.		Billets. Parades:-Work on Railway continued. Much progress has been made during the last week, as soil,owing to frost,has worked easier and traffic has been better arranged. The A.D.M.S. 1st Cavalry Division,inspected the billets. 9th Lancer detachment moved from TINCQUETTE to TINCQUES.	
TINCQUES	21st January. 1917.		Billets. Parades:- Work on Railway continued. A German aeroplane alighted in the village and the observer,an officer,was taken prisoner by the Wireless Company,R.E.,and handed over to the Town Major; the machine got away but eventually came to ground near SAVY,where the mechanic was also taken.	
TINCQUES	22nd January. 1917.		Billets. No work on Railway. Men had baths and employed on cleaning billets and various inspections The Director General of Railways inspected the work done on the railway and expressed satisfaction with the progress made.	
TINCQUES	23rd January. 1917.		Billets. Work on Railway continued. Four Officers and 15 Other Ranks joined Battalion,forming the new Headquarters of Battalion. One Interpreter joined Battalion. One Officer,(Lieutenant H.D.Wise,18th Hussars),2 Other Ranks and 2 Riding horses struck off strength Officers joining:-Lieutenant & Adjutant R.J.F.Chance,Lieutenant and Quarter-Master F.A.Dunham, 2/Lieutenant Emsell and 2/Lieutenant Clarke,all 4th Dragoon Guards.	
TINCQUES	24th January. 1917.		Billets.Work on Railway continued; work greatly hindered owing to lack of coal for the engines; ground very hard for digging owing to depth to which frost has penetrated.	
TINCQUES	25th January. 1917.		Billets. Work on Railway continued;work again curtailed owing to traffic on the main line,being, practically closed all day. Two Officers(Lieutenant & Quarter-Master W.H.Parsons,18th Hussars, and 2/Lieutenant A.N.Odling,4th Dragoon Guards),one Interpreter, and 13 Other Ranks rejoined their Regiments today and struck off strength. One Officer,(Lieutenant R.D.Busk,9th Lancers,and one Other Rank joined Battalion.	

Army Form C. 2118.

WAR DIARY
INTELLIGENCE SUMMARY
(Erase heading not required.)

Place	Date	Hour	Summary of Events and Information	Remarks and references to Appendices
TINCQUES.	26th January. 1917.		Billets. Work on Railway continued; but was again impeded owing to trafficon permanent line. The frost which was a benefit to us at the beginning now hinders railway work considerably, as ground is much harder and the Railway Engineering Company are unable to lay line and be independent of main line, owing to sleepers splitting when the rails are rivetted to them. One Other Rank from Hospital to Battalion; two Other Ranks to Hospital and two Other Ranks to rejoin Unit, are struck off strength of Battalion.	proceed
TINCQUES.	27th January. 1917.		Billets. Work on Railway continued;Ground very hard and many tools broken. One Officer,(2/Lieutenant F.W.Pink.18th Hussars),and two Other Ranks from Hospital rejoined battalion. Three Other Ranks to Hospital and struck off strength.(Captain W.Jeynson. and 2/Lieutenant F.W.Pink,18th Hussars,Captain H.C.Taylor-Whitehead,9th Lancers),and 7 Other Ranks rejoined their Units today and struck off strength of Battalion.	
TINCQUES.	28th January. 1917.		Billets. Work on Railway continued.Divine Service in the afternoon.One Officer (2/Lieutenant H.Turner.4th Dragoon Gds),and three Other Ranks rejoined their Units and struck off strength of Battalion. One Other Rank to Hospital and struck off strength.	
TINCQUES.	29th January. 1917.		Billets.No work on Railway;men employed at various inspections and cleaning up of Billets, Men unable to have baths on account of pipes being frozen. One Other Rank rejoined Unit and struck off strength of Battalion.	
TINCQUES.	30th January. 1917.		Billets. Work on Railway Continued.	
TINCQUES.	31st January. 1917.		Billets. Work on Railway continued. The progress for the last 10 days has not been so marked owing to the frost but the men have worked extremely well under very trying conditions.	

E.J.Thackwell
Major.
Commanding, 2nd Cavalry Brigade Pioneer Battalion.

Army Form C. 2118.

WAR DIARY
INTELLIGENCE SUMMARY
(Erase heading not required.)

War Diary
of
2nd Cavalry Brigade Pioneer Battalion
for the month of
February 1919.

C. J. Thornhill Major
Commanding 2nd Cavalry Brigade Pioneer Battalion.

Army Form C. 2118.

WAR DIARY
INTELLIGENCE SUMMARY

(Erase heading not required.)

Instructions regarding War Diaries and Intelligence Summaries are contained in F.S. Regs., Part II. and the Staff Manual respectively. Title Pages will be prepared in manuscript.

Place	Date	Hour	Summary of Events and Information	Remarks and references to Appendices
TINCQUES	1-2-14		Billets. Work on Railway continued; practically all work on cuttings has to be done by iron wedges, as the earth will not yield to a pick owing to severity of frost. One Other Rank to Hospital, and struck off strength.	
TINCQUES	2-2-14		Billets. Work on Railway continued. One Officer(Lieutenant Stobart,18th Hussars) and one Other Rank, joined Battalion and taken on strength. One Officer(Lieutenant Pillman,4th Dragoon Gds.),and one Other Rank, rejoined their Regiment and struck off strength of Battalion.	
TINCQUES	3-2-14		Billets. Work on Railway continued. Five Officers, viz, Capt.Fetherstonhaugh, 4th D.G. Lieutenants Hankey, Mather Jackson, and Severne, 9th Lancers, and Major Barcley. Chaplain to the Forces, having joined are taken on strength of Battalion: 4 Other Ranks also taken on strength. One Officer (Lieut. MacAlpine, 9th Lancers)and one Other Rank struck off strength of Battalion.	
TINCQUES	4-2-14		Billets. Work on Railway continued. Divine Service held during afternoon.	
TINCQUES	5-2-14		Billets. Work on Railway continued. Lieutenants Colvin and Porter, 9th Lancers, and 7 Other Ranks rejoined their Units and struck off strength.	
TINCQUES	6-2-14		Billets. Work on Railway continued. One Officer (2/Lieut.Turner,4th Dragoon Gds), and 6 Other Ranks, rejoined their Units and struck off strength of Battalion.	
TINCQUES	7-2-14		Billets. Work on Railway continued. The men had baths during the morning in reliefs. One Officer (2/Lieutenant Anson,18th Hussars,) and 5 Other Ranks rejoined their Regiments and struck off strength of Battalion.	
TINCQUES	8-2-14		Billets. Work on Railway continued: owing to severity of frost the work has to be done by wedges and hammers of which there is a great scarcity, consequently progress is slow. Two Other Ranks rejoined and taken on strength of Battalion.	
TINCQUES	9-2-14		Billets. Work on Railway continued. One Other Rank joined and taken on strength of Battalion.	

Army Form C. 2118

WAR DIARY
INTELLIGENCE SUMMARY
(Erase heading not required.)

Instructions regarding War Diaries and Intelligence Summaries are contained in F.S. Regs., Part II. and the Staff Manual respectively. Title Pages will be prepared in manuscript.

Place	Date	Hour	Summary of Events and Information	Remarks and references to Appendices
TINCQUES	10-2-15		Billets. Work on Railway continued. One Other Rank rejoined Battalion and 3 Other Ranks struck off strength.	
TINCQUES	11-2-15		Billets. Work on Railway continued; ground still extremely hard, but progress has been made. Divine Service in the afternoon. Three Other Ranks joined for duty and taken on strength.	
TINCQUES	12-2-15		Billets. Work on Railway continued. A partial thaw set in but ground is still like granite. G.S.1, 1st Cavalry Division, inspected the work done on the line. Three Other Ranks rejoined Unit and struck off the strength.	
TINCQUES	13-2-15		Billets. Work on Railway continued. A.D.M.S., 1st Cavalry Division visited Battn.	
TINCQUES	14-2-15		Billets. Work on Railway continued; hard frost again and the ground is as hard as ever. A.Q.M.G., 1st Cav. Division, visited Headquarters of Battalion. One Other Rank to Hospital and struck off strength of Battalion.	
TINCQUES	15-2-15		Billets. No work on Railway. Men had baths and employed at cleaning billets.	
TINCQUES	16-2-15		Billets. Work on Railway continued. G.O.C., 2nd Cavalry Brigade, inspected the work done on the Railway. A partial thaw set in and earth works somewhat easier. Two Other Ranks to Hospital and struck off strength.	
TINCQUES	17-2-15		Billets. Work on Railway continued: Three Officers(Capt.& Adjt.Eric Smith, 9th Lancers, Capt.Grant, 9th Lancers, Lieut.McNeill, 4th Dragoon Gds., one Interpreter, and Three Other Ranks joined and taken on strength. Four Officers,(Capt.& Adjt.R.Chance, 2/Lieut.Wright, 4th Dragoon Gds., Lieut.Mather Jackson, 9th Lancers, Major Rev.Barclay, and 8 Other Ranks, rejoined Units and struck off strength. Two Other Ranks to Hospital and struck off strength.	

Army Form C. 2118.

WAR DIARY
or
INTELLIGENCE SUMMARY

(Erase heading not required.)

Instructions regarding War Diaries and Intelligence Summaries are contained in F. S. Regs., Part II. and the Staff Manual respectively. Title Pages will be prepared in manuscript.

Place	Date	Hour	Summary of Events and Information	Remarks and references to Appendices
TINCQUES	18-2-19		Billets.Work on Railway continued.Ground a good bit easier to work,but frost is deep in the ground.One Interpreter struck off strength of Battalion.	
TINCQUES	19-2-19		Billets. Work on Railway continued. G.O.C.,1st Cav.Division.,visited Battalion Hd-Qrs. Three Other Ranks taken on strength,two Other Ranks rejoined Units and struck off strength.	
TINCQUES	20-2-19		Billets. Work on Railway continued;heavy rain throughout the day;soil heavy in consequence.	
TINCQUES	21-2-19		Billets. Work on Railway continued;One Other Rank to Hospital and struck off strength.	
TINCQUES	22-2-19		Billets.Work on Railway continued;good progress made the last few days. One Other Rank to Hospital and struck off strength.	
TINCQUES	23-2-19		Billets. No work on Railway with exception of off-loading one Ballast train. Men had baths and employed on various inspections. One Other Rank to Hospital and struck off strength.	
TINCQUES	24-2-19		Billets. Work on Railway continued;the big bulk of the work is now completed as both cuttings are finished;one Company now working at AUBIGNY with 4th Cav. Brigade.One Other Rank to Hospital and struck off strength.	
TINCQUES	25-2-19		Billets. Work on Railway continued;One Other Rank from Hospital and taken on strength.	
TINCQUES	26-2-19		Billets. Work on Railway continued;Five Other Ranks rejoined Unit and struck off strength.	

Army Form C. 2118.

WAR DIARY
INTELLIGENCE SUMMARY
(Erase heading not required.)

Instructions regarding War Diaries and Intelligence Summaries are contained in F. S. Regs., Part II. and the Staff Manual respectively. Title Pages will be prepared in manuscript.

Place	Date	Hour	Summary of Events and Information	Remarks and references to Appendices
TINCQUES	27-2-19		Billets. Work on Railway continued. Two Officers (2/Lieut.Collier, 4th Dragoon Gds., and 2/Lieut. Beart,18th Hussars,) and three Other Ranks joined Battalion and taken on strength. Two Officers (Lieut.McNeill, 4th Dragoon Gds. and 2/Lieut. Mitchelson,18th Hussars), and Three Other Ranks rejoined Regiments and struck off strength. One Horse (A.H.T.Coy.), evacuated to Mobile Veterinary Sections.	
TINCQUES	28-2-19		Billets. Work on Railway continued. Marked progress has been made during the last week, and practically all the heavy work has been completed. One Other Rank rejoined Regiment and struck off strength of Battalion.	

C.J. Mackwell Major.
Commanding 2nd Cavalry Brigade Pioneer Battalion.

Army Form C. 2118.

WAR DIARY
INTELLIGENCE SUMMARY
(Erase heading not required.)

Vol 3

War Diary
of
2nd Cavalry Brigade Pioneer Battalion
for the month of
March 1919.

E.W. Dorman, Major,
Commanding 2nd Cavalry Brigade Pioneer Battalion.

Army Form C. 2118.

WAR DIARY
—or—
INTELLIGENCE SUMMARY
(Erase heading not required.)

Instructions regarding War Diaries and Intelligence Summaries are contained in F. S. Regs., Part II. and the Staff Manual respectively. Title Pages will be prepared in manuscript.

Place	Date	Hour	Summary of Events and Information	Remarks and references to Appendices
TINCQUES.	1-3-17.		Billets. Work on Railway continued; all three companies now working in our own area. 2/Lieutenant Halliday.R.E., three Other Ranks and two horses rejoined units and struck off strength.	
TINCQUES.	2-3-1917.		Billets. Work on railway continued. One Other Rank joined Battalion and taken on strength. G.O.C.2nd Cavalry Brigade visited Headquarters and inspected the Transport lines.	
TINCQUES.	3-3-1917.		Billets. One company working on railway, remainder of Battalion having baths and employed on arms inspections, etc.. Two Other Ranks joined and taken on strength. Five Other Ranks and two horses to units and struck off strength.	
TINCQUES.	4-3-1917.		Billets. Work on railway continued. Four Other Ranks joined and taken on strength: four Other Ranks to Hospital and two Other Ranks to Hospital and struck off strength.	
TINCQUES.	5-3-1917.		Billets. Work on railway continued; snow fell heavily during the night. Major E.M.Dorman, 4th Dragoon Guards took over command vice Major G.J.Thackwell, 18th Hussars. 1 Other Rank joined, 1 Other Rank to unit and struck off.	
TINCQUES.	6-3-1917.		Billets. Work on railway continued. The following officers joined the Battalion:- Lieut. & Quarter-Master W.A.Letts, Lieut. L.E. McNeill, 2/Lieut.L.G.B.Rogers, 5 Other Ranks joined.	
TINCQUES.	7-3-1917.		Billets. Work on the railway by both 4th Dragoon Gds. and 18th Hussars. The 9th Lancers stood to, but did not turn out. The following officers and 3 Other Ranks, left the Battalion and rejoined their units:- Lieut.& Quarter-Master F.A.Dunham, 2/Lieut. R.A.Radclyffe, B.S.V.EMBELL, 4th Dragoon Gds.	
TINCQUES.	8-3-1917.		Billets. Work on Railway. Snow.	
TINCQUES.	9-3-1917.		Billets. Work on Railway. 2 Other Ranks to Hospital. 1 Other Rank rejoined from Hospital. Snow.	
TINCQUES.	10-3-1917.		Billets. Work on Railway. 1 Other Rank to Hospital. 1 Other Rank rejoined.	

Army Form C. 2118.

WAR DIARY
INTELLIGENCE SUMMARY

(Erase heading not required.)

Instructions regarding War Diaries and Intelligence Summaries are contained in F. S. Regs., Part II. and the Staff Manual respectively. Title Pages will be prepared in manuscript.

Place	Date	Hour	Summary of Events and Information	Remarks and references to Appendices
TINCQUES.	11-3-1917		Billets. Work on Railway beyond FREVIN CAPELLE for two Companys. 1 Other rank to Hospital. 14 Other Ranks, 6 Limbered G.S. Wagons, 1 Water Cart and 26 L.D. Horses rejoined their units.	
TINCQUES.	12-3-1917		Billets. Work on Railway - two Companys employed beyond FREVIN CAPELLE. Lieut: H.W.DURNFORD, 9th Lancers and 1 O.R. joined. Lieut. T.D.HANVEY, 9th Lancers and 2 O.R's to unit.	
TINCQUES.	13-3-1917		Billets. Work on railway. Battalion entrained at TINCQUES and left at 9-10 p.m.for MONTREUIL, which was reached at 5-0 p.m.on 14th instant.Transport proceeded by road.Battalion returned to billets of component units by motor lorry.	

EuDorman Major,
Commanding 2nd Cavalry Brigade Pioneer Battalion.

www.ingramcontent.com/pod-product-compliance
Lightning Source LLC
Chambersburg PA
CBHW081421300426
44108CB00016BA/2277